THE MINERS' ASSOCIATION

THE MINERS' ASSOCIATION

A Trade Union in the Age of the Chartists

by

Raymond Challinor

and

Brian Ripley

1968
LAWRENCE AND WISHART
LONDON

Printed in Great Britain by
The Camelot Press Ltd., London and Southampton

Foreword

OUR interest in the Miners' Association was kindled by accident. In Wigan Public Library, we happened to come across a valuable collection of original manuscripts. These, apparently, had only been used twice before. Once by Professor A. J. Taylor for an article that appeared in *Economica*, and on the other occasion by Miss Ellen Wilkinson for her book on Jarrow, *The Town that was Murdered*. So far nobody had devoted prolonged intensive research to the "Pitmen's Strike Collection".

Likewise, the Miners' Association itself appears to have been neglected. What was the most powerful trade union of its age receives only passing mention from historians of the Labour Movement. Our aim has been to repair this omission.

We think our account has intrinsic interest. The 1840s was one of the most intense, heroic periods of working-class struggle. Millions of people yearned for democratic rights and better conditions. Their attempts to achieve these objectives, the story of their fight, deserves not to be forgotten.

In this battle the miners took a prominent part. Lessons that can be derived from their experiences may have relevance to the present day. At a time when the law again threatens trade unionists with imprisonment, the legal battles of W. P. Roberts acquire fresh significance. The Lancashire strike tactic of the 1840s, involving the union in limited struggle, taking on one employer while remaining at peace with the rest, resembles the method used by the Draughtsman's Union of the 1960s. And the disunity and lack of solidarity that characterised the Miners' Association in decline at least contain a warning for today.

In our work, we received great assistance from Mr. Edward Thompson and Dr. V. L. Allen. They both read the entire manuscript and made many valuable suggestions. We would also like to thank the following for their comments, criticism and advice: Mr. George Barnsby, Dr. Henry Collins, Mr. Lawrence Daly, Mr. J. Hammond,

Dr. J. R. Harris, Mr. R. S. Neale, Mr. Stan Newens, and Mr. R. Samuels.

We are indebted to Mrs. Brenda Gleave, our typist, and to Mrs. L. M. G. Challinor for help with the correction of proofs and preparation of the Index.

R. C.
B. R

Wigan,
May 1968

Contents

I

The Miners' Association in Perspective

THE Miners' Association of Great Britain and Ireland, formally established at Wakefield on 7 November 1842, constitutes an important landmark in the history of British trade unions. Its size, structure and intention made it, in many ways, the prototype of the modern trade union, an advance on previous combinations of workmen.

The 1830s had already witnessed the rise of the concept of national trade unionism. The three main practising exponents were: the Grand General Union of all Operative Spinners of the United Kingdom, which survived till 1831; the Operative Builders' Union, which lasted a couple of years, till 1834; and the Grand National Consolidated Trades Union, with its brief ill-fated existence for a few months in 1834. These organisations, examples of trade-union federalism, were soon shattered by their inherent centrifugal tendencies. The absence of any clearly held idea of what their role should be, a growth of divergent local interests and the ferocity with which capital opposed them made their cohesion precarious and short-lived. Like meteors, they briefly dazzled the industrial firmament and their significance lay primarily as a portent of the future.

In contrast, the Miners' Association possessed greater strength and durability. It had a unitary organisation whereby the powers exercised by the constituent bodies were, on paper at least, those granted to them by national delegate conferences, usually convened every six months. Day-to-day activities were supervised by an executive committee. In size, too, the Miners' Association represented a breakthrough. The same authority that gave the Builders' a membership of 30,000 reckoned the Miners' to have 100,000:

> "In the very heat of the battle (September 1833) the Builders' Union held its annual delegate meeting at Manchester. It lasted six days; cost, it is said, over £3,000; and was attended by two hundred and seventy delegates representing thirty thousand operatives."[1]

[1] S. and B. Webb, *The History of Trade Unionism*, p. 130.

"The delegate meetings at Manchester and Glasgow in the year 1844 soon came to represent practically the whole of the mining districts of Great Britain; and the membership rose, it is said, to at least 100,000."[1]

This figure of 100,000 is certainly an exaggeration, despite support for it from Engels' *Condition of the Working Class in England in 1844*, Fynes' history of *The Miners of Northumberland and Durham*, and repeated references in the *Northern Star*. However, the smallest estimate of the Miners' Association membership in 1844 is 60,000, which is still considerably in excess of the Builders' figure, which may itself be an exaggeration.

The total membership of the Grand National can hardly be compared with that of the Miners' Association. Their functions were too dissimilar. Whereas the miners built a strong organisation, effective in industrial struggles, the Grand National remained a loose federation, a conglomeration of local bodies with disparate trades and practices. Consequently, it is difficult to determine its precise strength. As a contemporary historian points out: "the Grand National Consolidated Trades Union never became really national, and certainly fell a long way short of consolidation."[2]

The Miners' Association was an object of awe in its day. Its size and financial resources were spoken of in legendary terms by enemies as well as friends. We may well come to realise that the actual funds at its disposal were very much less than commentators imagined. Nevertheless, their general impression remains correct: the Miners' Association did represent a new departure. Its objects, perhaps more than anything else, distinguish it from its predecessors. They gave it a more modern outlook. The rules and regulations of the union set out the sole aim "to unite all Miners to equalise and diminish the hours of labour and to obtain the highest possible amount of wages for the labour of the miner".[3] A firm rejection of apocalyptic or utopian ends may partly reflect a prudent fear of authority, a reluctance to suffer again the repressions of 1834 and 1842, but it also signifies the emergence of a different type of trade unionism.

The syndicalism of Benbow and the utopian revolutionism of Owen, which had widespread influence in the unions of the 1830s, represented only a large-scale application of a more venerable attitude. Unions, as

[1] S. and B. Webb, op. cit., p. 182.
[2] G. D. H. Cole, *Attempts at General Union*, p. 156.
[3] Rules and Regulations of the Miners' Association of Great Britain and Ireland. Rule 1.

distinct from trade clubs and friendly societies, were viewed as temporary expedients for a particular end. The demise of a union was accordingly something to be expected once its objects had been achieved. Brevity of life was a characteristic feature: it happened to the successful unions as well as the failures. The Miners' Association, on the other hand, clearly intended to make itself a permanent and enduring organisation, representing the interests of miners throughout the land. Its durability made it more in accord with the Webbs' classic definition of a trade union as "a *continuous* association of wage-earners for the purpose of maintaining or improving the conditions of their working lives".[1]

The Miners' Association made other startling innovations. It was the first union to use the courts of law systematically to defend its members' interests. W. P. Roberts, an able and energetic solicitor, with strong labour sympathies, was engaged. "We resisted every individual act of oppression, even in cases where we were sure of losing," he subsequently explained.[2] To begin with, some miners had a naïve belief in the ultimate fairness of the law. They thought the coalowners, by guile and knavery, had succeeded in temporarily twisting the law to suit their own purpose; by employing Mr. Roberts, the pitmen would redress the balance. But soon it became clear that, despite the tremendous efforts of Roberts, this would not happen. The law possessed a built-in bias favouring the employers: the situation could only be altered by changing the law. Consequently, the Miners' Association was one of the first unions to be seriously involved in political and parliamentary action. It began a tradition among mineworkers that has continued right down to the present day.

Throughout its existence the Association kept friendly parliamentarians briefed and applied pressure whenever legislation affecting miners came before Parliament. David Swallow, its first general secretary, had given evidence to the Royal Commission in 1842.[3] Lord Shaftesbury was greatly impressed by the clear and competent manner with which a working miner addressed the Commissioners and, from then on, he remained in correspondence with Swallow. The Association passed many resolutions praising Lord Shaftesbury's work and continually plied him with data. On one occasion, Lord Shaftesbury replied, saying "he was only an instrument, and

[1] S. and B. Webb, op. cit., p. 1.
[2] *Flint Glass Makers' Magazine*, October 1951.
[3] Letter to David Swallow reported to Shaddon Hill meeting, 18 March 1843.

possessed little power unless the working classes stood at his back".[1]

The Association realised the importance of mass agitation. In 1844, a Bill enlarging the powers of magistrates to imprison workmen for "any misbehaviour concerning such service and employment" was brought before Parliament. Roberts was not slow to see the sweeping powers such a measure would give employers. On his advice, a miners' delegate meeting at Glasgow initiated a campaign that resulted in 200 petitions, on behalf of two million people, being sent to Parliament in protest. The Bill, which had already slipped through the second reading and committee stage without a division, now encountered stiff opposition and was defeated.

But the miners did not limit themselves to influencing Parliament; two of their leaders—William Dixon and W. P. Roberts—actually stood as candidates in the 1847 General Election. It appears to be the first time trade unionists stood for Parliament. Naturally, neither had any chance of getting elected. However, the hustings presented an excellent opportunity for staging a protest demonstration. At Wigan, Dixon harangued 5,000 cheering miners and weavers in the Market Place; made slashing attacks on the other two candidates (both local coalowners); and, when a show of hands went almost unanimously in his favour, he declared himself the duly-elected Member for Wigan. But the other candidates demanded a poll which, on the restricted franchise that then prevailed, inevitably meant victory for them. This, in turn, gave Dixon a good opening to express his Chartist beliefs and denounce the iniquitous electoral system that denied most working men the vote.

*   *   *

The Miners' Association was a trade union in the age of the Chartists. Generally speaking, historians have considered that the two movements exerted little, if any, influence on one another. A recent expression of this traditional view comes from Dr. Hobsbawm:

"Miners—whether of coal or metal—were an isolated body of men, often geographically separated from the rest of the working people and concerned less with politics than with their specialised economic struggles. Hence in most parts of the country they took surprisingly little part in the radical and Chartist agitations."[2]

[1] *Children's Employment Commission*, Appendix Part I, pp. 277–8.
[2] E. J. Hobsbawm, *Labouring Men*, p. 30.

It is an opinion that needs some modification. A detailed examination of the *Northern Star* shows that in mining areas a very large proportion of the population signed Chartist petitions and in 1842, the year the Association was formed, Chartist activity in the coalfields greatly intensified. But miners rarely played a leading role. Throughout 1842 the *Northern Star* contained the names of nominations to the Chartist General Council. Most branches made about ten nominations and usually mentioned their nominees' occupations. From the many hundreds of names that appear, we can gain some idea of who played a prominent part in Chartist agitation at local level. It shows that support came from an impressive cross-section of the people—small producers, labourers and artisans. But miners are conspicuously absent, even in lists coming from mining areas.

There are, however, two significant exceptions. The North Stafford-shire Chartists nominated five pitmen, including George Hemmings and Thomas Mayer, who were local leaders of the general strike that occurred in the summer of 1842. More significant are the sixteen nominations from Byker Hill, Northumberland: five of them were miners, including Martin Jude, who became treasurer of the Miners' Association, and John Hall, its second general secretary.

The North-east miners were strong supporters of Chartism. Most of the leaders of an earlier union—the Hepburn union, 1830–2—turned to Chartist activity once they had given up all hope of re-forming their shattered association. For Thomas Hepburn, it was the only outlet of protest left open. After the 1832 strike he was victimised, unable to find work and on the verge of starvation. Eventually, a coalowner offered him a job on condition he never again joined a trade union—and he accepted.

Richard Fynes, the historian, describes him in the following terms:

"Hepburn was not only a great leader amongst the miners, but his sympathies extended to the broad platform of politics. He was a man with a strong constitution, an intelligent mind, active and ever ready to lend a hand to any movement that had for its object the elevation of the people. . . . He was one of the most active men of the Chartist agitation. Fergus O'Connor, speaking of him, said, 'he is a noble specimen of human nature, and the people of the North of England have a right to be proud of him. . . .' When the miners' union was broken up, he spent a number of the remaining years of his laborious and useful life in agitating for Parliamentary Reform, and in educating the young ones with whom he came into contact."[1]

Many of Hepburn's young protégés were later to form the hard core of the Miners' Association. He educated them in the Chartist tradition. "He travelled long distances on many a dreary night, and addressed meetings to advocate the political rights of the people, advising his hearers to get knowledge. He taught and illustrated the great truth by his argument that, if the people of England once demanded their rights, no Government could withhold them."[2]

The North-east was not only one of the best organised regions of the Chartist movement, with strong links extending to villages throughout the area, but it was also dominated by advocates of physical force Chartism. Augustus Beaumont published his *Northern Liberator* from Newcastle, in which he regularly denounced the moderates: "Those men were well fed, and therefore they relied on moral force; but let them labour for one week, and be ill-fed and ill-clothed, and it would soon convert their moral force to physical force."[3] It was also the stamping ground for people who were regarded as extremists, like Julian Harney. Even he regarded the political atmosphere there, in the winter of 1838-9, as exhilarating. "In small villages lying out from Newcastle the exhortation to arms was being taken quite literally ... a strong tradition of owner-paternalism had been replaced by an extremely class-conscious Chartism, and fowling pieces, small cannon, stoneware grenades, pikes and 'craa's feet or caltrops—four-spiked irons which could be strewn in a road to disable cavalry horses—were being turned out in quantities. It was localities like this which, on hearing rumours that troops would be present at the great meeting in Newcastle on Christmas Day, sent couriers to find out if they were to bring arms with them."[4]

The numerous Chartist rallies in Northumberland and Durham were well-attended. Thousands of colliers and ironworkers marched miles, mingling with trade and benefit society members and carrying banners with inscriptions like "He that hath no sword, let him sell his shirt and buy one". The speakers, who always denounced the Birmingham and Edinburgh moderates, were equally violent. Dr. John Taylor said his last action would be "to write his epitaph upon the tyrant's brow, in characters of blood, with a pen of steel". Julian

[1] R. Fynes, *The Miners of Northumberland and Durham*, p. 244.   [2] Ibid.
[3] *Northern Liberator*, 28 December 1838.
[4] A. R. Schoyen, *The Chartist Challenge*, p. 42.

Harney advised his audience to carry "a musket in one hand and a petition in the other".[1]

Dr. Taylor and Harney were among the main speakers at Newcastle Town Moor, on 20 April 1839, at a great meeting convened to consider what action should be taken if the Government rejected "the People's Charter". But neither of them nor any of the other main speakers took the lead when the authorities tried to prevent the meeting continuing and read the Riot Act four times. Hepburn was the only one to defy authority. He stood up and shouted, "John Fife, Mayor of Newcastle, I tell you your proclamation is no law. You have no right to prevent us from holding our meetings." Hepburn's "eloquence and ability inspired people on that day," says Richard Fynes, "and established him as a great favourite among Chartist agitators."[2]

Later that year, when Dr. Taylor and others were arrested, workers in the North-east immediately responded with strike action. A letter from Newcastle to the Chartist Convention reported "nearly all the colliers in the North are laid in with a stern determination on the part of the men not to commence work again until they have gained their rights. We have done all in our power to try to get them to wait for the commands of the Convention. The answer is that long enough for aught they have to expect from their tyrants. They add, 'We are prepared to commence.' In fact, they have done so. . . ." The letter states there were 25,000 pitmen from Northumberland and Durham on strike, as well as some industrial workers from Newcastle itself. A postscript mentioned that another ten collieries, with a further 7,000 men, had also struck.[3]

With such a tradition of industrial struggle for Chartist objectives, it seems quite natural that, when the miners began organising their new trade union, they should turn to the same quarter for assistance. They invited Feargus O'Connor, T. S. Duncombe, M.P., and Thomas Hepburn to address the first mass recruitment rally in Northumberland, at Shadon Hill, on 13 May 1843. None of the invited speakers attended. Thomas Hepburn honoured the pledge he had given, in return for employment, never to join another union. As for the other two, perhaps they had other engagements or felt reluctant to associate themselves too closely with a venture that appeared to have little chance of success.

[1] He later claimed in court, somewhat improbably, that he had actually said, "a biscuit in one hand and the Charter in the other."
[2] R. Fynes, op. cit., p. 245.
[3] A letter from the Newcastle Political Union, dated 12 July 1839, published in *Charter*, of 21 July 1839.

Nevertheless, O'Connor, Duncombe and the Chartist Movement did help the Miners' Association.[1] It is doubtful if the union could have established itself, and certainly it would have been much less effective, without Chartist assistance.

The *Northern Star* gave the miners every encouragement. In an editorial it said, "We highly approve of the organisation now being adopted by the colliers. . . . For our part, we shall cheerfully publish the progress of their cause."[2] So the miners had ample space in its columns to state their case and report their meetings. This was especially valuable in the period before October 1843 (when they started their own paper) since it was the main link between coalfields, giving them a flow of information about each other's wages and working conditions that no previous pitmen's union had possessed:

> "We request that the men of every pit will appoint a man to write, or forward to us, addressed to the Colliers, Griffin Inn, Wakefield, every accident and all information concerning the miseries that oppress you: those facts, carefully collected and printed, will show the world such a picture as it never saw before."[3]

Also, the *Northern Star* acted as an organiser: disgruntled miners, wishing to join the union, had only to look in its columns to find where to apply. Coalowners quickly discovered the significance of this: a delegate meeting at Byker Hill was sarcastically told "good workmen were discharged for no fault than because they committed the most heinous crime of reading that poisonous journal, the *Northern Star*."[4]

Another way in which Chartism assisted the Miners' Association was to provide technical expertise. After the inaugural Wakefield conference, copies of the proposed rules were submitted to O'Connor and the Rev. W. Hill, editor of the *Northern Star*, for advice on their legality. They both "pronounced them in perfect accordance with the law."[5] O'Connor was also consulted—he addressed the Glasgow conference of the union—on the question of whether the Association should buy its own printing press and make the *Miners' Advocate* a stamped paper.

O'Connor's attitude to trade unions was of crucial importance, as it influenced many active Chartists. He adjured them "to keep your eye fixed upon the great Trades' Movement now manifesting itself. . . . Attend their meetings, swell their numbers, and give them your

[1] Duncombe visited Newcastle on 21 October 1843.
[2] *Northern Star*, 22 July 1843.   [3] Ibid., 31 December 1842.
[4] Ibid., 25 March, 1843.   [5] Ibid., 6 May 1843.

sympathy; but upon no account interpose the Charter as an obstacle to their proceedings. All labour and labourers must unite; and they will speedily discover that the Charter is the only standard under which they can successfully rally: but don't interpose it to interruption of their proceedings."[1]

Many Chartists, from taking a sympathetic attitude to the colliers' struggles, found themselves drawn into the Miners' Association and eventually playing a leading role in it. Chartism placed a vast reservoir of talent at the union's disposal. It swelled its ranks with people who, but for Chartism acting as intermediary, would never have dreamt of going anywhere near a pit. Moreover, besides bringing in recruits from outside the pits, Chartism provided, through its own activities, a training-ground where most of those who were later to become miners' leaders gained their first knowledge and experience. As a result, it becomes difficult to find any prominent union member who did not have, at some time or other, Chartist connections.

W. P. Roberts, a solicitor from Bath, was a personal friend of Feargus O'Connor. He also became legal adviser to the Chartist Land Bank and lost considerable money in it. After addressing stormy Chartist demonstrations at Trowbridge in 1839, he was imprisoned in Fisherton jail for two years. He suffered badly in jail and protested against being put in irons.[2] Roberts came to the Association via Chartism. William Beesley, who had met Roberts at Chartist functions, was dispatched by the miners to try and persuade him to be their legal adviser.

Although never a miner himself, William Beesley edited the first miners' paper. An Accrington chair-maker, he gained his journalistic experience through editing a Chartist journal in North Lancashire, where he was also the district secretary. He was quite prominent in the Chartist Movement at national level too, being appointed, among other things, to a committee of five who considered which petitions should be submitted to T. S. Duncombe, M.P. In 1845, Beesley became a founder member of the Fraternal Democrats, an organisation with which Karl Marx remained in friendly contact.[3]

---

[1] *Northern Star*, 16 November 1844.   [2] H.O. 40 (1839), 48.
[3] Henry Collins and Chimen Abramsky, in *Karl Marx and the British Labour Movement*, say that the Fraternal Democrats' "importance in giving organised expression to the idea of proletarian internationalism can hardly be exaggerated. To Harney and the Fraternal Democrats must go much of the credit for the fact that in the 1850s and 1860s the British workers were more responsive to international issues than at any time before or much of the time since." (p. 9.) William Beesley was one of the small group signing the first declaration of the Fraternal Democrats.

Besides Beesley, the only other editor of a miners' paper was William Daniels, who likewise had originally no direct connection with the coal industry. He was a carpet-weaver from Lasswade, near Edinburgh, and secretary of the Mental Improvement Society there. Before editing the *Advocate* his only previous journalistic experience appears to have come through Chartism: he wrote reports for the *Northern Star*.

In contrast, David Swallow, the union's first general secretary, was a self-educated miner. An organiser with exceptional talent, he journeyed through Northumberland, Durham, Lancashire and Staffordshire, the first person to raise the banner of the Miners' Association in these coal-fields. Even when the Association was merely a young tender sprig, not properly rooted, he took time off from union work to address Chartist meetings. At Newcastle, he publicly debated whether O'Connor's Land Scheme was a worth-while and realistic proposition. After Beesley had suggested that a million people should each give a penny towards the purchase of land, Swallow "rose to show the impracticability of the people in their present oppressed condition procuring the means of land and contended that we should endeavour to get the Charter at any cost first, and the means of locating the people on the soil would soon follow."[1]

David Swallow remained general secretary for only six months. He was too valuable to the miners as an organiser for them to allow him to devote his energies to routine secretarial work. In May 1843, he was replaced by John Hall, a flax-dresser from South Shields, whose administrative experience had been acquired as treasurer of the Northumberland and Durham Chartist Lecturers' Fund. He continued to hold the office until 1847 when William Grocott, a Manchester weaver, became general secretary. Grocott, a former secretary of the South Lancashire Chartists, remained active in the political as well as trade union movement. In 1848, after the Chartists had presented their third petition, the police unleashed a campaign of repression, and Grocott was among its many victims. He was tried, along with seventy-five other Chartists, at the South Lancashire Winter Assizes, and sentenced to a year's imprisonment. His incarceration in Kirkdale jail was a contributory factor in the demise of the Miners' Association.

The Association's treasurer and, throughout its existence, one of its most able and far-sighted members, was Martin Jude, who kept various public houses in Newcastle, which were often used for meetings. Jude

[1] *Northern Star*, 29 April 1843.

was a Chartist before the Association began and remained, for twenty-five years, prominent in the struggle for universal manhood suffrage. In 1847, he was Newcastle's delegate to the Chartist convention, and in the 1850s, when Chartism was a spent force, he continued to espouse the same ideas by actively supporting the Northern Reform Union, along with Joseph Cowan and Julian Harney.[1]

Martin Jude had originally worked down the pit.[2] But coalowners made a habit of sacking militants and a blacklist effectively debarred them from getting work elsewhere. So, like many working-class leaders, Jude was driven from his occupation. Tommy Hepburn was another example of this: after the 1832 debacle, he wandered around mining villages for five years, trying to sell tea.

Most of the top leaders of the Miners' Association (with the exception of Swallow and Jude) appear to have never worked in the coal industry. The fact that victimisation was so common makes this even more remarkable. A continual cry came from members for the appointment of miners, sacked for activity on behalf of the union and unlikely ever to gain employment down a mine again, to official posts within the organisation. That so few were appointed appears to indicate that most of them were unsuitable. The exploitation, ignorance and squalor that prevailed in the mining villages, the very conditions that created the need for a trade union, also gave the Miners' Association an impediment in its speech. To a large extent, it had to use others as its spokesmen. This is not to say miners themselves did not play a vital role in the union. But, generally, they became leaders at county level; national positions were almost all reserved for men coming from outside the industry, invariably with a Chartist background.

While the influx of Chartists helped to provide the union with talented and resourceful personnel, it also gave rise to grave problems. In the eyes of the established order, Chartism was an ogre, a wild beast to be slain: for the union to become too closely linked with it furnished the coalowners with an excellent pretext for smashing the union. This was especially true immediately preceding the general strike of 1842, when the authorities used draconic repression and savage sentences indiscriminately. Many victims were miners—the Midlands, Lancashire and Scottish coalfields had been centres of the most hard-fought class struggles—and the newly-formed Miners' Association realised that if

---

[1] The Cowan Collection, Newcastle-on-Tyne Public Library, contains some of Jude's letters to the Northern Reform Union.

[2] Jude later wrote, "I have been a coal miner ... in the worst days of coal mine slavery." (Northern Tribune, January–June 1854.)

it were to avoid strangulation at birth it had to be ultra-cautious and keep within the letter of the law.

Its leaders also realised that there was a danger not only from the authorities, but from their own membership as well. Any hasty ill-prepared action on the part of any of their supporters could have disastrous consequences for the whole union. Self-preservation dictated that all thought of using violence to achieve their ends be quietly dropped. Otherwise repression of the Miners' Association would be swift and decisive. Yet, strong support for physical-force Chartism existed in mining areas. As we have seen, Northumberland and Durham colliers cheered the revolutionary utterances of Taylor, Harney and others.[1] In South Wales, Frost's Newport rebellion of 1839 was supported mainly by miners. Ever since the Merthyr uprising of 1831, the strange and secret custom of "Scotch Cattle" has been prevalent among South Wales colliers. It acquired its name apparently from the red figure of a bull's head, the symbol of a clandestine organisation which blew up furnaces, beat up blacklegs and carried out numerous other acts of violence. In North Staffordshire, the period of unrest in 1839 saw miners building barricades, exchanging fire with the troops and indulging in fierce hand-to-hand fighting.[2]

Understandably, the leaders of the Miners' Association strove to restrain the members. The danger of violence erupting was a very real one. In a typical editorial, the Miners' Advocate urged men to remain peaceable. It reported a parliamentary debate where Lord Howick, son of Earl Grey, had asked the government to take action against the colliers' union. But Sir Robert Peel, the prime minister, had replied that "the colliers, as yet, have kept within the law". This remark was not lost on the Advocate: it counselled all miners to continue law-abiding. Not that the laws were made in the colliers' interests, but everything had to be done to avoid government interference. The editor went on to say the union's watchword should be "Prudence, Patience, Caution and Perseverance": "Let the Miners' Association only take these as a guide, oneness of purpose and singleness of soul, and then no power can prevent them from bringing their present movement to a speedy, successful and happy termination."[3]

[1] Thomas Burt: An Autobiography: "Many of the young Northumbrian miners were believers in the 'physical force' side of the movement." (p. 24.)

[2] F. C. Mather, Public Order in the Age of the Chartists, pp. 20–21, says the only occasion in this period when barricades were erected was at Stone (Staffs) in 1839. In fact, there was another instance at Lane Ends, near Newcastle-under-Lyme, which was fully reported in the press.

[3] Miners' Advocate, 27 January 1844.

Pleas for non-violence, however, often aroused heated controversy, as for example at the Scaffold Hill meeting, attended by 20,000 Northumberland colliers, in March 1843. The chairman, Benjamin Pyle, a veteran of the Hepburn union, reminded the audience it was not a Chartist meeting; in fact, it was the inaugural meeting for the Miners' Association in that area. He soon ran into difficulties. The second speaker, Benjamin Watson, condemned Pyle for attacking Chartism. The Chartists, he said, were not opposed to property, but only to working men receiving so little for their property—in other words, their labour. Whereupon "the Chairman explained he had been misunderstood. He did not say that the Chartists were destructive (cries of 'You did'). He had only warned them not to split upon politics, or they would never be firmly organised. They must use moral force and then they would be safe and powerful (Cries of 'We know all that, but you said the Chartists were destructive')."[1] After this altercation, the meeting was addressed by P. M. Brophy, a Chartist weaver from Dublin, who later became an organiser for the Association. While he warned the miners not to allow themselves to become divided on political issues, he told them it was no use petitioning Parliament as it was then constituted. "Providence was not the author of their distress but class legislation," he said.

Both Brophy and Beesley first went to the North-east to propagate Chartist ideas among miners. The *Northern Star* contained notes to readers such as this:

"To the Colliers of the Wear—will any of the colliers wishing to have the services of William Beesley, of Accrington, send their addresses to Mr. George Charlton, sail-maker, 2, Fitters Row, Sunderland, as soon as possible."[2]

During the 1842 general strike, Beesley had sought to get the colliers to strike for the Charter. Subsequently, he was arrested and tried at Lancaster, with Feargus O'Connor and fifty-seven others, for his part in the disturbances. It was alleged he advocated armed insurrection at a mass rally he addressed along with William Holdgate and others. At his trial, Beesley ended his speech to the Court: "You may lock me up in prison, but the moment I get out I will begin again advocating my principles. . . . Let ten thousand convictions be obtained against me and I will still be a Chartist."

Naturally, some miners were apprehensive when Beesley became a

[1] *Gateshead Observer*, 18 March 1843.   [2] *Northern Star*, 20 May 1843.

union organiser. The North Elswick branch wanted the decision rescinded. A leaflet, sent to other North-eastern branches on 10 July 1843, said:

> "In reviewing the past conduct of Mr. Beesley in the Lancashire strike case, as stated himself publicly in Newcastle on two occasions that, when he and others had got the colliers of the South to stop work for the Charter, the Colliers of the North would not follow it out, although he came here expressly for that purpose. We therefore think that we are perfectly justified in stating our opinion that Mr. Beesley's intentions are to influence the minds of unsuspecting miners and induce them to a premature strike, that he may accomplish his own ends although the Union might be severed to atoms thereby."[1]

It was agreed that a general delegate meeting reconsider Beesley's appointment; North Elswick proposed that he should be replaced by a victimised miner named Smith. Meanwhile, Beesley, addressing 20,000 miners at Black Fell, seconded a resolution that the union set up a law fund. Irrelevantly, he "introduced the subject of the people's Charter. This led to some division of feeling, but the majority sided with the speaker."[2] However, in spite of the way Beesley seized every opportunity to introduce Chartist ideas, the general delegate meeting decided he should continue to be a paid union official.

Even so, it is no doubt true the miners were afraid their close associations with Chartism might provide coalowners with a handy weapon. Not only could it be used to justify the employers' intransigence, their unwillingness to negotiate with the union, but also it gave them a means for sowing discord in the miners' ranks. They could play Chartist off against non-Chartist. This tactic was frequently employed, especially during the great strike of 1844 in Northumberland and Durham. The *Newcastle Journal* declared, "The fact is the pitmen are now divided into two great sections, one being of those who have imbibed Chartist principles, and are not unwilling to turn their strike into a political movement, and the other of those who have regard only to the matters of trade in hand and look for personal rather than national and remote, benefits."[3] In a later issue it went on to say, "The owners have never refused to meet the men at their own respective collieries and confer upon any of the proposed modifications of terms, but they have, and will continue, we trust, to refuse a conference with Chartist agitators who proceed from colliery to colliery,

[1] Leaflet contained in The Pitmen's Strike Collection, Wigan Public Library.
[2] *Gateshead Observer*, 15 July 1843.   [3] *Newcastle Journal*, 13 April 184.

sowing disaffection among the pitmen for their own selfish ends."[1]

In the eyes of the *Newcastle Journal* and many other hostile sources, the very formation of the Miners' Association could be attributed to Chartism. "The agitation of Chartism," the paper says, "brought to the surface of society a great deal of scum that usually putrifies in obscurity below."[2] After the defeat of Chartism in 1842, many leaders had to look for other occupations and came to miners' areas. "Beesley thrust himself upon the pitmen, who employed him as a runner amongst the various collieries for a few shillings per week. That was certainly better than starving." Instead of discarding his Chartist ideas, Beesley "set at once inoculating the miners with the virus of his malignant notions." He then proposed the miners should employ W. P. Roberts, a relative of John Frost. When installed as miners' attorney, Roberts was alleged by the *Newcastle Journal* to have received in six months £1,000, plus expenses and to have asked for Beesley's appointment as his clerk. Beesley "forthwith mounts the office stool, and plods through foolscap sheets the livelong day, except only such brief portions as lawyers usually devote to tooth picking, digit brushing and mahogany hewing. There being, in truth, but little to do for Mr. Roberts and his Man Friday, it was a most gross imposition on the gullibility of poor men." When Roberts established a miners' journal with Beesley as editor, "the colliers of Northumberland and Durham, or the majority of them, state they did not sanction or approve of the political aspect which Beesley and his master had endeavoured to give their movement. They regarded the difference between their employers and themselves as pertaining to business only, and their object in employing Mr. Roberts was not to extend Chartist doctrines, but to resist what they considered to be oppressive proceedings in their own case."[3]

This venomous account is significant since it represents what owners and editors really believed. They thought the Association was the product of Chartists gulling ignorant pitmen. This implied the grievances were manufactured by outsiders, not genuinely held by pitmen themselves, and consequently nothing had to be done about them. Moreover, to attribute all troubles to Chartist agitators was a diagnosis calculated to arouse widespread sympathy in upper- and middle-class circles. An added advantage was that it helped to disunite the miners.

To begin with, many miners' leaders sought to parry this charge by

[1] *Newcastle Journal*, 11 May 1844.   [2] Ibid., 13 April 1844.   [3] Ibid., 13 April 1844.

openly dissociating themselves from Chartism. Feargus O'Connor was rebuffed when he offered to address the Manchester conference in January 1844; a Chartist leaflet, mysteriously circulated at the Glasgow conference in March 1844, was disowned by all delegates; and speakers were repeatedly reminded to omit political remarks from their speeches.

Such evidence is used by Professor A. J. Taylor to adduce that the Miners' Association rejected the Chartist embrace.[1] But, in our opinion, this overlooks the context in which these actions took place. It only occurred at a time when it was definitely expedient for tactical reasons to dissociate the union from Chartism. A massive wave of repression had followed the 1842 general strike, sweeping many Chartists into prison. Miners had also found themselves imprisoned. It looked as if, given the least excuse, the State would pounce on the infant union, and every conceivable precaution had to be taken. We now know what the miners doubtless surmised: that the Home Secretary, Sir James Graham, asked for the union to be kept under constant surveillance and told the coalowners to report on any political activity in which it indulged.[2] A plain-clothes policeman posed as a delegate to the Manchester conference; at Glasgow, the authorities kept a watchful eye on the conference, asking the organisers for a full explanation of its objectives. Everything appeared poised for repression.

When the great strike of Northumberland and Durham colliers occurred in 1844, the full weight of the State apparatus came down firmly on the side of the coalowners. This taught the miners an important lesson: they saw that, whatever they did, they would still be stigmatised as Chartists. The military would still be used against them whether they nailed Chartist colours to the masthead or not. So after the great strike, a startling change occurred. The leaders became less shy of revealing their political beliefs. In fact, the Miners' Association was transformed into a Chartist union. That is not to say it took orders from O'Connor or subordinated itself to any outside body: the union retained its independence, making up its mind about problems. But no longer did it try to conceal its Chartist sympathies. Every miners' celebration was marked with toasts to W. P. Roberts and Feargus O'Connor. Whereas some trade unions grew hostile to Chartism in the late 1840s—the Steam Engine Makers' Society even

---

[1] A. J. Taylor, "The Miners' Association of Great Britain and Ireland, 1842-48". *Economica*, February 1955, p. 47.

[2] Record on an interview between Sir James Graham and coalowners' representative, 23 June 1844. Buddle Collection, North of England Institute of Mining Engineers.

suspended branches that supported Chartism—no such development happened within the miners' ranks. It may be, as Engels suggests, that leaders of other trade unions harked after respectability, acceptance by the established order, which could not be achieved if their names were linked to a revolutionary movement like Chartism.[1] Miners, on the other hand, were social outcasts, and therefore had nothing to lose from such connections.

The membership of the Miners' Association could be divided into three groups. First, those who had come from Chartism into the union, the Chartists-all-along brigade. Second, those who started with the limited objective of improving miners' conditions but who, in the course of the struggle, had come to see the wider social implications, broadening their horizons to include a critique of the political order. And, third, those miners who identified themselves with Chartism, not because they were particularly concerned about political rights, but as a gesture of defiance, an act of rebellion against their masters.

If the Miners' Association was deeply influenced by Chartism, then the converse is equally true. The Miners helped to influence the Chartist attitude to working-class organisations. Initially, most Chartist leaders had regarded trade unions with hostility, as a diversion from the real task of getting signatures for the petition. They thought it essential not to alienate middle-class support, to make the appeal of Chartism as wide as possible, aims which links with trade unions were likely to prejudice. Such an attitude, prevalent in the early days of Chartism, gradually lost its force as middle-class radicals defected. At the same time, Chartism became a more genuinely working-class movement, directing its message to the ranks of the proletariat:

"From the loom, the anvil and the plough, from the hut, and the garret and the cellar, will come forth—are even now coming forth —the apostles of fraternity and destined saviours of humanity."[2]

[1] Engels explains that "the Chartists' name was in bad odour with the bourgeoisie precisely because theirs had been the most outspoken proletarian party . . . rather than continue the glorious traditions of the Chartists, the 'labour leaders' preferred to deal with their aristocratic friends and be 'respectable', which in England means acting like a bourgeois." (*Marx and Engels on Britain*, p. 467.)

[2] *Northern Star*, 10 November 1849.

2

The General Strike of 1842

THE 1842 general strike, the first not only in Britain but in any capitalist country, played an important formative role in the development
of the trade union movement. For the first time, many thousands of
workers acted together, creating unity, cohesion and a feeling of
common interest that provided a basis for building working-class
organisations. The Potters' Union was born in 1843; likewise the
Cotton Spinners' Association. The Operative Stonemasons' membership swelled from 2,134 in 1842 to 4,861 in 1845. Also in 1845 the
printing trades united the various and growing local bodies under the
title of the National Typographical Association. Meanwhile, the tailors
and shoemakers were in the process of forming national societies. The
powerful United Flint Glass Makers' Society dates from this period,
and by 1846 the Steam-Engine Makers' Society was sufficiently strong
to withstand a legal onslaught that cost them £1,800. It was in this
context of emergent trade unionism that the Miners' Association was
born.

But the general strike itself was a cry of anguish and despair.
Economic conditions had steadily deteriorated. Unemployment was
extensive, in some towns reaching as much as half the population,
while even those fortunate enough to be employed were often on
short-time and subjected to frequent wage cuts. Almost all the working
class was on the verge of starvation. People from all walks of life
recognised that the labouring masses were suffering intensely. When
T. S. Duncombe rose in the House of Commons, on 21 July 1842, to
complain that Parliament was going to rise "when almost the whole
social system was on the eve of dissolution", the Home Secretary, in
reply, had to concede "the existence of great, severe and painful
distress over widespread districts". Describing the situation in the
Birmingham area, a *Manchester Guardian* correspondent stated, "It is
absolutely impossible to convey an idea of the amount of suffering
among the poor for thirty miles around. It is admitted on all sides to be
very great and, if not speedily remedied, will involve all classes in one

common ruin." The Midland miners, the report continues, said "they did not mind being hungry themselves, but when they heard their wives and children crying for bread, it cut them through and they couldn't stand it." They talked about walking to London to see the Queen and the Prime Minister, and thought the sight of a long column, marching six abreast, would be impressive. They believed that affairs in London were in some mysterious way the source of their problems.

A more practical suggestion came from Arthur O'Neill, a Chartist lecturer, who told a West Bromwich strike meeting in May "the whole district should be forthwith canvassed, united and organised to enable them to resist not only the present reduction but also future attempts".[1] His advice, in the short run, proved of no avail. The workers were forced to accept a 10 per cent wage cut and the authorities, helped by the police and military, smashed the rudimentary organisation of the workers. Eighteen leaders were arrested and many workers, unable to get their old jobs back, wandered around the countryside begging.[2]

But this was no more than a dress rehearsal. The strike had only been over a fortnight when between 10,000 and 14,000 iron and coal workers went on strike in the Black Country.[3] Then trouble spread to North Staffordshire, where a notorious Longton coalowner decided to impose another wage reduction: miners were to receive 7d. a day less as well as being expected to hew an extra daily yard of coal. They refused to submit to these new conditions, and were locked out.[4] Men at other pits expressed their solidarity, giving money to the strike fund. A meeting at Hanley, attended by 2,000, passed a resolution that it viewed "with disgust and indignation the attempts of Messrs. Sparrow to reduce the wages of their workmen and pledges itself to support, with all means in their power, in the struggle of might against right".[5] Others quickly became involved in the dispute. At the Earl of Granville's Collieries and Ironworks at Shelton, the employers tried to reduce wages by 6d. a day. The workers objected and the pits became idle. By the end of July, all the North Staffordshire mines were closed and the whole of the Midlands was engulfed. Industry ground to a halt.

A contemporary account, appearing in a journal called *The Union*,[6]

---

[1] *Manchester Guardian*, 20 April 1842. [2] Ibid., 10 May 1842.
[3] Ibid., 22 May 1842. [4] *North Staffordshire Mercury*, 18 June 1842.
[5] *Northern Star*, 25 June 1842. [6] *The Union*, September 1842.

says the strikes "began in the coal mines of Staffordshire. They have since spread over the principal manufacturing districts of England and created a great stagnation in every department of trade and commerce. The strikes of 1834, in England, and of 1837 in Scotland, were very formidable and of long continuance, but they were more local and confined to individual trades. That of 1842 has embraced almost every description of labour in the midland counties."

Then another trouble spot flared up. Millowners at Stalybridge reduced their operatives' wages, telling them that, if they did not like it, they could "go and play a bit". Workers greeted this with defiant cheers and marched to neighbouring factories, closing them down and bringing out the operatives. Soon all Lancashire and Yorkshire was paralysed. In Lanarkshire, too, the pattern was repeated: attempted wage cuts, followed by strikes or lockouts. By August 1842, almost all the industrial parts of Britain with the exception of the London area were involved in industrial strife.

The hardships of the people, already impoverished before the strike began, rapidly grew acute, especially in mining communities where opposition was the staunchest and most prolonged. Surprised by the tenacity shown by the colliers, *The Midland Mining Commission Report* inquired how they could hold out so long. "Their general answer was we did as we could." Some found casual work harvesting, others begged, "there being a general feeling," the *Report* concedes, "that there was justice in some of their demands." By these means, enough was scraped together to eke out a scanty subsistence, usually of potatoes and weak porridge. Even so, "many were nearly 'clammed' (i.e. starved) to death".[1] Thompson Cooper, a Wolverhampton surgeon, said:

> "Many miners were reduced to the greatest distress and almost to actual starvation. I could not but admire the staunchness with which they endured privations, which were very great indeed, though I considered their demands, as regards wages, extortionate. The women, particularly, were exceedingly inveterate in urging their husbands to hold out, saying they would rather live on potatoes and salt than give in. I have known the country for some years, but never saw the people in so distressed a state as they are now in. During the strike they sold everything they could turn into money, and I could take you to dozens of families who are lying on the floor, having no bedstead. Their furniture is nothing, clocks have vanished and everything converted into money."

[1] *The Midland Mining Commission Report*, xxv, 72.

One man told the Commissioners he had "as many pawn tickets as would fill a tea-cup".[1]

A similar picture emerges of conditions in Northern England. "So deep was the distress, so universal the hunger, that they had to eat the dead carcasses of cows dug up after they were buried."[2] Richard Pilling, a Stalybridge mill worker, was responsible for bringing out the workers in Ashton-under-Lyne. He was prosecuted at Lancaster Assizes, along with Feargus O'Connor, for fomenting the general strike. He told the Court how they had been subjected to repeated wage reductions; how his son, dying of consumption, had neither medical attention nor food (except for salted potatoes); and how the many hardships he had endured throughout his working life had prematurely aged him: "Gentlemen, I am somewhere about forty-three years of age. I was asked last night if I were not sixty." Soon after his son's death, Pilling heard that the employers intended to reduce wages by another 25 per cent. In desperation he went among his fellow workers, calling them out on strike.

It was a movement of spontaneous protest. In the textile towns large crowds of gaunt, famished, desperate-looking men wandered about emptying the factories and filling the streets. Armed with bludgeons they did not hesitate to use force to maintain and extend the strike. They pulled plugs from factory boilers, extinguishing the fires, stopping the engines and making an early resumption of work impossible. Thus in Lancashire and Yorkshire the strike became known as the Plug Plot Riots. Frequently the mere threat of violence, the intimidation caused by a sudden entry of thousands of angry strikers into a town, was sufficient to "persuade" the unconvinced that they had better stop working. Where this proved inadequate, as at Bingley in Yorkshire, strikers threatened to burn down any mill that continued activity. It helped to clarify the minds of any who remained recalcitrant. The use of force gave expression to the pent-up frustration and embitterment of the masses, giving them greater cohesion and a sense of their own power.

But miners, on the whole, appear to have opposed the use of violence. They understood it would provide the authorities with a pretext for massive reprisals. So, generally, they only turned to violence in self-defence, once the military had employed force against them, or when their leaders were being arrested. Thus, a *Morning*

---

[1] *The Midland Mining Commission Report*, xxv, 73.
[2] William Beesley, testimony at the Lancaster trial.

Herald report on North Staffordshire stated "the distress exceeds anything known in this district, but there is no disposition to break the
peace".[1] The *Northern Star* said that in the Potteries "they have
continued up to the present moment very peaceable, although it is
stated that 10,000 miners have organised themselves to withstand the
proposed reduction".[2] Self-discipline had replaced the need for
violence. Even when the authorities were provocative, no violence was
used. At the mass meeting at West Bromwich, on 1 August 1842,
attended by 20,000 miners, George Hemmings, the chairman, asked
them to offer no opposition to the cavalry present. Miners "should
conduct themselves in a peaceful and orderly manner," he said. If the
soldiers tried to push their way through the crowd, "they should open
a passage for them and allow them to pass".

The West Bromwich meeting was also significant because it passed
a resolution outlining the miners' demands. These included an eight-
hour day, 4s. a day wages, and an end of the truck system. They wanted
as well to stop the practice of what was known as "buildas" whereby
miners sometimes worked for a quarter or half a day and received only
a pint of beer as remuneration. The demand that "no man should go
down the pit except for a full day's work" was loudly cheered. Nevertheless, colliers were not averse to receiving a pint of beer from their
employers. Indeed, the resolution contained the demand that the coalowners should give them two quarts of beer daily.[3]

In some Midland pits all negotiation encountered an insurmountable
obstacle. Colonel Thorn informed the Home Secretary, on 29 July
1842: "There are several masters who will not inform their men on
what terms they are to be employed, and therefore it is not, I conceive,
fair to expect the colliers will go down into the pits until it is explained
to them what they are to be paid for the work they do."[4]

So, in some places, the colliers had to prepare for a long struggle. It
raised issues which were seriously discussed at the West Bromwich
mass meeting. Joseph Linney of Bilston reminded the strikers that, in
previous struggles, miners from his district had been left to fend for
themselves. Once miners in other districts had won their demands they
had returned to work, leaving Bilston on strike, isolated and alone.
This time Bilston miners had decided unanimously to stand firm until
all demands of the miners had been met, and "he hoped they would
afterwards assist their fellow countrymen to get the People's Charter".

[1] *Morning Herald*, 28 July 1842.   [2] Ibid. 23 July 1842.
[3] *Northern Star*, 6 August 1842.   [4] H.O. (1842), O.S., 260.

This last remark was greeted with cheers and "We will, lads."[1]
Representatives of colliers from Walsall, Wednesbury and Oldbury
then spoke pledging their areas to stand by all decisions reached. Thus
the long string of demands was used to strengthen solidarity and
increase co-ordination of the struggle throughout the South Staffordshire coalfield. The resolution was also printed in leaflet form, to bring
their grievances to the notice of the general public and of miners in
other coalfields. Undoubtedly, this was a sign of growing maturity:
the realisation that it was necessary to sink local differences and
collaborate with miners from other parts of the country was a pre-
condition for the formation of a national colliers' union.

Nevertheless, this step was achieved mainly from an impetus coming
from outside the body of miners themselves. A startling fact was the
extent of their dependency on people from other occupations to formulate their demands and state their case. At the West Bromwich meeting
it seems that only two speeches were actually made by colliers. The
first was from George Hemmings, bringing fraternal greetings from
their fellow miners in North Staffordshire, and the second came from
Joseph Linney, who was also a prominent Chartist and delegate to
the Chartist Convention of 1848.[2]

In a sense, the strike in South Staffordshire represents a turning-point:
never again, in any struggle, were the miners so dependent on outside
help. It took decades of slow progress, of education and cultural
advance, before miners had the requisite training and self-confidence
to make their voice heard throughout the country. In 1842, they had
to rely on the selfless devotion of people like O'Neill, raising money in
Birmingham for the cause and helping until he was sentenced at the
Stafford Assizes to a year's imprisonment for a seditious speech. George
White, too, was courageous. After ten miners had been arrested and
taken to Dudley Town Hall he went there to advise them. At first
refused admission, he eventually wheedled his way in. As he was
talking to the men, a Tory reporter began to read one of his speeches
in a loud voice. Immediately all the coalowners, butties and troops
recognised him. To shouts of "Take him into custody. He's the
ringleader", he was thrown down the Town Hall steps. Undaunted, he

[1] *Northern Star*, 6 August 1842.
[2] Other speakers were: Arthur O'Neill, a university-educated Scottish Chartist, representing the Oldbury colliers and foundrymen; George White, a foundation member of
the Leeds Working Men's Association, who became a physical force Chartist in 1839;
Fraser Pearson a Chartist lecturer; MacIntosh, a Socialist lecturer; Powell, a Chartist
shoe-maker; Griffith and Fairburn, both Chartists.

returned to advise the arrested men, and the police chief vowed, if he made another speech, he would join them.

Sometimes speakers mixed Christianity with their Chartism. At a Dudley strike meeting Samuel Cook, a draper, who was chairman, began proceedings with community hymn singing. The starving miners sung, "Praise God, from whom all blessings flow". After this indiscretion, Cook went on to say "he heard Dudley was a Tory town. He would therefore ask all those who approve of the Tories to hold up their hands. What, not a hand? Then he would ask all those who approve of Chartism and would help to get it, as the only means of protecting their labour, to hold up their hands. An immense forest was then raised, amidst loud cheers."[1]

*   *   *

Since Chartism gave the general strike its political orientation, the type of message conveyed by Chartist orators has significance. John Mason, speaking at Sedgley—"a little Tory-ridden village" in South Staffs, as the *Northern Star* described it—said "the laws of this country were made by the aristocracy; that the people had no voice in the election of their representatives; that the laws which were to be obeyed by all should be made by all; that the individuals who worked the hardest received the least, and that those who worked the least received the most." T. S. Duncombe, giving Parliament this precis of Mason's speech on 25 July 1842, said he personally agreed with every word and protested against Mason's six-month sentence for making it.

But the most memorable speech of the general strike was made by Thomas Cooper, a self-educated worker, to an immense crowd in the Potteries. Standing on Crown Bank, Hanley, he followed the usual practice of taking a Biblical text for his theme. In his autobiography, he describes what happened:

"I took for a text the sixth commandment: 'Thou shalt do no murder'—after we had sung Bramwich's hymn, 'Britannia's sons, though slaves ye be', and I had offered a short prayer.

"I showed how kings, in all ages, had enslaved the people, and spilt their blood in wars of conquest, thus violating the precept, 'Thou shalt do no murder'.

"I described how the conquerors of America had nearly exterminated the native races, and thus violated the precept, 'Thou shalt do no murder'.

[1] *Northern Star*, 15 August 1842. The colliers of the Black Country were enthusiastic Chartists. See *The Working Class Movement in the Black Country 1815–67* by G. Barnsby (Birmingham Univ. M.A. Thesis).

"I recounted how English and French and Spanish and German wars, in modern history, had swollen the list of slaughtered and had violated the precept, 'Thou shalt do no murder'.

"I described our own guilty Colonial rule, and still guiltier rule in Ireland; and asserted that British rulers had most awfully violated the precept, 'Thou shalt do no murder'.

"I showed how the immense taxation we were forced to endure, to enable our rulers to maintain the long and ruinous war with France and Napoleon, had entailed indescribable suffering on millions, and that thus had violated the precept, 'Thou shalt do no murder'.

"I asserted that the imposition of the Bread Tax was a violation of the same precept; and that such was the enactment of the Game Laws; that such was the custom of primogeniture and keeping of land in the possession of the privileged classes; and that such was the enactment of the infamous new Poor Law.

"The general murmur of applause now began to swell into loud cries; and these were mingled with execrations of the authors of the Poor Law. I went on.

"I showed that low wages for wretched agricultural labourers, and the brutal ignorance in which generation after generation were left by the landlords, was a violation of the precept, 'Thou shalt do no murder'.

"I asserted that the attempts to lessen the wages of the toilers underground, who were in hourly and momentary danger of their lives, and to disable them from getting the necessary food for themselves and families, were violations of the precept, 'Thou shalt do no murder'.

"I declared that all who were instrumental in maintaining the system of labour which reduced poor stockingers to the starvation I had witnessed in Leicester, and which was witnessed among the poor handloom weavers of Lancashire, and poor nailmakers of the Black Country, were violating the precept, 'Thou shall do no murder'.

"And now the multitude shouted; and their looks told of vengeance—but I went on, for I felt as if I could die on the spot in fulfilling a great duty—the exposure of human wrong and consequent human suffering. My strength was great at that time, and my voice could be heard, like the peal of a trumpet, even on the verge of a crowd composed of thousands."[1]

At the end of the meeting he announced another at nine o'clock next morning, when he would address the striking miners. Eight thousand

[1] *The Life of Thomas Cooper, written by himself*, pp. 271–2.

were present. John Richards, then seventy years old, a member of the first Convention and the most prominent Chartist in the Potteries, moved the resolution "that all labour cease until the People's Charter becomes the law of the land". "When I put the resolution to the crowd," says Cooper, "all hands seemed to be held up for it, and not one hand was held up when I said, 'On the contrary!'" The crowd then marched to Longton, bringing out on their way the few potters who still remained at work.

Cooper was torn between conflicting duties: to stay in the Potteries to lead the struggle there or to go to Manchester, where a National Assembly of Chartists was arranged for 16 August. Eventually, he adopted the latter course. At the Executive, he seconded a resolution, moved by M'Douall, pledging the Chartist Movement to support and extend the strike. A manifesto, written by M'Douall, was drawn up and issued:

"Nature, God and reason, have condemned the inequality, and in the thunders of a people's voice it must perish for ever. He knows that labour, the real property of society, the sole origin of accumulated property, the first cause of all national wealth, and the only supporter, defender, and contributor to the greatness of our country, is not possessed of the same legal protection which is given to those lifeless effects, the houses, ships, and machinery which labour alone have created. He knows that if labour has no protection wages cannot be upheld, nor in the slightest degree regulated until every workman of 21 years of age and of sane mind is on the same political level as the employer. He knows that the Charter would remove, by universal will and universal suffrage, the heavy load of taxes which now crush the existence of the labourer, and cripple the efforts of commerce; that it would give cheap government as well as cheap food, high wages as well as low taxes, bring happiness to the hearth-stone plenty of the table, protection to the old, education to the young, permanent prosperity to the country, long-continued protective political power to labour, and peace, blessed peace, to exhausted humanity and approving nations; therefore it is that we have solemnly sworn, and one and all declared, that the golden opportunity now within our grasp shall not pass away fruitless, that the chance of centuries afforded to us by a wise and all-seeing God, shall not be lost; but that we do now universally resolve never to resume labour until labour's grievances are destroyed, and protection assured to ourselves, our suffering wives, and helpless children, by the enactment of the People's Charter."

*   *   *

Mass revolt combined with revolutionary ideas constituted a formidable challenge to the established order. Sir James Graham, the Home Secretary, was in charge of dealing with the disturbances. Throughout, his central aims appear to have been to maintain law and order; defend private property; and use force in such a way as to demoralise and coerce the strikers. But the State apparatus was a ramshackle affair, ill-suited for dealing with civil commotions of 1842 dimensions. Lord Lieutenants, responsible in the shires for maintaining law and order, were in many cases decrepit nobles, in normal times decorative on ceremonial occasions but in times of emergency complete incompetents. Under them, at grass roots level, was the numerically inadequate police force. In Airdrie, a typical turbulent Scottish town, one superintendent and four constables attempted to control a mining community which, with surrounding areas, numbered 33,000 people. As James Lawson, the Airdrie superintendent, later said:

"In many cases, we have been obliged to let prisoners go, on account of the smallness of our numbers, and frequently assaults have been committed on ourselves . . . within the last three years, it has twice occurred that large mobs have had things all their own way in this town. On the last occasion they attempted to set fire to a house in which the constables had got some prisoners in custody; they were colliers who had been arrested for desertion of service. The rioters were colliers also, some of them residing in the town, but mostly from Dundyvan and Coatbridge, and other villages. The prisoners were rescued."[1]

A similar situation existed in other towns. The Midland Mining Commission reports that the total police force for the whole of Staffordshire was only 184. Consequently citizens likely to remain loyal to the powers-that-be were enlisted as special constables during the emergency.[2] In the eyes of South Staffordshire Chartists and miners, it was a hilarious spectacle when "the courageous conservators of the peace, with fear and trembling, ordered out the troops. Of course, meaning thereby a pretty considerable quantity of huge, ill-shapen country butchers, farmers and pot-bellied shopkeepers, mounted on miserable carthorses."[3] Even two men driving a manure cart were pressed into service.

[1] *The State of the Population of Mining Districts*, 1844, p. 19.
[2] Some special policemen's loyalty was highly dubious: William Beesley was one of them. He represented the police at the Manchester meeting of Trades.
[3] *Northern Star*, 13 August 1842.

The inadequacy of the police force meant it was impossible to have a graduated deterrent. When the authorities were confronted with a challenge they were inevitably pushed into taking the most extreme counter-measures. For example, it was reported that four sheep were stolen and a field of potatoes on an estate at Drumpeller "cleared without the customary digging operations". So the Sheriff of Lanarkshire proclaimed: "A military force, composed of cavalry and infantry, *to be supported, if necessary, by artillery,* will be forthwith stationed at Airdrie and Coatbridge."

Scottish and English miners alike indulged in poaching and stealing of vegetables. As the *Manchester Guardian* observed, "the colliers would seem to be abed the greater part of the day and bestir themselves at night to a very bad purpose". So the authorities, intent on a policy of starving strikers into submission, sought to cut off their food supplies. In Cheshire, a special mounted force, centred on Nether Knutsford, patrolled the country charged to ensure that information about attacks on farms should be quickly transmitted to the military. In Staffordshire, farmers and their labourers, enlisted as special constables, augmenting the regular force. At least, they prevented large gangs, of between twenty and fifty men, from stealing and begging in country districts, a feature that characterised the early stages of the strike.

It was these counter-moves that aroused the colliers' anger. Until then, things had remained peaceful. Granted in many mining communities it had become fashionable to catch a blackleg and duck him in the nearest pond—"to convince him of the impropriety of his conduct"; but no serious disorders occurred.[1] The first riot in North Staffordshire, scene of the most destructive rioting, was occasioned by the arrest on 6 August of three colliers for begging. A large crowd, hearing of their imprisonment, surged through Burslem. Quickly they broke into the police station, released the men, and went on to destroy all the windows of the Town Hall, where the magistrates' Court met. A second riot, which lasted two days, happened after Thomas Cooper's speech at Crown Bank on 15 August. The Home Secretary had written to magistrates throughout the country, telling them to suppress all large meetings, regardless of their character; let the troops "act with vigour and without parley", he said. So Sneyd, a local magistrate and coalowner, was merely carrying out his instruc-

---

[1] A slight variation of this procedure occurred when two men who had been working at Lord Granville's pits at Shelton were ducked in a cesspool. (*North Staffordshire Mercury*, 16 July 1842.)

tions when he marched into Hanley, at the head of a body of cavalry and infantry, to tell the crowds to disperse. He arrived as another coal-owner, Ridgway, was holding a meeting of his own to hear about the workers' grievances and to counsel moderation. An enlightened and well-respected master, Ridgway had abolished the truck system at his Ubberley pits, near Hanley. He paid high wages, had instituted a sick club for his workmen and subscribed to the local infirmary on their behalf. Being popular with the men, Ridgway requested the right to continue the meeting to conciliate. But Sneyd read the Riot Act—and nearly 300 were clamped in prison.

Next day Thomas Powys, a Burslem magistrate and deputy lord lieutenant of the county, ordered troops to fire on a procession of strikers in Burslem market square. One was killed and many wounded. Incensed, a crowd of 500 set off to retaliate by burning Powys' house. The whole situation got out of hand. The agent of Lord Granville's pits had his house pillaged and office burnt; the Rev. Aitken's house was plundered and set alight; Squire Allen's house was partly destroyed, his money stolen and his wine drunk. Many other acts of vandalism and retribution were done: coalowners, clergy and magistrates were singled out for special attention.

Queen Victoria herself was worried. She wrote to Sir Robert Peel, the Prime Minister, that "she is surprised at the little (or no) opposition to the dreadful riots in the Potteries . . . at the passiveness of the troops . . . they ought to act, and these meetings ought to be prevented . . . everything ought to be done to apprehend Cooper and all the delegates at Manchester."[1] The Queen remained in communication with the Prime Minister and Home Secretary during the riots. In his book, *Public Order in the Age of the Chartists*, Mr. F. C. Mather says, "The weight of Queen Victoria's influence was thrown on the side of energetic repression."

The Queen's orders were carried out with savage vengeance. For burning down the Rev. Dr. Vale's house—he was a clergyman and a coalowner—six men were transported for twenty-one years each and, with sentences passed on others for complicity in the same offence, a total of 189 years' imprisonment were imposed. "Measured in terms of human suffering," says Dr. Wearmouth, "the Rev. Dr. Vale had lived in a most costly house." For pillaging and burning the Rev. Aitken's home, terms of imprisonment totalling ninety-three years

---

[1] Peel papers, British Museum. Quoted F. C. Mather, *Public Order in the Age of the Chartists*, p. 33.

were imposed. All told, in other parts of the country as well as Stafford-shire, more than 1,000 arrests were made and 749 were imprisoned. Many who had nothing to do with the riots received harsh sentences; to have spoken at a public meeting was sometimes a sufficient cause for a person to be arrested.

The repression resulted in many personal tragedies. Take the case of Joseph Capper, a well-known Chartist and Methodist local preacher; he had played no part in the riots, yet they still arrested him. He practised civil disobedience and refused to get in the police-wagon. So the police had to carry him, much to the disgust of the crowd, who sympathised with the harmless old man. He was sentenced to two years' imprisonment for rioting. After serving six months, he faced fresh charges—conspiracy and sedition—and the *North Staffordshire Mercury*, of 25 March 1843, describes Capper's condition at his second trial: "The prison diet had made his inside so raw that at one time he thought he should have died. . . . During the first day or two he was often in tears and was much affected when he caught sight of his relations or friends whom he had not seen since his incarceration. It was a very touching scene to see the old man with his children and grand-children around him."

Thomas Cooper, tried with Capper, was made of sterner stuff. Originally arrested in August 1842 in Leicester, where he was leader of the Shakespearean Chartists, he was taken to Hanley, and from thence to Newcastle-under-Lyme, under an escort of sixteen soldiers with fixed bayonets. Committed to Stafford jail, he spent his time awaiting trial reciting poems to himself. He knew the whole of *Paradise Lost*, *Hamlet* and many other works. Charged with inciting the Potteries riots, Cooper made what the *Northern Star* described as a "most soul-stirring and thrilling defence".[1] He declared himself a Christian, in the fullest sense of the word, a lover of peace, an enemy of drunkenness, outrage and burning. The Court acquitted him. At his second trial, facing charges of conspiracy and sedition, he was not so fortunate. Again he conducted his own defence with unbounded enthusiasm and, while awaiting the verdict, assured friends, "the 10-day trial had only made him eager to be tried again". However, he was sentenced to two years' imprisonment. In jail, his passion with self-education remained undimmed. He read theological works and the scriptures in nine languages, as well as writing, "The Purgatory of Suicides".

In 1850, Cooper had the satisfaction to hear that Earl Talbot, the

---

[1] *Northern Star*, 15 October 1842.

Lord Lieutenant of Staffordshire, had addressed a public meeting at which a riot ensued. In an open letter to the noble Earl, he wrote:

"Unwarned by the frequent social convulsions of Staffordshire during the past few years, you believed that the numerous hangings had intimidated the people or that the new immense fortified gaol overawed them. You were deceived. . . .

The bread-taxing propensities of yourself and your co-magnates were thwarted, your hirelings were thoroughly beaten, and as for *you*—you were treated as if the shoemakers believed a lord was worse than live lumber. They rivalled each other in visiting your right honourable person most vigorously in the very quarter where the visitation would inflict the greatest indignity. They pelted you, at last out of town.

It seems, then, that you can cause riots in Staffordshire. It has now come to be your turn. . . .

A few poor men addressed the Staffordshire people seven years ago, on their grievances, and a riot took place—when those who delivered the addresses, although they had no share either in plotting or enacting the violence—were imprisoned or transported. You can be permitted to raise violence and to 'floor' your men in the open street (for they say you fist it valiantly) and you are to escape simply with black eyes and a little kicking. By my fay, shares are not fairly dealt in this world."[1]

About the unfairness of the administration of the law many liberals and humanitarians agreed with Cooper in 1842–3. They were appalled by the severity with which the authorities dealt with anybody remotely connected with the disturbances. However, from the government's viewpoint, the draconic punishments meted out had an important function. It was necessary to teach the agitators a lesson; if it were made particularly painful, then they would not do it again.

But, besides disturbing a section of the middle class, the government's retaliatory actions had a profound effect on the working class, and not entirely in the way the government anticipated. It helped to make workers discard their narrow mental horizons; a bond of suffering united them with their brothers in other parts of the country. Thus, the repression helped to develop a feeling of class consciousness. This was especially true among miners. They bore the brunt of the strike itself and of the subsequent jail sentences. As a result, when miners heard of their fellow miners, from other coalfields, being

[1] *Cooper's Journal*, February 1850.

arrested and imprisoned, they did not regard it as a matter of no concern to themselves. They held protest meetings, collected money for the victims, and—crucially important for the formation of the Miners' Association—began to think of themselves as a separate and distinct entity in society.

Moreover, many workers thought the general strike had not been altogether a failure. In Tipton, colliers' wages were reduced from 3s. 6d. to 3s. a day. But in Oldbury and the rest of the South Staffordshire coalfield the employers' attempt to reduce wages was effectively resisted. At a meeting with Earl Dartmouth and their master at West Bromwich in September, miners received the assurance that the truck and "buildas" systems would gradually be eliminated.[1] Spurious as this promise later proved to be, it still gave the colliers a sense of satisfaction. Their efforts had not been in vain. Similarly in North Staffordshire wages, on the whole, were maintained at the pre-strike level, and the miners were far from cowed into submission. "A finger raised would draw hundreds out of the pits where work had been resumed. The explosive elements in the industrial atmosphere came from the mines and not from the potbanks." In the following year, when the potters published The Potters' Examiner, it was conceded that the workers had benefited from the general strike.

From the situation in Lancashire the same conclusion could be drawn. At his trial, Richard Pilling told the Court "that if it had not been for the late struggle, I firmly believe thousands would have starved to death". Many Ashton employers re-opened their mills and withdrew the wage-cuts. The Manchester correspondent of the North of England Magazine admitted that the Bolton spinners had won an increase, while most workers had resumed work at their previous rates of pay and in a few instances with a trifling reduction.[2]

The final result of the general strike was far from what the employers anticipated. They found themselves unable to impose the large-scale wage reductions—sometimes as much as 25 per cent—that they had originally intended. Inescapably, workers drew the lesson that by their efforts and through their strike they had gained at least a partial victory. What could not be achieved if they had an organisation on a sound and permanent basis? Having gained a crumb of comfort from class action, they could see the loaf nearly within their grasp. A powerful impetus was given towards the creation of trade unions.

[1] Staffordshire Advertiser, 10 September 1842.
[2] North of England Magazine, 26 September 1842.

This could only be done if unions avoided brushes with the law. Hence, not surprisingly, the Miners' Association remained pre-occupied with the need for strict legality in all its actions. Never again did it want to see a union smashed, its leaders arrested and its members hounded because of some infringement of the law. They realised that the authorities, hostile anyway, would be ever vigilant, looking for some loophole which they could use. The answer was to employ the utmost care and discretion. Sir James Graham's repression cruelly taught them that lesson.

*   *   *

Besides having a seminal influence on trade unions, the general strike also changed the direction and orientation of Chartism. Until then, some Chartists, especially among its middle-class leaders, were hostile to trade unions. They regarded them as a diversion from the real struggle; all efforts should be channelled into campaigning for the Charter. To this end the maximum unity was required, and this necessarily involved making an appeal to respectable citizenry, who would be alienated if the movement became closely associated with trade unions and strikes. Of course, many of the working-class Chartists never held this position: to them, economic and political struggles for better conditions were inseparable. During the general strike these people, without any prodding, aligned themselves with the masses because they themselves were part of the masses. Contemporary newspaper and official reports all emphasise the role Chartists played in giving the strike, at local level, force and direction. But this leadership came from below, not from the top of the Chartist Movement.

As early as June, before the strike had begun, a meeting of workers at Preston had decided to convene a conference at Colne on 3 July. The intention was to unite Chartists and trade unionists. A permanent committee was to be formed so "that the working class (could) lay all their grievances through this body before the nation and all their appeals to Government". The *Northern Star* of 2 July contained a report of Feargus O'Connor holding a big demonstration at Colne. In the same issue a letter from William Beesley, as secretary of the North Lancs area, officially advised all Chartists not to attend the Colne conference. As Beesley was always very much influenced by O'Connor, it seems probable that he was following O'Connor's advice when he said the proposed permanent committee "would create division and discontent". He reminded them that the Chartists had "just elected an

Executive for the government of our agitation"; a new body would try to usurp its functions. The South Lancashire Chartists unanimously adopted the same position and agreed to boycott the Colne conference.

Yet, a month later, in the midst of the general strike, the Chartists made a complete *volte face*. A trade union conference, very much on the same lines as that envisaged at Colne, was held in Manchester with their blessing. From believing that such a conference should do nothing, they now believed it should do everything. The Chartist executive never sought to organise the strike. It simply limited itself to issuing a manifesto supporting the cessation of labour until the Charter was gained. It threw back responsibility for the vital task of organising the strike to the trade unions, who had no central body to accomplish this all-important end.

Confusion reigned in the top echelons of the Chartist Movement. Only M'Douall, and perhaps Cooper, had any conception of what was necessary in a revolutionary situation. Others, like O'Connor, vacillated, at one time supporting the strike, at another time opposing it. Julian Harney, regarded as the most extreme leader, was at least consistent: he was against the strike. So was the Rev. W. Hill, editor of the *Northern Star*. He described it "as the wasting overflow of a corrupt fountain". In an editorial he said, "We regret that the Chartist Movement should have been mixed up with the strike. We fear it will eventually be found to have served the purpose of the enemy."[1]

In the aftermath of the strike Chartism was affected by demoralisation, its leaders imprisoned, its forces scattered, its objectives unattained. No wonder many deserted. But these were mainly middle-class supporters; working-class supporters, like Dixon and Brophy, who had addressed many meetings during the strike, remained staunch. For them, a new road had been opened. They saw in the development of the labour movement a fresh way of achieving their objectives, and gradually they were able to transform the whole outlook of the Chartist Movement until it, too, strove to build up the trade unions.

This change is, perhaps, best shown by the *Northern Star*. It changed its name to the *Northern Star and National Trades Journal*. At the same time, its content altered. It became a genuine working-class organ, devoting much more space to trade union affairs. The circulation among miners can be gauged from the fact that some district committees of the union still sent their reports to the *Northern Star* rather than the *Miners' Advocate*. Repeated appeals had to be made, even when

[1] *Northern Star*, 20 August 1842.

the *Miners' Advocate* had reached a 10,000 circulation, for miners to support their own union paper rather than any other. Active unionists could evidently be presumed to read the *Northern Star*.[1]

Like the *Northern Star*, some prominent Chartists changed dramatically after the general strike. The most important of these, from the miners' standpoint, was W. P. Roberts. He was, at one time, under the influence of Sturge and accused of wanting to dilute the Charter's principles. In February 1842, Roberts talked of the need to pay attention to the conditions of the middle class. A year later, however, he was to be too busy devoting all his attention to the conditions of the working class ever to worry about this earlier preoccupation again. What wrought this transformation in Roberts? We know he suffered in prison and when he came out he always had sympathy for the oppressed. Probably it was the jail sentences inflicted after the strike that aroused his interest in miners, both those in prison and those outside. He acted as the legal adviser to Cooper at his Stafford trials. There he must have seen the retribution inflicted by Judge Tindall on the workers. As the *Staffordshire Examiner* said, anybody must have a very cold heart who "is not deeply moved by the family bereavements which the Special Commission has spread among us". Roberts could be accused of many things, but never of having a cold heart.[2]

Feargus O'Connor's outlook also changed. After 1842 his interest in trade unions greatly increased. He advised his followers to join them and do everything to promote their growth. He sought, as well, to develop a feeling of class solidarity as an antidote to the sectarian approach prevalent in the craft unions:

"By union, and by union alone, can the 'poor oppressed' contend against the injustice of the 'rich oppressor'. And let not the printers, if well paid, suppose that any injustice against the tailors, if badly paid, will not sooner or later come home to their own doors! Let

[1] A circular to the membership of the Association sent by the Executive on 1 March 1844, refers to an article in the *Northern Star*, and goes on "which you will no doubt have seen".

[2] W. P. Roberts was the nephew of Sir Nicolas Tindall, the Lord Chief Justice. Three years previously Tindall presided over John Frost's trial, who was sentened to death, later commuted to transportation for life. On that occasion, Roberts tried to help Frost. Although in trouble himself—he was out on bail pending his own trial for the Trowbridge disturbances—Roberts journeyed to South Wales. He was arrested at Blackwood in the company of two of Frost's daughters, "disguised as servants". Brought before the same magistrates court that was conducting the preliminary hearing of Frost's case, Roberts was dismissed. (David Williams, *John Frost*, p. 250.) Roberts also defended Chartists from Bath implicated in the Newport uprising. (See *Bath and Cheltenham Gazette*, 19 November 1839, *Bath Chronicle*, 14 November 1839, quoted in R. S. Neale's thesis, *Class and Ideology in Bath 1800–1850*.)

not the spinners, if better paid than the handloom weavers, lose sight of the fact that a 'surplus' of handloom weavers will constitute a reservoir for the masters to fall back upon, as a means of reducing the wages of the spinners. Let not the bricklayers imagine that a reduction in the wages of their labourers will not be followed by a reduction in their own wages. A blow successfully struck at one order of labour will as successfully wound all others."

Utterances such as these made O'Connor popular with the labouring masses. He was accepted as the champion of the horny hands and the fustian jackets. But their attempts to build unions "to contend against the injustice of the 'rich oppressor'" frequently ended in failure; only in the 1890s, with the general unions, did the labourers finally become organised. In the 1840s many valiant yet abortive attempts were made. However historians, such as the Webbs, have tended to concentrate their attention on the craft unions, which were more stable and enduring. Chartism, with its pseudo-revolutionary doctrines, was anathema to craft unions, striving for a respectable position in the established order. Its strength lay among the labourers, and consequently historians have usually underestimated the links between Chartism and trade unions. Indeed, they have sometimes regarded them as conflicting movements. A typical judgment comes from Mr. A. R. Schoyen:

"A more lasting consequence of the General Strike of 1842 was the turning away of trade unionists from Chartism. . . . (They)blamed the formal Chartist leadership for a course of action which it did not initiate, and a powerful element of Chartist strength fell away."[1]

This, however, suggests that Chartism and the trade unions were competing rather than complementary forces. It is our contention that the significance of 1842 was that it merely transformed a movement of protest, placing the emphasis on industrial not political action.[2]

We are inclined to agree with the verdict of Frederick Engels. He considered the main result of the general strike "was the decisive separation of the proletariat from the bourgeosie". The result of the turbulence and violence of the strike was that the respectable middle classes dissociated themselves from Chartism. Sturge established his rival, more moderate, organisation in January 1843. "From this moment," declared Engels, "Chartism was purely a working-man's cause, freed from all bourgeois elements." He noted the difference this

---

[1] A. R. Schoyen, *The Chartist Challenge*, p. 118.
[2] See Chapter 15, Politics and the Union.

made: "The 'knife and fork' question of the preacher Stephens was a truth for a part of the Chartists only in 1838; it is a truth for all of them in 1845."

So, the general strike of 1842 played a dual role: it helped to create the conditions for the growth of trade unions like the Miners' Association and, at the same time, it made Chartism more favourable, more responsive, more helpful to the trade unions than it would otherwise have been.

3

Social and Industrial Conditions

THROUGHOUT the first half of the nineteenth century a growing interest was taken in the miners and their problems. This was, in part, due to the increasing number of miners. They constituted a greater proportion of the labour force. They lived, moreover, in tightly-knit communities with a strong sense of solidarity. In times of trouble they acted together, often violently. Throughout the eighteenth century onwards Home Office files contain references to troops being used to quell strikes, riots and civil commotions in mining districts. The colliers constituted a threat to the social order.

Yet it was not merely self-preservation that caused members of the upper classes to be concerned about the miners' lot. Social reformers, like Lord Shaftesbury, were shocked by what they discovered. They sought to publicise the facts of the brutality and degradation of the collier's existence as a step towards the achievement of legislation. But even many politicians who considered it improper, or futile, for Parliament to regulate conditions in the pits, still thought the miners were pitifully treated. At the height of the general strike the Home Secretary, Sir James Graham, told Talbot, Lord Lieutenant of Staffordshire, "to faithfully represent the Government by marking a kind of sympathy with the feeling and just claims of workmen".[1] Indeed, Sir Robert Peel, the Prime Minister, was sufficiently convinced of the colliers' grievances as to institute an official enquiry.[2] While remaining trapped by the limitations of a *laissez faire* outlook, dubious of the efficacy of State action, Sir Robert still believed that factual reports could play an important role by changing the general climate of opinion. He wrote to the Home Secretary about "the practical grievances . . . the employed have just reason to complain", and averred that "what the law cannot effect, perhaps exposure might".

---

[1] 25 August 1842. H.O. 79/4.
[2] When the Report—*The Midlands Mining Commission*—was published, W. P. Roberts reviewed it at length in his *Miners' Magazine*. He conceded that it had been written "in a fair spirit", that most of it was accurate, and that it only had a slight bias to the coal-owners.

The eighteen-forties witnessed an unparalleled volume of documents describing coal-mining conditions. They shocked the public conscience, and led to a clamour for something to be done to eradicate the worst evils. However, this exposure, which Sir Robert and others favoured, was a two-edged weapon: it did not have an effect only among the general public but also among the mining communities. Even the least class-conscious miner was made to realise that his conditions were appalling and that something should be done about them. So why should not he, along with his work-mates, try to improve their conditions themselves? The publicity stimulated trade unionism. It gave miners a feeling of self-confidence, of justice in their demands, and, at the same time, helped to jog them out of their local preoccupations, so giving them a concern about mining conditions throughout the country. This transformation of mental outlook—viewing problems from a national rather than local standpoint—was a prerequisite for the forming of a national trade union.

Undoubtedly, the greatest furore was caused by the publication of the First Report of the Commission on Children and Young Persons in 1842. It revealed that boys were employed in every coalfield, but girls were used mainly in Lancashire, Cheshire, Yorkshire, South Wales and Scotland. Children were employed as trappers, to open and shut the doors necessary to ventilate the mine; as fillers, to load the tubs and skips after the men had hewn the coal; and as pushers (or hurriers) to push the tubs from the coal-face to the foot of the shaft.[1] Instead of pushing, some pits used another method: "A girdle is put round the naked waist, to which a chain from the carriage is hooked and passed between the legs, and the boys crawl on their hands and knees, drawing the carriage after them."[2] Women and girls were likewise employed. In the West Riding, the Report described girl pushers:

"Chained, belted, harnessed like dogs in a go-cart, black, saturated with wet, and more than half naked—crawling upon their hands and feet, and dragging their heavy loads behind them—they present an appearance indescribably disgusting and unnatural."[3]

Trappers were usually between the ages of five and eight. They generally sat in a hole near the door, at the pit-bottom, opening and shutting it by means of a piece of string.

[1] John Monk Forster, a Wigan collier, stated in his book, *Children of Darkness*, that boys often used their heads to push the tubs and consequently lost their hair. He himself was bald at the front of his head by the age of twelve.
[2] Children's Employment Commission, First report, *Mines*, 1842, p. 67.
[3] Ibid., p. 67.

"The poor little fellow has no exertion to keep his body in warmth; the place where he is stationed is cold and often damp, and the blood in his veins is almost frozen from want of exertion; physical and mental development, necessary in youth, needs exercise; and the result is an early grave, a debilitated frame and an impaired intellect. . . ."[1]

They were the first down in the morning and the last out at night. Most of the time they were in the dark, but sometimes a kindly collier would give them a bit of candle. A girl of eight said:

"I'm a trapper in the Gamber Pit. I have to trap without a light, and I'm scared. I go at four and sometimes half-past three in the morning and come out at five and half-past. I never go to sleep. Sometimes I sing when I've light, but not in the dark: I dare not sing then."[2]

Such conditions inevitably had a psychological effect on some children. One sub-commissioner reported: "I can never forget the first unfortunate creature (of this class) that I met with: it was a boy of eight years old, who looked at me as I passed through with an expression of countenance most abject and idiotic—like a thing, a creeping thing peculiar to the place."[3] At Halifax a sub-commissioner met a boy crying and bleeding from a gashed cheek. His master explained "that the child was one of the slow ones, who would only move when he saw blood, and that by throwing a piece of coal at him for that purpose he had accomplished his object, and that he often adopted the like means."[4] In Lancashire the customary way of punishing pit-boys and girls was "purring", a local term used to describe a kicking administered in heavy clogs. The 1842 Report confirmed the findings of an earlier investigation: Lancashire pit-lads "seldom slept with a whole skin".[5]

Children began to work at an early age. A worker in the West Riding told the commissioners he took his child to the mine before he was three years old. "When the child was exhausted, it was carried home, stripped, and put to bed."[6] The Report also mentions a three-year-old who was forced to follow his father to a Halifax pit "to hold the candle, and when exhausted with fatigue was cradled upon the

[1] Reynolds' Political Instructor, 2 March 1850. "Voice from the Coal Mines", by "One Who Has Suffered".
[2] Children's Employment Commission, p. 71.
[3] Ibid. First Report, Mines, 1842, p. 75.
[4] Ibid. p. 130.
[5] Ibid.   [6] Ibid., p. 12.

coals until his return at night". [1] In most places, however, children went down at the age of four or five. Their working hours ranged from twelve to eighteen. Some received no pay, but most received between 2s. 6d. and 3s., according to age. But the Report's revelations on child labour were not universally accepted. Lord Londonderry, a half-brother to Lord Castlereagh and a large coalowner in Durham, said the Commissioners were not persons of the calibre required to give an accurate report. Their methods were "underhand" and their "disgusting pictorial illustrations" had given a false impression:

"Their instructions were to examine the children themselves, and the mode in which they collected their evidence—communicating with artful boys and ignorant girls, and putting questions in a manner which in many cases seemed to suggest the answer, was anything but a fair and impartial mode."

Whereas the Report said that "were it not for the passing and repassing of the coal-carriages" a trapper's existence would "amount to solitary confinement of the worst order", Lord Londonderry gave the House of Lords a different impression. Instead of depicting the trappers cringing in total blackness for long hours, His Lordship thought they had an idyllic existence:

"The trapper is generally cheerful and contented and to be found, like other children of his age, occupied with some childish amusement—as cutting sticks, making models of windmills, wagons, etc., and frequently in drawing figures with chalk on his door, modelling figures of men and animals in clay, etc."

As J. L. and Barbara Hammond comment, "Lord Londonderry's mines must have resembled the caves of Altamira whose decorated walls have preserved the imaginations of primitive man for the delight and mystification of later ages." [2]

*　　　　*　　　　*

The 1842 Report also denounced the employment of women in the pits. It cites cases of women and men, completely naked, working side by side; examples of immorality in mines; and women who actually gave birth while underground. For instance, Betty Wardle told the Commissioners:

"I have worked in a pit since I was six years old, I have four children,

[1] Ibid., p. 14.
[2] J. L. and Barbara Hammond, Lord Shaftesbury, pp. 77-8.

D

two of them were born while I worked in the pit. I have worked in the pit whilst I was in the family way. I had a child born in the pits, and I brought it up the pit shaft in my skirt; it was born the day after I were married."[1]

Matthew Lindley, of Barnsley, admitted he had "worked a great deal where girls were employed. . . . I have had children by them myself, and frequently had connexion with them in the pits."[2] The Report states that many women as a result of their employment became crooked and deformed. They became as rough and uncouth as the men, fighting and swearing like them. Many bastards were born in colliery villages. All this confirmed the findings of a previous inquiry:

"Mr. Binney says that he has visited many collieries in Lancashire and Cheshire, and he finds the moral and intellectual condition of working colliers in a much worse state where females are employed in mines than in those parts where the proprietors will not allow them to work in their pits."

Mr Binney went on to complain that:

"The disgusting nature of the employment of these poor creatures was bad enough in itself, but to hear the awful swearing, obscene conversation and filthy songs would lead any person to believe that he was in a land of savages rather than in civilised England."[3]

What the Commissioners found when they investigated female employment in mines shocked and revolted them. But they would have been better prepared for what shocked their upper-class morality most if they had been more in touch with conditions generally prevailing among the working class. As a coalowner pointed out, it was customary for whole families to live in one room in a situation which made it impossible to preserve privacy or decorum: "Let us remember that these poor people have passed the night in small apartments, in which the father, mother, adult brothers and sisters have slept and dressed in company.'[4] As this state of affairs was quite common in other sections of the working class, besides miners, he felt the Report placed undue emphasis on the fact that men and women sometimes worked underground in various stages of undress. The coalowner also contended there was no evidence for maintaining that

[1] Children's Employment Commission, First Report, 1842, p. 27.
[2] Ibid., p. 32.   [3] Appendix to the 7th Report on Public Petitions, pp. 88–90.
[4] Manchester Guardian, 15 June 1842.

immorality was greater among miners than other types of workers.

In reality, naked exploitation was a greater evil than naked bodies. Women were a source of cheap labour. They could be made to work for long hours for little pay. At the Earl of Balcarres' pits, near Wigan, for instance, they received one penny for every three tons of coal they drew to the surface.[1]

*   *   *

The most telling indictment of the Report—a thing that applied equally to men, women and children—concerned the appalling conditions underground. As the century progressed these grew worse, because it became necessary to go deeper and deeper to get the coal. Ventilation and safety precautions failed to keep pace with the expansion of the industry. The result was a catalogue of accidents and ill-health. "Great numbers employed in the labour of the coal mines suffer from loss of appetite, pains in the stomach, nausea, and chronic pains in the back." Many were ruptured while others suffered from tuberculosis. No less painful were the prevalent complaints of rheumatism and inflammation of the joints. "While some miners were capable of prodigious muscular exertion," the Report observed, "in a few years their strength diminishes and many lose their robust appearance; these then became pallid . . . short of breath, sometimes crooked and crippled."[2] Too often the miner was "a disabled man with the marks of old age upon him when other men were scarcely past their prime." An assistant commissioner said that it did not surprise him to be told that "old age comes prematurely upon them and that they were mashed up at 40 or 45; indeed the careworn countenances, grey hair and furrowed brows of those I met with at that age were sufficient indications of the fact."[3] One doctor, accustomed to treating miners, declared he knew "of no old miners".

Confirmation for this view came from David Swallow, who made his own personal investigation in eleven Fifeshire pits. One collier there told him, "We have some men amongst us that have not arrived at 40 years of age, with constitutions completely shattered and quite unable to work where there is not a good current of air." Swallow's statistics showed the work was so exacting no man over sixty years of age worked in any of the eleven pits.

[1] *Manchester Guardian*, 22 July 1843.
[2] Ibid., p. 194.   [3] Ibid., p. 63.

Number of workmen
Below

20 years	20–30 yrs	30–40 yrs	40–50 yrs	50–60 yrs	60 +
303	215	172	18	10	0

Swallow also discovered that forty men who had worked in those collieries had been disabled and that 137 women living in the area had been married to men who had died in pit accidents.[1]

Casualties in the Northumberland and Durham coalfields are listed in William Mitchell's pamphlet, *What do the Pitmen Want?* Giving the name of each colliery and the number of lives lost, he calculated that 1,446 miners had been killed in the two counties in 1800–40.

Generally human life was regarded as a cheap commodity, easily expendable. Thus owners frequently required men to work in dangerous seams where roof-falls and explosions were likely. When accidents occurred, employers sometimes exhibited a contempt for their workmen's lives. At Seaton Delaval miners were expected to work in a colliery where an explosion had occurred and which still remained on fire. At Wingate Grange, pitmen were expected to descend the shaft using the same winding rope that had already broken once.[2] At Sholton Moor pit a man and a horse were injured. The underviewer told the rescue team to leave the man and concentrate their efforts on saving the more valuable horse.[3] At Winstanley, after women had been excluded from the pits under the 1842 Act, they were used as enginedrivers. They ran the coal from the colliery to Wigan pier. On one occasion a small child was knocked down by the train and killed. Company records show that £1 10s. compensation was paid, but when a few months later, a cow was killed £10 compensation was paid.[4]

*   *   *

Along with bad working conditions went equally bad social conditions. In many places miners lived a life of barbaric isolation in hovels far worse than those any other section of the community would tolerate. The Commissioners for the Mines described in their 1844 Report a typical colliery house in the Lothians:

"It is rather a hovel than a cottage, having nothing but ground floor. Some consist of only one, others of two rooms, from 10 to 14

[1] Swallow's report appears in the *Miners' Advocate*, October 1845.
[2] See below, p. 96.   [3] *Miners' Advocate*, 3 March 1844.
[4] Bankes, J. H. M., "The Nineteenth Century Colliery Railway", *Trans. of His. Soc. of Lancs. & Ches.*, vol. 114, p. 174.

feet square each. Many of the older ones have no ceiling: vacancies in the roof let in the wind and rain, and the floor is damp, being often little more than the natural ground. No domestic care could give an appearance or a feeling of comfort to habitations such as these."[1]

Not being able to take any interest in the appearance of his house, the miner tended to treat himself with the same scant respect. The Commissioners continue:

"The collier, as a general rule, when he comes home from his day's labour, as black from head to foot as the coal he has been working, sits down on a stool before the fire and washes his face, neck and breast, his arms, and his shoulders, and his legs to his knees—often not so far; he washes his head on Saturdays. The whole of the rest of his person remains untouched by water. I found during casual visits to their cottages from time to time after the hours of labour, some hundreds of men in the act of washing; the backs of every one of them were quite black, and every one of them gave the same reason in the same words for not washing his back, namely, 'that it would weaken it'. The universality of this habit was allowed by all the managers and persons in authority, whom I questioned upon the subject."[2]

The lack of personal hygiene gave miners a fragrance all their own:

"Such habits of dirt and neglect must have greatly contributed to keeping the colliers a separate race, apart from the labouring masses, and to perpetuating the disadvantages of such isolation. There can be no doubt of its injurious consequences to their health, especially of its increasing their liability to those distressing internal complaints to which so many of them fall an early sacrifice. The exterior also of a colliery village too often presents features as unfavourable as the interior of the cottages themselves. Immediately outside the doors, up to the very threshold, every species of repulsive filth is scattered or collected."[3]

The Commissioners went on to complain about the prevalence of drunkenness. They instanced Coatbridge, a town of 9,000 people, with 126 shops. Out of these, 25 were grocer and spirit dealers, 33 spirit dealers, 4 stores selling spirits—in all, 66 shops in which spirits were sold, besides three inns. In Scotland the mining districts were the places where the consumption of alcohol was highest. But the same picture

[1] *Report of the Commissioner of Mines, 1844*, p. 10.   [2] Ibid. *1844*, p. 10.
[3] Ibid., p. 10.

of drunken squalor could be found in most English coalfields as well. Reporting on North Staffordshire, the Commissioners say:

> "the hamlet of Goldenhill had fallen under the deteriorating influence of high wages, numerous beer-houses, and the absence of all adequate means of education and spiritual superintendance. In a mining population of 1,300 there were 14 beer shops and continued scenes of riot and drunkenness."[1]

Often drinking sprees were accompanied by such pastimes as dog-fighting, pigeon-flying, and heavy gambling on races and fights.[2] Several songs mention the difficulties miners encountered with the general public, who considered them wild, feckless and unclean. It inevitably led to courtship problems, as the song "The Bonnie Pit Laddy" relates. Meeting a lovely country maid on his way home from the mine, the young collier explains to her:

> "You may see I'm a Pitman, as black as sloe,
> And all the night long I am working down below."

He goes on to tell her "the Pit Lads are the best of boys". When they are in the ale-house, they "spend their money freely and pay before they go".

> "So come all pretty maidens, wherever you be,
> A Pit Lad do not despise in any degree,
> Fer if that you do use them well, they'll do the same to thee."

Sometimes miners themselves had clog-fights, kicking at each other's bare shins until one of them was unable to stand. Describing this "game", a St. Helens pitman explained:

> "It is all up and down fighting here. They fought quite naked, excepting their clogs. When one has the other down on the ground, he first endeavours to choke him by squeezing his throat, then he kicks him on the head with his clogs. Sometimes they are very severely injured."[3]

As mining districts often displayed such violence and lack of civilised conduct, the rest of the community usually tried to avoid contact with them. A forceful illustration of this fact came when the union dispatched its organisers into North Wales, an area in which the Associa-

---

[1] Ibid., p. 66.

[2] A Lancashire saying was that a collier's coat-of-arms consisted of "a stark naked child and a game cock on a dunghill". Quoted P. E. H. Hair, *The Social History of the British Coalminers, 1800–1850*.

[3] Barker and Harris, *A Merseyside Town in the Industrial Revolution*, p. 278.

tion had no contacts in the summer of 1843. Benjamin Watson, one of the lecturers, reported to the Newcastle conference:

"When the agents of the Society went to North Wales and began to inquire for some of the colliers, the other inhabitants expressed their surprise that any man should inquire for a collier, stating if they were seen in company with them, that decent people would avoid their company."[1]

It was only when social apartheid began to break down that a more humane outlook entered into mining areas. In 1865 Samuel Bishop, a St. Helens glass manufacturer, said:

"Colliers have a bad name; they used to live isolated from every one, and were rough and ignorant: to some extent they are so still, but towns have grown up round coalpits of late years . . . the colliers have now been forced to mix more with their fellows and have improved accordingly."[2]

Other influences also tended to produce social amelioration. First, there was the desire of many miners for self-improvement. Some of them, realising how uneducated they were, went to great lengths to learn how to read and write. In Northumberland and Durham grown men were to be found sitting next to children in school-class. Second, there were the trade union activists, who appreciated that, to improve the workers' lot, it was necessary to transform their whole attitude towards life. So long as "the typical miner was drunken, dissolute and brutalised"—to use Sidney Webb's description—then he would be "tyrannised over by his employers and their underlings".[3] The acquisition of self-respect had to go hand in hand with a desire for social and material improvement. And, third, there was the influence of social reformers and Methodism. These had an uneven effect, great in some places, non-existent in others. It helped magnify the great disparities between the coalfields. The Methodists' influence, for example, was almost entirely confined to North Staffordshire and the North-east coalfields. In the latter district, Fynes described how the miner "took to going to chapel and, finding it necessary to appear decent there, he got new clothes and became what is termed respectable".[4] Religion induced a new attitude, a new way of life. "They took away his gun, his dog, and his fighting cock. They gave him a frock coat for his posy

[1] *Northern Star*, 9 September 1843.   [2] Barker and Harris, op. cit., p. 270.
[3] S. Webb, *The Story of the Durham Miners*, p. 20.
[4] R. Fynes, op. cit., p. 282–3.

jacket, hymns for his public house ditties, prayer meetings for his pay-day frolics."[1] Sometimes a man's religious conversion aroused hostility among his workmates. The *Miners' Advocate* cites the case of a collier who played in the colliery band. After joining a Methodist sect, he abandons this form of frivolity as unbecoming a Christian. His fellow workers, incensed, successfully ask the management to dismiss him. The Editor of the *Advocate* commented: "This is a most disgraceful piece of business and reflects little credit on the party, or parties, who turned the poor fellow out because he became religious."[2]

*   *   *

Wages and conditions differed as greatly as miners' attitudes to life. The poverty in some coalfields was matched by comparative affluence in others. It is impossible to state, with accuracy, what wages and hours actually were. They varied from coalfield to coalfield, from pit to pit, fluctuated seasonally, changed with variations in market conditions, as well as differing between workers in any given pit. Moreover, to complicate matters further, masters and men usually gave conflicting figures. In the North-east coalfield the position was further obscured by managers still continuing to use a medieval system of accounting. They put "the consumption of oats by race-horses with the payment of wages to coal-miners in one single tally, which effectively concealed his real financial position from the owner even if it served to square the accounts".[3]

It is possible to cite individual instances of poor wages. For example, when Richard Heathcoat, a pitman working at Lord Egerton's Worsley colliery, was killed, the *Northern Star* commented: "Who would be a collier to be exposed to hourly death; to have his head split in two; his brain dashed out; and all for fourpence a day?"[4] The same issue contained a report from David Swallow in Lancashire: "I can name several places here where they do not get ten shillings a fortnight and for 11 days work, too! . . . The colliers in this part of the country live chiefly on a little oatmeal mixed amongst boiling water. This is their main food, when eaten with buttermilk." At Westhoughton, Lancs, miners plaintively appealed to their employer, W. F. Hulton, J.P., for a wage increase:

> "We ask it on behalf of our once blooming wives, but now hunger stricken and emaciated wives and children; we ask it on behalf of

[1] S. Webb, op. cit., p. 20.   [2] *Miners' Advocate*, 23 March 1844.
[3] F. M. L. Thompson, *English Landed Society in the 19th Century*, p. 153.
[4] *Northern Star*, 19 August 1843.

ourselves who in many instances have to descend into the pit without a breakfast, for no other purpose but that ye be enabled to grow rich while we sink by slow degrees into a premature grave, victims to over-exertion, nauseous gases and starvation."[1]

Yet the *Manchester Guardian*, writing about Lancashire miners' pay, said: "The colliers in this county are able to earn excellent wages."[2]

Similarly, conflicting and contradictory statements about wages can be given for any coalfield. In Northumberland and Durham coal-owners and their supporters claimed, before the 1844 strike, that a hard-working collier could earn upwards of five or six shillings a day. Miners, on the other hand, said wages rarely rose above three shillings a day.

From the figures perhaps only one fact clearly emerges: namely, that wide divergences existed between one part of the country and another. As the Miners' Association foresaw, these glaring disparities would, unless checked, create built-in divisions within the union's ranks. Hence it had, as its first and foremost aim, "to *equalise* and diminish the hours of labour and to obtain the highest possible amount of wages".

*   *   *

The union's difficulties in making and maintaining unity within its ranks were aggravated further by each coalfield having its own special problems. As we have seen, child and female labour were used in some coalfields but not in others. The same was true of the truck system. This primarily existed in Staffordshire, Derbyshire, some parts of York-shire, and Scotland. Where it did exist, however, colliers were pre-occupied with its abolition almost to the exclusion of other objectives. Cloughan said conditions in Scotland were 50 per cent worse than in Northumberland and Durham, and he attributed this to the prevalence of the truck system; W. P. Roberts, addressing a Derby court, said he would withdraw his prosecution if employers in the county discarded the truck system; and in South Staffordshire miners were reluctant to support strikes since they were likely to increase their indebtedness and hence the scourge of truck.

The Midlands Mining Commission described how it worked:

"One of the essentials of the tommy system is to pay the wages only

---

[1] H.O. 45. O.S. 350 1843.   [2] *Manchester Guardian*, 6 December 1843.

once in a month or five, six or even seven weeks. Now, as the men cannot go without any fresh supplies for so long a period, their only resource is to apply to the masters' shops, and get goods in lieu of part of what they would otherwise receive from the butty at the reckoning."

The butty was a sub-contractor, an intermediary between master and men. The coalowner employed the butty who, in turn, employed the colliers. Sometimes an owner deferred paying his butties so that they were unable to pay their men, who consequently had to rely on tommy shops for essential food. Sometimes, the butties themselves owned the tommy shops and compelled men, as a condition of employment, to spend so much of their wages in the shop. Another variation occurred when the butties owned beer shops, where, on pay day, wages were paid out with the overt stipulation that the miners must spend a given amount on drink. As we have already seen, in South Staffs the practice of paying a proportion of the wages in beer—known as "buildas"—existed.

One effect of the truck system was that it seriously curtailed workers' power. So long as they remained indebted at the tommy shop—"owed my soul to the company stores", as the American mining song has it—it greatly limited their freedom of action, their ability to seek to remedy grievances or come out on strike. Furthermore, the system was objectionable because the tommy shop sold poor quality goods—hence the expression "tommy-rot". Another grumble was that prices were higher in the tommy shop than in ordinary shops. The Midland Mining Commission was told:

"The prices now are 8d. a lb. for cheese, we could get quite as good for 5d.; bacon, 8d., it is only 5½d. and 6d. at Wolverhampton; salt butter is 1s. instead of 9d.; tea 5d. an ounce, I could get the same for 3½d. . . . I think the flour and sugar are about the best articles they sell. The sugar is about a halfpenny dearer than in the town."

Leaders of the Miners' Association in Lanarkshire said tommy shop prices were 15 to 20 per cent higher than elsewhere.[1] In Staffordshire, Shropshire and Derbyshire, the union claims the difference was 25 to 30 per cent.[2] They appealed to coalowners who did not use the truck system and ordinary shopkeepers, adversely affected by this unfair competition, to assist the Association in its endeavours to abolish truck. By contrast, Commissioner Tremenheere estimated owners only

---

[1] *Manchester Guardian*, 24 February 1844.   [2] Ibid., 6 April 1844.

gained a cost advantage of 7 per cent by possession of a tommy shop. Mr. G. W. Hilton suggests this "is probably the most authoritative estimate of the mid-nineteenth century"[1] Certainly, where the opportunity arose, the best workmen would seek employment at a colliery where the truck system was not practised, and having a better quality labour force did counterbalance, in some instances, the advantages other owners achieved through their tommy shops. One owner, putting this view, said, "Let them tommy; I get all the best workmen by that means, and save more by this than other parties gain by their shop."[2]

The masters had the power, even when they dispensed with the truck system, to make exactions from colliers' wages. In Northumberland and Durham the Bond gave them the ability to fine at will. In other coalfields, while not legitimised by elaborate legal documents like the Bond, owners still fined extensively. Moreover, they also made large deductions from wages for equipment colliers used in the course of their work. With these two means, it was possible for owners to reduce net earnings while leaving the miner's gross earnings untouched. Alternatively, gross earnings could be slashed. Where a miner was paid for the amount of coal he hewed, the owner could use faulty weighing-machines or refuse to pay for a proportion of the coal "laid out" on the pretext that it was of poor quality or contained stone, shale, etc. So the owners had considerable room for manœuvre when they wanted to reduce labour costs.

To give some examples how this was done. George Williams, a union organiser in South Wales, wrote in the *Miners' Magazine* that colliers' wages were between 8s. and 10s. He cites the plight of William Taylor, who was left with £1 1s. 6d. to feed and clothe his family of six for a month:

	£	s.	d.
Gross month's wage for hewing 10 tons at 4s. 5d. a ton	2	4	2
Minus			
8 lb. of powder at 6d.		4	0
8 lb. of candles at 6½d.		4	4
Stoppages		8	4
Rent		6	0
	1	1	6

[1] G. W. Hilton, *The Truck System*, p. 40.   [2] *Midland Mining Commission*, p. 36.

Miners regarded these deductions as unjust exactions. Besides complaining about the high prices charged for candles and powder, the Stainboro colliers of Yorkshire grumbled:

"For a shovel shaft there is 1s. stopped; for a peggy shaft there is 6d. stopped, which used to be only 2d.; but now if a stone falls and takes a man's finger off—if the shovel shaft be broken at the same time, there is 1s. stopped out of his wage for it, if he has earned as much. . ."

At another Yorkshire pit—Blacker Hill near Barnsley—men smarted with a different type of grievance. While the owners, Messrs Vizard & Co., had promised the same pay as neighbouring pits, they only paid 9d. to 1s. whereas in other pits men received 1s. 2d. for that quantity of coal. To make matters worse, the owners sought to impede production by getting the banksmen to destroy the colliers' wooden tokens ("motties"):

"We are not only robbed as above, but we suffer by the banksmen having unlimited power in their unmerciful hands; they throw down our motties, and if they cannot get rid of them fast enough, they put them under the boiler to keep up the steam; some are hid, and others are sent in the waggons down to the vessels, and are found floating in the canal."[1]

Likewise, "when the picks have been sent out on the corves, they would not take them off, but have been wantonly sent down to Hull and elsewhere on the vessels." The Blacker Hill colliers ended their catalogue of woe with a common complaint: they were not being paid for all the coal they hewed.

In the North-east, colliers composed a special prayer that began:

"Unto thy care and protection, O most unmerciful master, I commit myself this day. Preserve me from all fines, cheatery, deductions, either by weight or measure, or from anything contrary to the justice of my labour, by thy graceless assistants, enable me to receive my pay without any subtraction, division or reduction from its true and rightful amount. . . ."

Sometimes, even when the actual wage sum was not in dispute, colliers had other grievances. Miners at Elemore complained:

---

[1] Miners savagely punished fellow workers who stole other workers' tokens, thus defrauding them on their legitimate wages. In Cumberland the practice developed of seizing offenders, tying their arms behind their backs, and writing their 'crime' on a piece of board, which was placed above their heads. In this manner, the culprits were driven through the town by the men they had tried to defraud. (*Whitehaven Herald*, 22 October 1847.)

"The rule at this colliery is to pay fortnightly every Friday. Last pay-day they would not pay us on the Friday, but said they would pay us next morning. We went for our money at 7 o'clock in the morning and we were kept waiting till 5 o'clock in the afternoon, while they knew our wives had a great way to go to buy a bit of meat. The viewer at this colliery was not very long ago a coal hewer. He appears to have forgot himself. Oh, God! how long are the miners to suffer this oppression?"

*   *   *

From a study of social and industrial conditions, it seems impossible not to agree with the verdict reached by Carleton Tufnell. He was appointed as a factory inspector under the 1833 Act. In carrying out his duties, he visited a few pits in Lancashire and wrote in his Report:

"I cannot much err in coming to the conclusion, both from what I saw and the evidence of witnesses given on oath, that it must appear to every impartial judge of the occupation, that the hardest labour in the worst factory is less hard, less cruel, and less demoralising than the best of coal mines."

It was as a reaction to these appalling conditions that the union came into existence. But because of the wide range of grievances, the many evils against which the men pitted their strength, the Association had many voices, not one. The very things that called the union into being also destroyed it.

4

The Formation of the Union

HISTORICAL accounts of the actual formation of the Miners' Association, up till now, have been somewhat confused. The Webbs bear some of the responsibility for this: in their *History of Trade Unionism* they claim it was formed in 1841, a year too early. And Sydney Webb, in his book on the Durham miners, goes on to compound his error by attributing the key role at the inaugural Wakefield conference to Martin Jude, who almost certainly was not there.[1] The Webbs' monumental work created a pattern of confusion other labour historians followed.

The Webbs probably gained the idea the Association was formed in 1841 from reading Fynes' book.[2] But while Fynes wrote a fascinating first-hand account, his knowledge was almost entirely of the Northumberland and Durham coalfields; elsewhere, at best, it was fragmentary. When he mentions the date, 1841, he must have been referring to the first faltering steps being taken towards organisation at individual pits. Perhaps informal discussions took place between miners from one colliery and another. There may even have been rudimentary county associations—this is particularly true of Scotland and Lancashire. But at the beginning of 1842 no national union of mineworkers existed.

In the North-east, the pitmen of the Tyne and Wear held their first delegate meeting at Chester-le-Street on 22 January 1842. The *Northern Star*, on 15 January 1842, contained a letter from George Binns, appealing to Northumberland and Durham miners: "Let every colliery obey the summons of that meeting." An advertisement, appearing in the same issue, signed by Thomas Birrell, "by order of the Thornley Colliery Union", stated that the meeting was called "to adopt measures for resistance to the tyranny of the coal owners and their viewers". That a single colliery union convened the meeting would seem to suggest there was, at that time, no Northumberland and Durham union. The weakness of the organisation was conceded by the miners'

---

[1] S. Webb, *History of the Durham Miners*, p. 29.   [2] R. Fynes, op. cit., p. 37.

leaders themselves: they admitted that only a few delegates attended the meeting. Those present agreed, however, that they had no alternative but to struggle against "servile vassalage". They expressed the hope that pitmen would "not be led away again by evil advisers from their duty to their families". They requested all colliers to restrict their labour to eight hours a day. And they placed the organisation on a permanent basis. The secretary appointed was Thomas Hall, a Thornley pitman, who was asked to convene a further delegate meeting at Thomas Hutchinson's house, Monk Wearmouth, on 5 February.

It is interesting to note that Benjamin Embleton, of Wingate colliery, chaired this first meeting. He was a veteran of earlier struggles and had joined his first trade union, an illegal combination, thirty-two years previously. Embleton had participated in the "binding" strike of 1810, when the pitmen had defied the owners for seven weeks. Fynes recounts how, on that occasion, the miners "were hunted about from place to place by the owners and magistrates, assisted by military, and committed to prison in such large numbers till the prisons would hold no more."[1] The overflow, nearly 300 men, were billeted in the Bishop of Durham's stables. Encountering such fierce repression, both the strike and the union were crushed. Despite his experiences in 1810, Embleton remained undaunted. When the miners again started to form a union, in 1831, he became one of its leaders, along with Tommy Hepburn. But, once more, the union crumbled before superior might, and for five years Embleton was unemployed. The coalowners, he later explained, "made a scapegoat out of me . . . pointed me out as an example to keep their poor slaves in subjection". With no possibility of trade union employment, Embleton then turned to Chartism, addressing many pithead meetings in the North-east. He even continued doing this after the new union of Tyne and Wear pitmen was formed. In August 1842 he addressed a Chartist rally at Thornley colliery, and next day the miners went on strike. As the *Northern Star* explained, "the colliery, in some part of its workings, had been in a very foul state and the men have, even in some of the most dangerous parts, been kept working with candles instead of lamps. By this proceeding, the lives of the workmen have been in imminent peril."[2]

Another Chartist meeting, held at Newcastle-on-Tyne in August 1842, was addressed by Cockburn, a working pitman. Along with others, he protested against the mass arrests and heavy sentences imposed by the authorities to crush the general strike. "It is undeniable

[1] Fynes, op. cit., p. 13.   [2] *Leeds Mercury*, 6 August 1842.

innocent blood has been shed," he said, "'neither age nor sex spared by the powers-that-be; that armed, trained and disciplined ruffians have been sent to butcher the people without any right or cause whatever."

*   *   *

In spite of these moves in the North-east, little progress towards creating a miners' union appears to have been made there after the initial burst of enthusiasm in January and February of 1842. The main impetus towards the creation of the Miners' Association came from Yorkshire. On 1 August 1842, "about eight hundred miners or up-wards" crowded in the street of Halifax, "a sight which astonished the townfolk as they could not guess at, or get information respecting, the object contemplated by the miners".[1] Eventually, they assembled in the Oddfellows' Hall. Although they met in secret, turning away unauthorised visitors, the most important decision of the meeting—a resolution calling for the formation of a national union—was made public: that "in order to facilitate the object desired, we form ourselves into Societies, these Societies into Districts, and those Districts into one grand body as speedily as possible, to consist of the whole of the coal miners of England". But along with this new conception of an indus-trial union went the old Benbow conception of a general strike: "A fund be established for the support of a general strike by the whole of those employed in the coal mining department throughout England, and we all cease from labour for one day."

Apparently, some colliers doubted the efficacy or feasibility of a general strike. For a second meeting, at Wakefield on 15 August 1842, sought to achieve their objectives through industrial co-operation, not strife. They wished to establish a community of interest between masters and men. To do this, it was necessary to act with caution and diplo-macy, to show a "cordial feeling" to the coalowners. But, alas, the hand of friendship was rudely rebuffed. No owner showed any interest in the miners' plan to raise the price of coal to manufacturers and large consumers, who paid considerably less than householders. And some masters even dismissed men associated with the newly-formed union.

Reappraising the situation, delegates thought they would adopt a new tactic. As no reply had come from the masters, they hoped to evoke a more favourable response from the public. A committee was set up for the purpose of writing an appeal to the general public, describing the plight of coal miners and asking for help:

[1] *Leeds Mercury*, 6 August 1842.

"Our masters have ears only for the sound of gold, smiling eyes for their customers, and feelings for them. We who send more gold into their pockets than any other trade are left to starve."[1]

The appeal went on to complain that miners' families were perishing for lack of food; that the miners themselves worked short-time, yet they had to hew as much coal in two days as they previously did in three; and that they were paid by measure and corves were often enlarged without any increase in pay. It claimed that no section of society stood in greater need of education and religion "for no one is more suddenly snatched out of time into eternity";

"Unacquainted with the will of God and the laws of man, ignorant, stupid and wicked, as he lives so he dies, and his blood will be on your hands. Look at our children—who takes care of them? Who gives them the food and education they are entitled to? Where are their Schools? Where can they learn of their Creator and the love of man? They are brought up in slavery and ignorance."[2]

They asked consumers to pay an extra threepence a ton for coal in order that wages could be increased. Alas, the public, like the owners, remained unmoved by the eloquence of their appeal. No higher price was forthcoming.

So, having nobody else to whom they could turn, the miners realised they would have to rely upon their own efforts to secure improvement in wages and conditions. A further meeting was held at Wakefield, on 7 November 1842. Every pit was asked to appoint delegates and urged to make "unity, peace, law and order" its motto. The conference, ostensibly called "for the purpose of taking into consideration the distress of coal miners and adopting a petition to Parliament", did more than issue another appeal. It appointed an executive committee; it planned to start a journal; and it sought, by asking all colliers throughout Britain to contact the Miners' Philanthropic Society at the Griffin Inn, Wakefield, to lay the foundations for a national organisation. A public meeting for local miners, held on the spare ground at Wood Street that evening, heard the gist of the day's deliberations. It re-affirmed the resolutions passed by the conference. The two most important were: first, "that the present state of wages paid to colliers is not a fair remuneration for the labour"; and, second, "that it is the opinion of this meeting that we shall never better our condition, social or moral, until we unite for the protection of our labour."

[1] *Northern Star*, 1 October 1842.   [2] Ibid.

E

In the period immediately following the Wakefield conference, the union made little headway. A note of despair crept into a further appeal, issued by the Executive Committee of the Yorkshire Colliers on 21 December 1842, "to the colliers of England, Scotland, Ireland and Wales":

> "Fellow workers, we earnestly address these few lines to you, hoping that you will boldly come forward and assert your rights and not allow yourself to be trampled on any longer by the greatest tyrants on earth. They are doing all they possibly can to crush you and yet you stand quietly by with your hands folded lamenting your fate."[1]

David Swallow, the full-time general secretary, remained in Wakefield awaiting some response to this new proclamation. So far no progress had been made outside Yorkshire. But then it came: on 21 January 1843 the men of Cowpen, Cramlington and Seaton Delaval decided to correspond with "the colliers of Wakefield". Swallow, an organiser of genius, snapped up the opportunity. He rushed to meet them and addressed numerous meetings throughout the North-east. In early February he spoke at Scaffold Hill to a large audience of Tyne and Wear pitmen, some of whom had walked forty miles in stormy weather to hear him. Swallow "was received with warm approbation" and "entered into minute detail of the encroachments which the master class made upon the miners throughout Britain."[2] He could already report his activities had received an enthusiastic reception in various districts and many had joined the Miners' Philanthropic Society. The meeting passed a resolution: "That the only remedy for our present distress is a cordial union of our order throughout the whole United Kingdom." A delegate meeting, held after the public one, resolved to ask Swallow to stay another fortnight and arranged for Ben Embleton to escort him around the coalfield.

Since the union continued to make steady progress in Northumberland and Durham, Swallow decided to extend his stay beyond the requested extra fortnight. A disaster at the Stormont Main colliery, where twenty-seven men lost their lives, may have had some influence on his decision. The *Northern Star*, of 15 April 1843, reported:

> "Mr. W. Lockey Harle, solicitor, was in attendance on behalf of the Pitmens' General Union, Mr. Swallow, of Wakefield, Secretary of the Union, was also present, both in his official character and at

---

[1] *Northern Star*, 31 December 1842.   [2] Ibid., 11 February 1842.

the request of the relatives and friends of the deceased, and the men of the colliery."

But Swallow also remained in the North-east to organise what it was hoped would be the first truly national meeting of British miners. It was to be held at the house of Hamlet Booth, the Rose and Crown, Shields New Road, Newcastle, on 1 May 1843. In a letter addressed to all colliers throughout the country, Swallow explained, "On account of the rapid and extensive increase in the Miners' Philanthropic Society in the principal districts throughout England and Scotland, it is resolved to hold a delegate meeting of all grades of miners." His letter exuded militant confidence: "Colliers! Arouse youselves! be up and doing; the harvest is really ready. . . . Fellow men, be determined! Do not be apathetic any longer and spaniel-like, licking the hand that smites you."

Most of the delegates to the conference came from Northumberland and Durham, with a sprinkling from the Scottish and Yorkshire coal-fields. Only one came from Lancashire (Pemberton), and none from the Midlands, Wales, or elsewhere. The union could hardly be described, even at that stage, as attaining national dimensions.

The main item of business was to consider the Constitution. The Wakefield conference had approved a draft, which had been submitted to Feargus O'Connor and the Editor of the *Northern Star* for their observations. They had both pronounced it perfectly legal and in order. But Martin Jude and W. P. Brophy remained unconvinced; each submitted his own alternative draft. A committee of nine subsequently spent a whole day during the conference considering the three drafts, although they contained only minute differences.[1] The tremendous importance attached to small differences of wording may appear, at first glance, mere formalism, but in fact it shows how painfully concerned everybody was to keep within the letter of the law.

The conference laid down the broad, general policy of the union. It asked all miners to restrict their earnings to 3s. a day. It empowered district delegate meetings to appoint "lecturers" (i.e. organisers) and plan their itineraries. It arranged a mass recruitment rally at Shadon Hill on May 15. There followed a furore of activity, a spate of union and Chartist meetings, in all parts of the North-east. Swallow, Davis and Watson spoke at the Newcastle Chartist Hall. Brophy and Beesley lectured in many places. On 10 June, Beesley, along with Embleton and Richmond, spoke at Thornley and, according to the *Northern*

[1] This accounts for the small variations between the printed versions in Newcastle and Wigan Public Libraries and the manuscript version in P.R.O. H.O. 45 O.S. 434.

Star, "were rapturously applauded". Next day Beesley and George
Charlton spoke at a Chartist camp rally at Bolden Hill. Meanwhile, at
Bishop Auckland, after "only seven days previous agitation by Mr.
Swallow", 1,500 miners attended a meeting and, a fortnight later, a
further meeting was held to consolidate the union's gains. Undoubtedly, the tempo of development quickened. On 1 July, despite being
restricted to one delegate per pit, 120 delegates attended the Northumberland and Durham meeting at the Black Swan, Newcastle. Almost
all the North-east colliers were already organised, so the meeting was
able to concern itself with weaknesses in other coalfields: William
Daniels and W. Hammond, a veteran miner from Sunderland, were
appointed as lecturers for Scotland.

They had reached a turning-point in the fortunes of the union, its
growth from a tiny sect into a significant force. In the period between
the Wakefield and Newcastle conferences—that is, between November
1842 and May 1843—membership had remained small and almost
entirely confined to Yorkshire and the North-east. On 3 May 1843 it
had only 4,802 members, but by August 1843 it had shot up to 50,000.[1]
Moreover, John Hall, the secretary, could report by this time that
fourteen full-time lecturers had been engaged: progress was being
made in Derbyshire, Staffordshire, Wales, Cumberland, Yorkshire
and Scotland. The union was becoming a truly national organisation.

*   *   *

The executive committee seriously considered proselytising into
other coalfields only when the Miners' Association had become firmly
established in Northumberland and Durham. It required men of special
qualities, able to undergo great hardship and provocation, to plant the
union banner in hitherto unexplored, and usually hostile, regions. In
this by far their most successful man was David Swallow. On 10 June
1843, the Association decided to send him to Lancashire. He was
accompanied by Daniel Thompson, a miner sacked because of his
union activities and engaged by the union in a full-time capacity.
Swallow wrote to the Lancashire miners, saying he hoped to arrive at
Oldham by 27 June and his services could be obtained by writing to
him via the *Northern Star*. He added, "Brethren, we are entirely
strangers to your district." By early August, Hall in Newcastle had

[1] Membership figures, given at union conferences, appear to have been accurate. A
heavy fine was imposed on any person purporting to represent more men than he did.
Figures, so far as they can be cross-checked, have proved to be correct.
[2] *Miners' Advocate*, 13 January 1844.

received a report from Thompson telling him that the two of them "are doing wonders in Lancashire":

> "But we are watched at every step by the creatures of the masters, acting as spies upon our actions. They even get into our sleeping rooms to listen to our private conversation; but as our work is done openly and above board, we have nothing to fear and defy their malice."

A more open manifestation of malice came when Swallow wanted to hold a meeting at Hulton Lane Ends, near Bolton. Not a single publican would allow him a room in which to hold a meeting. Yet their premises were packed with miners consuming free beer bought by the coal owners. To show that cordiality between the classes reigned supreme, some masters ostentatiously played bowls with their men. But most owners were content merely to be present, keeping a wary eye to see their men had nothing to do with the union. So Swallow, denied a room, decided to hold an open-air meeting. When he attempted to speak, a magistrate, W. F. Hulton, the largest local coal-owner, strutted over to stop him. Swallow protested he was causing no obstruction. Hulton replied that if he was not gone in a few minutes he would be sent to prison.

"Have you not threatened the publicans if they allowed us to meet?" Swallow asked. "And does not your whole conduct prove that you dread the diffusion of intelligence among your vassals?"

"Well, you have no occasion to come here and teach us," answered Hulton. "We know more than you do."

"I do not know quite as much about Peterloo," conceded Swallow. "I had to go and work in a coal-pit when very young to help aggrandise such men as you."

Whereupon two colliers, paid by Hulton, lumbered over to Swallow and said, "Dun you noa the consequence oa takin' abeawt Peterloo to th' Squoire?" They had a short way with union organisers—they threw him forcibly from their midst.[1]

Notwithstanding this hostility, Swallow made tremendous progress in many parts of Lancashire. After three weeks he reported he had attained a higher rate of recruitment than achieved in Northumberland and Durham. Informal ties between collieries, based on a tradition of local unionism, assisted him in his task. It was, to some extent, a question of strengthening, and making more durable, already existing links.

[1] *Northern Star*, 12 August 1843.

On 31 July a colliers' meeting was held on Kersal Moor. The military and police were alerted, but their precautions were unnecessary. It was only a delegate meeting. The *Manchester Guardian* reported 150 present, about a hundred of whom were colliers. After Swallow had spoken, a resolution was unanimously passed to support the national union. Then Daniel Thompson went on to discuss the inadequacy of partial strikes. In the disturbances the year previous dangerous means had been used to stop machinery. A general strike would be much more effective without entailing the risk of scalding hands pulling out plugs.

The meeting's chairman, John Lomax, of Radcliffe Bridge, and Henry Dennett, of Wigan, both became union lecturers. Besides augmenting Swallow's organising force, these were men with valuable local knowledge. Dennett had been a leader of the 1831 union. He had been on the delegation that met the Lancashire and Cheshire coal-owners, winning an advance in wages. When the union collapsed, he maintained his contacts and became an active Chartist. Soon another veteran John Berry, joined the ranks of full-time organisers. Born at Standish, near Wigan, on 30 November 1807, he began work at a local pit at the age of six. When he was twenty-three, Berry started rambling from coalfield to coalfield, in much the same way as, in a later age, the Wobblies did in America. Before joining the Miners' Association he had already worked in ten coalfields and belonged to four local unions, including the 1831 and 1834 Lancashire unions and Hepburn's 1832 union in the North-east.[1]

The five lecturers worked hard in Lancashire, making members, establishing branches and area committees. From time to time they also held public meetings, usually well-attended by enthusiastic pitmen and ending with a unanimous declaration of support for the Miners' Association. On 15 September, Swallow went to Westhoughton, close to Hulton Lane Ends. He enrolled many miners into the union, a step the owners there had so desperately sought to stop a few weeks previously. Dennett and Berry worked in the Wigan-St. Helens area, Thompson at Oldham, while the Accrington-Burnley district was covered by a newcomer from Yorkshire—John Auty.[2] Meanwhile, William Grocott relinquished his post in the Chartist Movement to become county secretary.

[1] A pen portrait of John Berry. *Miners' Advocate*, March 1847.
[2] John Auty had been Paymaster General of the Friendly Society of Coal Miners, the first Yorkshire pitmen's union, formed at Wakefield in 1833. His name was printed on the membership card, a courageously reckless act which guaranteed his victimisation by all the Yorkshire coalowners. (Cf. F. Machin, *The Yorkshire Miners*, pp. 40-1). It is note-worthy that Auty, Swallow and the Miners' Association all came from Wakefield.

As the union seemed firmly established in the North-west, it was time for Swallow to move on. He went with Lomax to work in Staffordshire, where the Miners' Association remained very weak. They were sent by the Lancashire miners, who agreed to pay their wages and expenses. Quickly accounts start to appear of branches springing up in the Potteries—at Longton, at Lane End, two at Burslem. They made 468 members in the first fortnight; the figure rose to 1,500 in five weeks.

A strange thing happened when Swallow went to Cheadle, near Longton. William Bower, junior, a partner in Woodhead colliery, agreed to chair the meeting. "Mr. D. Swallow spoke on the advantage of men and masters being united and proved to the satisfaction of both that the hours of labour must be greatly reduced before men could be well paid and masters have a fair return for their capital. Both men and masters joined in the applause."[1] The chairman then announced a wage increase. "The men gave the master three cheers and he afterwards treated them most liberally with good, old English cheer."

Industrial harmony, however, did not pervade much of the Potteries. Many miners were dismissed for belonging to the union. In the *Miners' Advocate* Swallow cites the example of Samuel Wilson, who got only 19s. 7½d. for three weeks' work, out of which he had to pay 2s. 6d. a week rent, 1s. 6d. a week for drink and 2d. a week for the doctor. "This leaves him with seven shillings to support himself and his family, pay taxes, etc., for three weeks. And yet he is discharged for trying to better his condition." Wilson was given a pound to help him go to look for work in Lancashire.

With North Staffordshire reasonably well organised, Swallow journeyed to South Staffordshire. Colliers in this coalfield, tired by hard-fought strikes in 1842 and 1843, were reluctant to join the union. Wage reductions had sparked off the strikes of the summer of 1843. Whereas in the previous struggle they could turn to Chartists, like O'Niell and Mason, the repression of the 1842 general strike had crushed their leadership: "The unfortunate men appear to have no leaders; and, in the absence of any specific plan of agitation or resistance, talk nothing but wild revenge,"[2] Predictably, their struggle ended in defeat, leaving a strong feeling among the miners that all strikes were futile. It was in this atmosphere that, in the autumn of 1843, the first glimmer of trade union organisation appeared. The most prominent member of the new body was William Thomason, who

[1] *Miners' Advocate*, 2 December 1843.   [2] *Manchester Guardian*, 16 July 1843.

had come from the Vale of Leven in Fifeshire. He was a follower of
Sturge, a believer in free trade, and a fierce opponent of strikes.[1] The
Northern Star devoted an editorial to saying why they thought he was
not a fit and proper person to be a lecturer for the miners.[2]

David Swallow's views on Thomason are not recorded. All that is
known is that he started, as he always did, to recruit new members for
the union. Three hundred joined during his first week there, but still
a large proportion remained non-unionist. Soon after his arrival, he
reported that only 3,000 out of 25,000 miners throughout Staffordshire were in the Miners' Association. Probably he exaggerated the
total number of miners: it is likely there were only 4,000 in North
Staffs and 16,000 in South Staffs. When Swallow left Staffordshire
three months later, North Staffs had 4,000 members and South Staffs
had 1,000 members.

*   *   *

If the Miners' Association was to be a truly British trade union, it
had to gain a substantial membership in Scotland. It was an area with a
tradition for trade union organisation all of its own. Granted there
were differences between the various Scottish coalfields, each at its
own stage of development, but it seems that, generally speaking, the
Scottish miners had been able to place their organisations on a more
durable footing and to achieve their aims more frequently than their
English counterparts. The Mines Inspector reported:

> "In fact, the whole of the colliers in Lanarkshire, with few excep-
> tions, amounting to 16,000 men, have *for many years past* (since the
> repeal of the Combination Laws in 1825) placed themselves under
> regulations as to the amount of their labour . . . for the maintenance
> of wages at a fair level; for their protection against overwork; and
> against the overstocking of the market for labour and the market for
> coal."[3]

Workers stipulated for one another a certain amount of work,
which they called "the darg". Anybody trying to exceed "the darg"
was liable to have his pit-light blown out, be harried by his fellow

---

[1] Thomason, a prominent Edinburgh Chartist, played a very minor role in the Association. At the Newcastle conference, November 1843, he stood as a candidate for the
editorship of the *Miners' Advocate*. Voting was: Daniels 12,450, Dixon 9,014, Thomason
1,305. As delegate from South Staff, he had 1,200 votes. Soon afterwards he resigned from
being lecturer, and popped up again, for a short time, during the great strike in the
North-east when he recommended the men to return to work.
[2] *Northern Star*, 5 August 1843.   [3] *Inspector of Mines Report*, 1844, pp. 31-2.

miners, and even have them impose a heavy fine upon him. For, as Dundas Simpson, an overman, explained, "There are leaders in every pit who regulate these matters."[1]

The class struggle, consequently, was fought over the size of "the darg" and the payment for it. Employers would, of course, have liked to smash "the darg", thereby lifting the worker-imposed restriction on productivity and output. But even after the fierce struggle of 1837, when 4,000 strangers were brought in from other areas to break the twelve-week strike, "the darg" still remained. The fluctuations since it began in 1825 were:

1825–7	2 carts at 2s. 6d. each
1827–42	4 carts at 1s. 0d. each
1842	3 carts at 1s. 0d. each
1843	2 carts at 1s. 0d. each

The reduction in income, despite a degree of organisation, made Lanarkshire a place of great discontent in 1842. A strike broke out in August 1842; 97 pits in Airdrie were idle, 32 pits in Holytown, 43 at Coatbridge and 28 in the Glasgow area. The miners met at Meadowhead, near Airdrie, and, after hearing speeches from Gibson, a Chartist lecturer, and Lee, heard a resolution for a four shilling a day minimum moved by John M'Lay. It was carried unanimously. A delegation, set up to negotiate with the masters, ran into the insuperable obstacle that they did not meet as a body.

After Lanarkshire went back, trouble continued to rumble through Scotland. October 1842 saw a dispute in the Mid and East Lothian coalfield. An ugly incident developed when police stopped strikers carrying away potatoes. A fight ensued; the miners struggled free; they reached home. But then the whole police force was mobilised. A striker was arrested and clapped in irons, only to be liberated from the police station by his comrades. In the battle, a policeman was seriously injured. Then, in November 1842, the Ayrshire miners turned out. This was later followed by a second strike in Lanarkshire. Many miners and their families were evicted from their homes during the coldest part of the winter. In February, William Daniels wrote a letter, describing the plight of the Scottish miners and appealing for financial assistance; "I hope that the English colliers will stand by and support their unfortunate Scottish brethren."[2]

---

[1] Ibid., p. 33.   [2] *Northern Star*, 17 February 1843.

Their own misfortunes made the Scottish miners anxious to contact their English brethren. William Cloughan, their most talented leader, came down to the North-east. He addressed the mass rally at Scaffold Hill on 15 March 1843. He told them that, while there were many evils to fight in the North-east, "they also had many comforts and advantages of which to boast in comparison with the colliers of his native county. When he saw their clean houses and comely wives, and observed how well they were clad, he thought with a sigh of the contrast which Scotland presented, and envied their lot."[1] Immediately before Cloughan, Brophy had spoken of the plight of women in the North-east:

"There were many wives and daughters—he knew of instances in Newcastle—who submitted to prostitution to keep those that were near and dear to them out of the odious workhouse."

Obviously, if conditions in Scotland were worse than these (as Cloughan said) then they were in urgent need of assistance. Collections were made in Northumberland and Durham to provide relief for the Scottish miners.

In some respects, besides enforcing "the darg", the Scottish colliers were, so far as trade union development was concerned, far more advanced than the English. First, they had their own paper—*The Colliers' and Miners' Journal*—of which Cloughan was the editor. Already, by July 1842, six issues had been published; it was fifteen months later that the English miners published their paper. Second, as early as July 1842, Scottish miners were holding delegate meetings; again, well before any English coalfield. And, significantly, the Scottish were the first to use the term "Miners' Association".[2]

But there is a difference between informal links and close organisational ties. The Scottish, as Hammond and Daniels discovered, valued their independence and did not want an organisation centred in England. Hammond had been in Lanarkshire for eight weeks when, at the Holytown district meeting, he asked them if they were in favour of a national union. Cloughan stalled the question, saying it would be considered at their next meeting. What happened at their next meeting is not reported, but Cloughan and some of the Lanarkshire colliers did join the Miners' Association. However, the impression is given that they did it with reluctance, leaving the door open for a hasty exit. It may well be that the Miners' Association held its national conference

[1] *Gateshead Observer*, 18 March 1843.   [2] *Northern Star*, 16 July 1842.

at Glasgow, in March 1844, deliberately to impress wavering Scotsmen. But one interesting fact, contained in the Glasgow conference membership returns, is that only about a quarter of the Lanarkshire miners were represented at this conference on their doorstep.

Other Scottish miners, in coalfields less well-organised by indigenous effort, were more amenable to outside help. William Daniels quickly became secretary of the Fifeshire miners until he moved to Newcastle to edit the *Miners' Advocate*. Stirlingshire, Ayrshire, Mid and South Lothian colliers all, to varying degrees, assembled under the banner of the Miners' Association. Even so, the difficulties of communication, the inherent tendency towards separatism, in the long-run proved too strong. Nevertheless, for the major portion of 1844 the Miners' Association achieved the miracle of becoming a genuinely national trade union.

5

The Structure of the Union

As the Miners' Association developed in the various coalfields, its central organisation became stronger and sought to exercise a unified control. The Newcastle conference, in May 1843, had finally resolved the issue of the union's constitution. Henceforth, an executive committee of eleven members would be in charge of the day-to-day running. A strict check was to be kept on membership and money. At meetings it was frequently said that the fatal flaw in previous combinations had been their failure to remain on a firm financial basis. Consequently, Rule 5 of the constitution required the general secretary to keep a list of all members, colliery by colliery, district by district, and to furnish officials with a monthly balance sheet. It also determined that the treasurer should receive all monies, "after having given such security as the association may deem necessary" (Rule 6).

Any coal, lead or ironstone miner was entitled to join the Association. Rule 7 laid down that members would be expected to pay 6d. entrance fee, 1d. for a membership card, and 1d. a week from then on. Half the money could be kept by the local mine or district association, to defray expenses, and half had to be sent to the general treasurer (Rule 10). So that no member should suspect that his money was being misused or misappropriated, highly detailed printed balance sheets were issued and, as a further safeguard, Rule 13 decreed: "That on a written notice of three days being given to the general secretary, signed by any five members of the Association, he shall upon such notice tender to them his books for examination." Also, auditors, appointed by each general delegate meeting, had to examine the secretary's and treasurer's books and report to the following meeting.

The executive committee controlled branches and districts through Rule 9. This stated that all integral bodies' constitutions—known as "bye-laws"—"shall be strictly in accordance with the general rules of the association". Rule 12 added another caveat: "That this Association will not support or defend any member who shall in any way violate the laws of the country."

Despite the executive's power on paper, in practice it was much less. Undoubtedly it played an important role in the formulation of general policy, but, within the broad outline laid down, considerable scope existed for local initiative. Power tended to be with the man on the spot rather than in the Newcastle headquarters. Executive members, consequently, were continually resigning to take up appointments as lecturers, the really key people, who spearheaded the union's advance. Salaries also provide an important pointer to the significance the union attached to the various duties. Lecturers received 18s. or 21s. a week, depending on whether they were working in their home district or elsewhere; William Daniels, for editing the *Miners' Advocate*, received 21s. a week; and John Hall, as general secretary, received 21s. as well. But the Manchester conference, which decided these last two salaries, did so after considerable controversy; many thought Daniels should receive 25s. and Hall only 18s. The grudging payment made to the general secretary may signify a belief in the principle of equality; probably, as well, it was due to his task being construed in almost a literal way as secretarial, adding up figures, answering letters, with little or no control over union affairs. Used as we now are to highly central-ised trade unions, whose general secretaries are the most powerful people in them, it may be difficult for us to visualise a period when power was more diffuse. Perhaps this accounts for the tendency of historians to attribute much greater significance to the work of Martin Jude (national treasurer) than to that of David Swallow.

The union relied on its lecturers—men like Swallow—to maintain its organisation at grass-roots level. Often persecution by the owners was so intense that merely to hold a union membership card was enough to get a miner the sack and eviction from his cottage. So men had to be discreet about professing their beliefs. It was only the lecturers, with nothing to lose, who could come out in open defiance of the masters. By the power of personal example, lecturers banished timidity and imbued workers with the will to resist. They were the backbone of the organisation.

Conditions of service for lecturers were laid down, amended and enlarged by successive conferences. At a Newcastle delegate meeting, on 24 July 1843, it was decided that lecturers should devote eleven days a fortnight to the Association; that the executive draw up the itinerary for travelling lecturers; that they be required to give an account to the secretary of their labours. The next delegate meeting in Newcastle, on 4 November 1843, stipulated that the executive should allocate lecturers according to the size and requirements of coalfields, and that no lecturer should remain more than six months in one place. Lecturers were warned not to mix politics with their speeches and told that wilful neglect of their duties would lead to expulsion.

In a statement to the membership, on 18 November 1843, the Executive said:

> "Lecturers and others have not been overpaid; nay, our hearts have been made to bleed at the privations which some of the Lecturers have had to undergo, and when it is considered, as it ought to be, those persons ought to have the highest place in your estimation and respect. They, be it remembered, are placed in critical situations, their devotion to the cause will most assuredly bring down upon them the antipathy of the masters, and not one of them in all likelihood, will ever get leave to work down a pit again. . . ."

Delegate meetings appointed and dismissed lecturers. The *Manchester Guardian* described how this occurred at the Manchester conference (2 to 7 January 1844), which was fairly typical. In their choice of appointment, "delegates seemed to be guided by the good moral character of the various candidates, their oratorical powers, and their having suffered in the cause of the Union, or from what was called 'King Coal Tyranny'." Evidently a candidate's personal qualities were of the utmost importance, for the *Manchester Guardian* editor, in his own comments that succeed the report, remarks that delegates made "scrutinising inquiries into the moral character and integrity of the individuals whom they selected from amongst their body to act as lecturers. 'If,' said one of the Staffordshire delegates, in recommending a candidate for election, 'the lecturer is of good moral character, the Staffordshire men do not inquire much about the rest; but we must have men of good moral character to do this work.'"

Even so, some of the lecturers were occasionally guilty of backsliding. At the same Manchester conference, for example, they dismissed Andrew Fleming, who "had been found playing at cards in a public house instead of attending to his duty". Daniel Thompson, as well, was sacked because he "had obtained four pounds per week for five weeks from the miners of the district of St. Helens by falsely representing himself and his family to have been turned out of their house and to be in great distress". Whenever accusations were levelled at a lecturer, he had a right to be heard in his own defence. Benjamin Watson, who had been lecturing in South and Mid Lothian, was also up for dismissal before the Manchester conference. The union paid nine weeks' arrears of wages and his coach fare down from Scotland— £3 2s.—after the charges had been found groundless. They also inserted in the *Miners' Advocate* a letter from the Lothian miners, describing in glowing terms his fine qualities.

Lecturers' duties became more onerous after the Burslem conference, 15–19 July 1844, when they were told:

"Then by all legal means endeavour to properly throw open their minds to the pursuit of knowledge, as it is that alone which will enable us properly to remove the causes which at present impede our progress."

The statement also said:

"We require knowledge of a superior description to any which it has been the fortune of the majority of us to receive, and above all things we should endeavour to obtain and disseminate this knowledge, as it will enable us generally to discover the necessity for Union of mind and action to relieve us from the difficulties and hardship by which we are surrounded. Each lecturer must, therefore, collect every kind of information appertaining to the interests of the Miners in particular and society in general, especially statistics regarding the wages of labour, the habits and conditions of workingmen, and all those causes that mainly contribute to the present state of things, and when meeting with men to use the simplest means for the purpose of digesting the information acquired, and to mature the plans laid by the Association."[1]

The lecturers were, therefore, supposed to be tutors in adult education, social investigators, statisticians—as well as being trade union organisers.

*   *   *

An insight into the workings of a typical branch of the union is gained from an examination of "The Bye-Laws of the Miners' Association of Castle Eden", contained in the Wigan Public Library Collection. Castle Eden, situated in Northumberland, had 300 members in 1844, of whom Thomas Pratt, a Primitive Methodist preacher, was the leading figure.

After specifying the officers the bye-laws charge the union committee to meet twice weekly, each committee member to receive $1\frac{1}{2}d.$ per

[1] *Miners' Advocate*, July 1844.

meeting expenses. Apparently, all union documents and funds were kept in a special box, which could only be opened by using three different keys for its three different locks. Each of the principal officers possessed one of these keys, so the box could only be opened when all three were present. As a result of the considerable inconvenience that would be occasioned by an official's absence, the bye-laws decreed he would be fined 6d. if not there at the appointed time—and 1s. if the key was not available.

Members paid their subscriptions every second Friday. This consisted of 3d. for the union's fund and 2d. or 3d. for weight. The deviation in these payments from those prescribed in the national rules arose because in Northumberland and Durham miners paid an extra halfpenny a week to maintain a legal officer. The 3d. for weight was probably paid because the local branch employed its own checkweightman to see that the owner paid the right money for the amount of coal hewn. Members who did not pay their dues at the correct time were fined 3d. for the second offence, 6d. for the third offence, "and for the fourth to be expelled, or suffer such a fine as the committee thinks fit".

A system of fines governed the running of the Castle Eden branch. Union officers were to be changed quarterly and to be appointed at a meeting called for the purpose. Any member refusing to fulfil the office to which he had been appointed was fined 2s. 6d. unless "he can give satisfaction of his not being qualified". Other fines imposed on members were:

Challenging another to a fight—fined 1s.
Swearing or using abusive language—fined 6d. per offence
Attending a union meeting intoxicated or leaving before time—
    fined 1s.
Not possessing, or not being able to produce "a copy of all laws by
    which he is to be governed"—fined 6d. for neglect.

The two most serious breaches of discipline were defined in Rule 15: "Should any member disobey any resolution which may be passed in connection with the work of the colliery, he shall be expelled and not again admitted without paying a fine of five shillings—and giving security for his good behaviour." And in Rule 17: "Should any member take the conduct of another into question, and not prove the same before committee appointed for that purpose, he shall be fined five shillings for every such offence."

The wide variety of offences for which the union imposed fines naturally aroused comment from newspapers. They argued that the miners were more severe with one another, fining one another more heavily, than were the masters. An editorial in the *Durham Chronicle* put it like this:

"We ought also to remind the pitmen that they act in a more tyrannical manner towards each other than the viewers or masters can possibly do. If a man were to earn six shillings per day, three shillings and twopence of that sum would be forcibly taken from him. Or, if he were to neglect attending a meeting at Pittington, Shadon Hill, or any other place, he would be fined five shillings by his fellow men. And why? Because the Union will it! This, too, is 'tyranny'; and is done with a view to giving delegates a controlling despotic absolute power over the Pitmen."

But this is malicious falsification. At Thornley colliery the owners imposed such heavy fines that some men, after a fortnight's work, came out of the pit having been fined more than they had earned. No examples can be cited of the union making fines of this magnitude.

Moreover, the colliers fought like tigers against the masters' right to fine while, at the same time, they struggled against fearful odds to maintain their union, the organisation that made exactions on them. The money paid to the owners was regarded as oppressive and unjustified; whereas for the union it was vital to preserve discipline and unity.

Nevertheless, the Castle Eden bye-laws show how deeply the concept of fining, first used by the employers, had been accepted by the workers themselves. They had imitated the employers' practices.[1]

But there was another side to it. The union was concerned, not only with improving wages and conditions, but also with the miner himself—his whole moral, mental and spiritual outlook. They wanted him to adopt higher standards of personal behaviour which, in their turn, would make it even more difficult for the employers to continue their oppression. The system of fines represented an effort to improve the miner's personal conduct, as well as ensure the smooth-running of the branch.

The importance attached to personal behaviour can be seen from an

[1] The practice of imposing fines has a long ancestry in the North-east. "The Law Book of the Crowley Iron Works" shows that this iron works, situated near Newcastle-on-Tyne, had a highly complicated system of fines. The custom was then adopted by Friendly Societies. See E. P. Thompson, *The Making of the English Working Class*, p. 419–21.

incident that occurred at Castle Eden in 1843. Robert Pearson, a pitman, threw his wife out of his house and started to live with his mistress, Catherine Wearmouth. Mrs. Pearson, having nowhere to live, went to the workhouse. But the guardians refused to help her, and told her to return to her husband, whose duty it was to support her. She returned home, sleeping in the same bed as her husband and his mistress. Next morning she was murdered. The union reacted to this scandal by getting its own printer, T. Dodds, of 77, The Side, Newcastle, to publish the shameful facts in leaflet form. Then an admonitory poem was composed, the moral being printed in the eighth, and final, verse, supposedly spoken by the condemned man:

> "Young men with speed your lives amend,
> And shun all wicked ways,
> Lest like me your lot should be
> In shame to end your days.
> My old companions all I pray,
> Take warning by my fate.
> Beware of passion's fatal sway
> Before it is too late."

Numerous appeals can be cited like that of John Madine, general secretary of the Cumberland district, which ended:

"Miners! then be sober—be united—for Union is indeed strength. Drunkenness and Card Playing is weakness and unworthy of those calling themselves MEN."[1]

Perhaps the union really did have a good effect on their conduct For, reporting a Miners' Association dinner at Little Lever, in Lancashire, the *Miners' Advocate* said:

"All passed off as merry as 'marriage bells', notwithstanding the prognostications of some that miners could not meet at a convivial feast without a fight. But they knew better now; the union has knitted them together, made them better men, better neighbours, better husbands."[2]

★   ★   ★

The only other important body within the Miners' Association was the national delegate conference. It was usually held half-yearly, but sometimes, when pressing business arose, more often. Its precise powers were not laid down in the constitution. Nevertheless, its resolutions

---

[1] *Miners' Magazine*, March/April 1844.   [2] *Miners' Advocate*, October 1845.

were implemented, whenever practical, by the executive committee. Hence it could properly be described as the supreme policy-making body of the union. Representation at national delegate conference was by branch or, where branches were numerous, by district. The delegates carried a block vote, each casting as many votes as the number of the membership he represented. If a delegate claimed to represent more members than in fact he did, he was fined 2s. 6d.

Conferences usually lasted five days and, besides the normal work of formulating policy, the delegates devoted spare-time in the evenings to strengthening the union's membership in the area. Indeed, after the 1844 strike in Northumberland and Durham, it became the common practice to hold the conference where the Association needed a short burst of intensive activity to revive its waning branches. Of course, this had dangers. Entrusting the work of conference organisation to an area where the union was weak might lead to the preparatory work being indifferently done—or not done at all. This might explain the abortive Rhosymedre conference in 1845.

Conference delegates, especially in the early days of the union, displayed a scant knowledge of procedure. Sometimes amendments were moved to motions that had not been seconded; men raised matters which they deemed urgent with no regard to the order of business; and delegates jumped up and down like Jack-in-a-boxes, speaking many times on the same motion. One of the conferences was described by the *Manchester Guardian*:

"In their discussions, the most distinguishing feature was, as might be expected, an utter disregard of those 'points of order', which are found so essential, and are so carefully enforced, in meetings of the more educated classes; each speaker seeming to consider it his undoubted right to rise as often, and speak as long, as his enthusiasm or his sympathy prompted him. But, with this neglect of 'order', there were often displayed a candour, an honesty, and apparent singleness of purpose, which would have done great credit to an assembly of men much more elevated in station. That they were not ignorant men was evident from the information displayed in their discussions, and from the fact that all of them appeared to be able to take notes of the proceedings; and a very large proportion were provided with memorandum books and pencils for this purpose, and dotted down their notes of the various propositions as they were submitted to the assembly."[1]

[1] *Manchester Guardian*, 10 January 1844.

The report also mentions that three or four of the delegates were Primitive Methodist and Baptist preachers, adding that the conference also had its humorists, ever ready to set the proceedings in mirthful uproar.

*   *   *

As one of the duties of the national delegate conference was to consider a financial statement, it might be worth while at this stage to delve into this perplexing and somewhat obscure subject. Contemporary sources, whether friend or foe, spoke with awe and admiration about the funds of the Miners' Association. Many thought its annual income was about £50,000 and the *Manchester Guardian*, at the end of 1843, said its funds were sufficient to sustain a general strike for two months.[1] Frederick Engels claimed funds were so large that for several months 20,000 men and boys received weekly strike pay of 2s. 6d. per family.[2] This same view has been maintained in the present century. In his classic work on coal-mining. Galloway repeats these claims while the American economist P. M. Sweezy says that in early 1844 the Association had "about £24,000 in the bank".[3]

Such as the evidence is, it fails to substantiate these claims. Six balance sheets of the Association that remain extant show a rather different picture:

	Income £ s. d.			Expenditure £ s. d.		
30th Sept.–11th Nov. 1843	254	14	8	230	12	8
11th Nov.–16th Dec. 1843	198	6	11½	202	11	1½
16th Dec.–10th Feb. 1844	485	10	5½	405	9	4
10th Feb.–13th Apr. 1844	527	6	10½	532	11	10
8th June–3rd August. 1844	316	18	8½	406	2	11½
5th Aug.–22nd Oct. 1844	496	12	7	601	16	10½

Making allowances for the gaps, these balance sheets cover a combined total of days almost amounting to a year. During this time, when the union's fortunes were at their zenith, the national income of the Miners' Association came to only £2,279 10s. 3d. And it is significant that, even before the tremendous struggle in the North-east coalfields began in April 1844, the union was only just paying its way. The union

[1] *Manchester Guardian*, 6 December 1843.
[2] F. Engels, *The Condition of the Working Class in England in 1844*, p. 170.
[3] R. Galloway, *Annals of Coal Mining*, Vol. 2, p. 176, and P. M. Sweezy, *Monopoly and Competition in the English Coal Trade, 1550–1850*, p. 43.

was always either on the verge of, or in, a balance of payments crisis. In an executive statement to members, issued on 18 November 1843, it was reported only £37 7s. 0d. remained in the general fund. For sending lecturers to the various coalfields £564—which they call a "vast amount of money"—had been used. Round about the same time, John Hall appealed to the Northumberland and Durham miners:

"Mr. Roberts is determined to break down the tyranny under which you have been so long groaning: no effort or energy on his part will be spared; his labours have already been successful. But it is YOU who must furnish the SINEWS OF WAR!! Much that ought to be done *is now prevented by want of money*. This ought not to be!" (Emphasis in the original.)

Hall wanted £1,000 to be raised. It does not appear that he got it.

Then, on 5 August 1844, towards the end of the great strike, the executive dispatched a letter to district secretaries about the union's severe financial plight:

"Our lecturers and all other officers with their families, positively, at this moment, are starving, many of them from their homes without the shadow of a chance of the means to relieve themselves, and get to their homes again. All this is caused by the districts not forwarding their portion to the General Fund while the Association is from £80 to £100 in debt."

The funds of districts remain shrouded in mystery. Not only was there the ever-present temptation to keep more than half the subscriptions, but also, in times of affluence in the industry, to raise dues above the sum stipulated in the constitution. Just as the owners charged for coal whatever price the market would stand, so district officials tended to think members' contributions should be determined by the same criterion. If the miners were enjoying a prosperous period, due to the exertions of the union, then they should show their appreciation by paying larger sums of money to it. Customarily, the districts tried to conceal this practice from headquarters. If their true financial position became known, then the national executive would claim more. In these circumstances, it is only possible to estimate roughly how much went into district coffers: probably, in 1844, the peak year, between £4,000 and £5,000.

Of course, the union had other funds. The *Miners' Advocate* between 2 December 1843 and 19 October 1844 had an income of £460 3s. 5d. But expenditure exceeded income, for the journal never fulfilled the optimistic estimate, repeatedly being made, that its income would help buttress the general fund. Then there was the legal fund which, between 3 August 1844 and 26 October 1844 amounted to £24 1s. 4½d. And, finally, from time to time, appeals for disaster victims and the unemployed were made. So, totalling the revenue from all sources, it would seem that the Miners' Association did not have an income of more than £8,000 in 1844.

       *   *   *

Discussions of the financial state of the union are bedevilled by the high propensity of all concerned to tell the most outrageous lies. Union supporters often did nothing to counteract stories about the vast wealth of the Miners' Association. Reports of vast hidden resources tended to magnify the importance and power of the union in the eyes of the public. Moreover, being eternal optimists, they sincerely believed that if the money had not been raised today, then it would be raised tomorrow. Even when the union was in its death throes, everybody believed it would be sure to grow. As Brother Micawber says, something is bound to turn up. From the opposite standpoint, the hostile press inflated the size of union funds so they could talk, more convincingly, about misappropriation. They liked to depict the leaders living a life of luxury on the members' hard-earned money. During the 1844 strike, leaders were described savouring the delights of beer and 'bacca while the ordinary pitman starved. It was an effective weapon with which to drive a wedge into the Association's solidarity. In reality, of course, the union leaders sacrificed as much—probably more—than the rank-and-file. When the general fund went into the red, Martin Jude lent the Association his life-savings of £100 which appears never to have been repaid. He was destined to die in abject poverty.

The man who is usually the most venomously portrayed—a sensuous Shylock, living off the miners' sufferings—is W. P. Roberts. In fact he was a remarkable man, a mountain of energy, who flung himself headlong into the miners' struggles, identifying himself with them and making many sacrifices on their behalf. But because the story that he received £1,000 per annum gained general currency, posterity has not given him due credit.

The decision to approach Roberts to be attorney for the Tyne and Wear miners was made at a delegate meeting at Newcastle on July 1st,

1843. The salary first mooted was £300 a year.[1] But subsequently, Thomas Barrow, a miner, wrote to a local newspaper in the North-east saying the terms agreed were £1,000 for the first year and £500 a year after that.[2] Then the *Northern Star* reported that he had been appointed at the salary of £1,000 per annum:

> "To those who do not understand profit and loss, this sum may appear large; while we have no hesitation in asserting that within any given period legal hawks would have plucked their clients of more than forty times that amount."[3]

It may well be that initially Roberts might have been tempted by the money. Son of a wealthy Cheltenham vicar, a former public schoolboy, he had no natural affinity with the miners. From Bath, where he practised as a solicitor, the struggles in the coalfields must have seemed very remote. But whatever inducement was used to entice him north-wards, he quickly entered the fight against oppression and exploitation; the monetary reward became a trivial issue.

The same papers that continually mentioned Roberts' salary of £1,000 were the first, the most gleeful, to describe his financial distress after the great strikes. On 15 March 1845, the *Gateshead Observer* wrote, "Roberts is still lurking about the district, so miserably clad and dirty in person, that he might be taken for a hewer in his second best." The *Newcastle Journal*, of 4 April 1845, reported a speech of Roberts to Northumberland miners, adding its own bitter comments in parenthesis:

> "Robert delivered a most lachrymose harangue, which in substance was as follows: The contributions of the union fund (alas!) were failing; and consequently it was incumbent on them to come forward more heartily to support the cause, as a means of adding to (query? subtracting from?) their future comforts. *He was very desirous of making them aware that their present contributions hardly admitted of thirty shillings a week being paid to himself.* (There's a rub. What is to come of the fast-trotting ponies?) Besides, he had con-siderable expenses brought against him which in justice (!), he was bound to find out of his own pocket (?). Having no other pockets to dip into, under existing circumstances, he assured them he would be compelled to resign his unwearied labour (happy circumstance!) for the benefit of the colliers of the two counties. . . . In conclusion, he said he should be extremely sorry to be compelled to leave them

---

[1] *Gateshead Observer*, 26 August 1843.
[2] Ibid., 5 September 1843.   [3] Ibid., 19 August 1843.

(doubtless!) without having the character of having on all occasions contributed to their welfare (which is not quite so clear). He had expended nearly £1,000 of his own (the immeasurable ——!) and would not like to remain in his present position till he was quite reduced (read—till he has found other gulls to practice upon)."

Roberts must have suffered considerable financial hardship. He had assistants, an office in Newcastle to maintain, and published his own paper, the *Miners' Magazine*. When the strike in the North-east started in April 1844, funds from the Northumberland and Durham miners, who were his employers, must have rapidly dried up. At the Burslem conference, in July 1844, to improve the situation, he was appointed Attorney to the whole union. But as we have already seen, the amount accruing to the legal fund in two and a half months, 3 August to 26 October 1844, was only £24 1s. 4½d., hardly a princely sum.

For the whole period, from the end of the great strike in August 1844 till 12 February 1845, the law fund totalled £130 10s. 11½d.[1]

When the Association was no longer in a position to retain his services, Roberts still continued to work for it. Later, in 1854, he reminded the miners: "After my time with you had expired, I remained with you—sometimes going to Manchester—for considerably more than six months; throughout that time doing the same work, attending inquests, meetings, disputes before magistrates etc., the same as before with this difference, however, that I was not paid at all, not even any expenses out of pocket."

Roberts wrote this in a letter to the 1864 Leeds conference, and there is no report of anyone contesting the accuracy of his statements. This is despite the fact that the main point behind his letter was to scotch stories of his personal self-aggrandisement, devised by the employers and sometimes spread by witless colliers. Roberts challenged them:

"If at any time you desire me to give any information about any-thing—what I eat, drink, or did, what I was paid, how I lived and where I went—anything, in fact, and will write me a line of inquiry, I will at once clear up any doubt or difficulty, either by a private letter in *The Miner*, or in any other newspaper, excluding, of course, such as live by slandering me. I cannot indeed, notice every lie—the liars are too numerous—but I will crush a few now and then."

Fynes, who prints Roberts' letter in full, entirely agreed with the points made. He paints this picture of the "Pitmen's Attorney General":

[1] Balance Sheet, Miners' Strike Collection.

"Those who have known Mr. Roberts from the outset of his connection with the miners until its close, know how to appreciate his honesty and manly character, and it is only those whose knowledge of his real character is a nullity, and who are morbidly suspicious of every good man, who could take any part in assailing him. The most galling part of the matter was that a charge of interested motives came from the very men he had laboured so disinterestedly all his life to raise. They charged him with wanting to extort money from the miners, when the fact was that the miners never did, nor never could, pay him one tithe of what they were indebted to him for the the many valuable services he rendered them."[1]

Fynes goes on to say: "He was a man who loved to be thought well of by his fellow men, but how much in hard cash did he put into his pocket over the transaction? Will any of his detractors say that he was anything like adequately paid for his labours by the miserable fees which he charged?"

*   *   *

The place of the legal department within the structure of the union is very difficult to define. Nothing was formally written, giving the precise power of Roberts and his clerks *vis-à-vis* the central organisation. It was more like a battlefield, with a large no-man's-land, through which Roberts and his men rampaged repeatedly while the unfortunate executive wondered how they could control this ferocious war-horse. In theory, from August 1843 until July 1844, Roberts was employed by the Northumberland and Durham miners, and hence under their direction. Any other coalfield, wanting Roberts' services, had to contact them and pay the expenses entailed. This meant that Roberts went round the country, visiting coalfields and developing closer contact with colliers in many localities than the executive itself possessed. It seemed, to the executive, he was almost usurping their function. They were jealous of the power he wielded, annoyed by the forthright manner he put forward his views, even when at variance with the executive's, and suspicious of this highly voluble man who had descended from high society to be the miners' messiah. Roberts' fiery temperament, his wild statements, his belief in his own infallibility—all helped to make his relations with the executive even more strained.

In the honeymoon period, from August 1843 until the end of that

[1] R. Fynes, op. cit., pp. 241–2.

year, harmony existed between Roberts and the executive. At the Manchester conference, in January, he entered amid cheering, and there was talk of making him Attorney-General for the whole union, not merely the two counties.

But on 2 February 1844, a leaflet was published, addressed "to the miners of Northumberland and Durham", attacking Roberts and Beesley. It was signed "An unsophisticated unionist and hater of humbug", and was obviously written by somebody with intimate knowledge of the day-to-day workings of the Association.[1] Significantly, it was printed by T. Dobb, the printer and publisher of the *Miners' Advocate* and most union material. The leaflet attacked Roberts for acting unconstitutionally:

> "I am sorry to say its (i.e. the Legal Department's) days are numbered, unless it be placed in the position in which it was first intended, and be made subservient to the rules of the society instead of the rules being laid aside by that establishment."

It went on to say that Roberts had actively encouraged strikes at single collieries, a contravention of Rule 11 of the constitution. The leaflet then questioned the high cost of maintaining a legal department. It also attacked the decision to make Beesley Roberts' articled clerk at a cost of £140 a year. A postscript claimed that Beesley had already shown his unsuitability for the post by being drunk in South Shields when he should have been at Jarrow colliery. It ended by alleging that the inebriated Beesley "then drove his pony with such violence as to precipitate pony, carriage, his companions, and himself over a wall, the consequence being much injury both to the carriage and his own bones".

The fascinating fact is that Beesley had been a fanatical supporter of temperance a few years previously. He had even edited a Chartist paper with the intriguing title of the *North Lancashire and Teetotal Letter-bag*. At the Chartist convention of 1842, Feargus O'Connor had proposed delegates should abstain from alcoholic drinks for the duration of the convention. But Beesley objected. If it was wrong to drink, it was wrong to drink at any time. Delegates should abstain not only during the convention but always. W. P. Roberts, also present, tried to smooth over the disagreement by saying he knew teetotallers and men who drank who were equally good men. The matter should be left to the individual's own judgment.

---

[1] The original document, in *The History of the Coal Trade* at the Picton Library, Liverpool, shows the author was Antony Stores, of North Elswick.

Whether Beesley had changed his way of life through closer contact with hard-drinking miners and with Roberts, we do not know. Nevertheless, there is no doubt that the leaflet depicts him as a man with unsteady habits, making "his devotions to the jolly god Bacchus".

The executive committee, on receiving the leaflet, enclosed copies of it with all bundles of the *Miners' Advocate* going out to members. Thus the accusations against Roberts and Beesley became known to the entire membership.

The leaflet came as a shock to Roberts, who had just returned from London. He dashed off a letter and had it circulated, along with the hostile leaflet, to all collieries in Northumberland and Durham:

"Mr. Roberts wishes the Secretary to whom this letter is directed, IMMEDIATELY to call a meeting of all hewers, etc., in his colliery—to read the enclosed handbill slowly and distinctly—and to invite the most full and complete comment on each charge. So that the delegate at the district meeting to be held at Durham on Friday next, may be able correctly to represent the feelings of the Pitmen who have elected him.

Mr. Roberts wishes the men of each Colliery to come to a vote on the subject—that is to say—whether Mr. Roberts is guilty of the within charges or not?"

They quickly jumped to Roberts' defence. The Durham delegate meeting gave him a unanimous vote of confidence, published its own handbill to rebut the charges made against him, and went on to call for the resignation of the executive council for circulating the original leaflet. The *Northern Star*, also came to Roberts' aid.[1] In an editorial it accused the Association's executive council of being in league with the masters to destroy the union.

The executive council—H. Birrell, Martin Jude, William Woodworth, John Stoker and John Hall—replied in a printed statement addressed to the membership. It said "a great portion of the members felt dissatisfied at the conducting of, and enormous expense of, the law establishment". Some pitmen had approached them with a handbill, requesting that a copy be enclosed with each bundle of the *Miners' Advocate*. They did not know they were doing wrong in circulating it. Nevertheless, at the Durham delegate meeting members of the executive were "examined, cross-examined, and teased, taunted and grossly insulted; and although they expressed their regret and sorrow at having taken any trouble with the bill, seeing it was without a

[1] *Northern Star*, 24 February 1844.

name, yet the candour and courtesy of the delegates did not prevent them from passing a vote of censure on all concerned in the circulation of same."

Matters could not be left there. Contending sides wanted a decision reached, and this was done at the next national conference of the union at Glasgow, 25 to 28 March. The Northumberland and Durham miners regarded the executive's attitude as one of unwarranted interference; Roberts was their employee and answerable to them. The executive, on the other hand, thought its own rights—and the constitution—had been violated by Roberts' actions.

At first sitting of conference, before the issue had been reached on the agenda, the tension over Roberts expressed itself. The *Miners' Advocate* says there was "a very long discussion on Mr. Roberts' right to repeatedly address the conference."[1] Scottish delegates, led by Cloughan, said he was not a member of the Miners' Association or a delegate to the conference. They had just debarred another nonmember from taking part in the proceedings, the same resolution should apply to Roberts. A Roberts' supporter then moved the previous resolution be rescinded, but Cloughan replied that, to do so, would go against the wishes of the majority. Finally, it was resolved Roberts should not take part unless specially asked for his opinions.

Further rumblings over Roberts occurred when an anonymous handbill, purporting to advertise a Chartist meeting to be addressed by Roberts and Beesley, was circulated in the conference. This appears to have been an openly provocative act, done to suggest that the union was being used to serve Chartist ends. From the strong way delegates reacted to it, the leaflet may well have been written in inflammatory language. The *Newcastle Journal* says, "The conference was therefore advised to take care." The report continues:

"On the reading of this bill by the chairman, an unruly person rose, and was proceeding to make some observations when he was called to order, as not being a member of the conference, and, consequently, having no right to address the meeting. Considerable confusion was occasioned by the interruptions, but the man was ultimately put down by the good sense of the meeting, and order was immediately afterwards restored."[2]

Next morning the matter was again raised. John Hunter, of Cumberland, protested against the circulation of the handbill. But, as the

---

[1] *Miners' Advocate*, 6 April 1844.   [2] *Newcastle Journal*, 6 April 1844.

authorship remained unknown, the conference allowed the matter to drop.

Roberts' role in the union took up the whole of the fourth morning of conference. Embodied in four resolutions before conference was the question: should he be made law officer for the whole Association or remain simply in the employ of Northumberland and Durham? Many delegates spoke for and against the motion. Miners from the North-east stoutly contended that Roberts was their man and insisted he should reside in Newcastle. Others thought it would be more convenient if he lived in Manchester. Eventually, Roberts himself addressed the conference. First of all, he ran over his triumphs in the North-east. Before he came among them the masters were contemplating making wage reductions; they had been compelled to abandon the attempt. He thought his efforts had saved the miners £24,000 to £25,000 in wages alone. He then recalled his legal triumphs—Thornley, Wingate, Jarrow, etc.—and said he would be prepared to serve the Miners' Association as a whole. "He was loudly cheered on resuming his seat," says the *Newcastle Journal*.

Cloughan, however, thought his legal triumphs had been won more by standing on legal formalities than on the merits of the cases. Roberts replied he always endeavoured to fight his cases on their merits. He had taught the magistrates law, and how to make legal warrants. The whole Association had benefited from making the law work in the miners' interests. Notwithstanding Roberts' defence of himself, after lunch the conference agreed, on a resolution moved by Edward Richardson and seconded by John Berry, that existing arrangements continue until the next conference. This meant any district wanting Roberts' services still had to apply to Northumberland and Durham, paying all expenses. A second resolution passed said "that no law agent, employed by any district, in any way could interfere with the affairs of the Association unless called on to do so".

Most of Friday, the fifth day of conference, was again taken up discussing Mr. Roberts—this time in connection with the contro-versial leaflet in which he had been attacked. Martin Jude tried to avoid this, saying it would be a waste of time to have a prolonged discussion and a vote should be taken immediately. But that did not satisfy Roberts. He jumped up and accused the executive of malpractices. They had "thwarted his exertions to benefit the Association". "They had sent letters to different parts of the empire, impugning his motives, stating it was love of money that actuated him." They had said "he wished to turn the *Miners' Association* into a political movement".

At this juncture, with Roberts still in full flood, conference passed a resolution calling upon the author of the leaflet to "stand forth and prove the statements contained therein". Whereupon Birrell, of the executive, while not accepting authorship of the leaflet, claimed parts of it were true. Roberts had violated the constitution by fostering partial strikes. Roberts had also done wrong by circulating leaflets against the executive.[1] John Hall and John Stoker followed by supporting their fellow executive member. Roberts replied to them by saying he had not interfered in Association business. He had objected to Scott and Brophy leaving South Staffs because he wanted them to gain information on the truck system, to be submitted to Parliament. Anyway, the local miners wanted them to remain there as lecturers. He also defended his right to solicit reports for his own journal since he saw nothing wrong in this. He admitted saying lecturers were useless unless they transmitted reports on legal matters to him. He conceded he had advised men at Hunswick colliery not to work as he thought the winding-gear dangerous. If this were a violation of the union's constitution, opposing partial strikes, then he pleaded guilty and, under like circumstances, would do it again. His character was a hot one; "he might be a hard-spoken man; but he meant no injury to anyone".

In the afternoon, after Roberts and delegates had made further speeches, the conference passed a four-point resolution:

First, to censure the writer of the leaflet and discount its content.

Second, to condemn circulation of it as an error, not to be repeated.

Third, to get Mr. Roberts and the executive to draw up a bill of agreement, to be laid before the Northumberland and Durham miners for approval.

Four, to appoint a committee of nine to draw up plans so that the Executive and Mr. Roberts "may not come into collision again".

Even this was not the end of the affair. On the sixth, and final day it cropped up again when John Pratt, a Roberts' supporter, tried to move, unsuccessfully, that John Hall no longer be general secretary.

*   *   *

As well as considering the role of Roberts, the Glasgow conference re-formulated the functions of the executive council. At the previous conference, at Manchester, the number of members was reduced from

---

[1] At a colliers' meeting at Black Fell "Mr Roberts said that the executive were under the pay of the masters and that he would advise the men to send them (the executive) to the masters altogether." (*History of the Coal Trade*, Picton.)

the original figure of eleven to six. However, as the Scots were unwilling to nominate another to the executive at the conference and did not do so subsequently, the number remained five. But a number of matters were left undecided, as they had not yet ascertained the exact legal position. At Glasgow, the *Advocate* reports, "a long discussion took place as to whether there should be an Executive Council or not, or whether the said Council should be permanent or not". Eventually, by a vote of 40,491 to 10,042, it was agreed to have a five-man permanent executive. Three of the five members were intended to journey about the country, inspecting agents, books and reports, while the treasurer and secretary remained in Newcastle. Fortnightly reports were to be sent to the *Advocate*. Also, the executive should meet as a whole every two months. Executive members should receive the usual wages. As each conference was convened, the duties of the executive ended. It was dissolved. The conference elected a fresh executive, which was to function until the next conference.

In the statement outlining the duties of the executive, it is significant that the first-mentioned function should be a negative one—that of not retailing "public scandal". Doubtless delegates, in drafting the document, had the recent controversy over Roberts in mind. But it is also indicative of the general tendency to regard the concept of centralised control with suspicion; initiative was to remain in the districts and branches, with periodic conferences to gather majority opinion among the membership.

The fluidity of the union, so far as its structure is concerned, is clearly shown by the fact that it had existed for seventeen months before the exact role of the executive within the organisation had been finalised.

6

Mr. Roberts versus The Bond

THE practice of having a yearly Bond, an agreement between masters and men, legally binding on both sides, existed in Northumberland and Durham as well as in a few other parts of the country. Technically an agreement freely negotiated between equals, the state of the labour market made this a grisly fiction. The effect of the Bond was to tether the worker to his job, limit his initiative, and stultify attempts at self-betterment.

Right from the inception of the union, miners in the North-east coalfields complained vociferously about the iniquities of the Bond. How it worked is described by Benjamin Embleton:

"The coalowners . . . have a standing union with regular meetings for combined action. At these meetings they ascertain how many unbound men each of them have in his employ, and five or six weeks before binding, the unbound men were discharged. Of course, they soon had empty pockets and hungry bellies. The consequence was (as the coalowners expected) that when the binding morning came, the unbound men were such as to be close 'clagged' up against the office door and ready to accept whatever terms were offered. They didn't venture to go upon the colliery, among the men; for they felt ashamed of themselves, at the same time they were forced to look about them for a living. It was thus out of the power of pit-men to have a voice in the terms of the bond. The bond was concocted in the coal trade office and the coalowners took good care to have the binding all their own way.

"When binding morning was come, and the viewer, peeping out of his office window, saw the hungry, unbound men coming up the road and clustering round the office door, to compete with the men of the colliery, he saw at once he was going to have his own way, and began his speech by saying, "We're not going to bind so many this year as last." Then, the poor hewers pressed still nearer to the door, and cared little what was in the bond when they heard it read. How should they object, when all objections would be no use? If some hewer, more independent than the rest, dared to object to any regulation of the bond, the answer was, "Oh, well, if you do not choose to sign, we don't mind: you can go somewhere else." This was enough to keep the rest quiet."[1]

The right of a miner to "go somewhere else" seems to have been severely limited. For binding was a subtle weapon, used not only for imposing onerous conditions on the necessarily acquiescent mass of colliers, but also weeding out the agitators. Co-operation between coalowners effectively prevented all protests being made. "The reason why we could not raise ourselves from this forlorn and degraded state was owing to our employers having such an understanding and communication with each other," Martin Jude explained in an undated letter, written to T. S. Duncombe. "If any of us objected to any part of the proposed articles, they immediately sent the names of such individuals round the district. Let such a person go where he would, his name and character was there before him, or, if he did get work, and it came to the ears of his late employers, a letter was immediately sent and he was discharged accordingly. Thus, Sir, you will see we were compelled to endure such oppressions as our employers thought proper to impose upon us."[2]

The Bond was buttressed by an elaborate system of fines, aimed at imposing the strictest possible industrial discipline. Masters had the power to make deductions from miners' wages virtually at will. Moreover, protests against these exactions could easily be strangled simply by increasing the level of fines. If workers found conditions intolerable and went on strike, then they would be breaking the Bond and hence the law, and rendered themselves liable to a three months' sentence. For any miner to go on strike, or to counsel others to go on strike, was an extremely hazardous action, likely to lead directly to the nearest prison.

The Bond also imperilled men's lives. A terrible instance of this happened when Mr. Buddle's management sought to connect Heaton Main with the disused Jesmond colliery to take the last of the coal. Two veteran miners, who knew the old workings, realised the danger as the water-level began to rise. "The men resolved to act on their own responsibility. They knew they incurred the risk of imprisonment, according to the bond, for quitting their employment. They consulted together and concluded that, as the danger was a matter of opinion, they were not warranted in alarming other workmen in the

---

[1] *Gateshead Observer*, 18 March 1843.   [2] Bell Collection.

colliery."[1] The two were saved; ninety-seven were drowned.

At Wingate Grange colliery the wire rope, used on the haulage, broke. The management patched up the same rope and expected everybody to continue as if nothing had happened. In places, there were twenty-two out of the ninety-six strands still broken. So the men refused to be lowered by the rope—and consequently violated their bond. One of the men, John Barkhouse, was imprisoned for refusing to work. At his trial, in July 1843, he was undefended: Roberts had not yet been appointed.

But Roberts was there when a somewhat similar event happened at Seaton Delaval colliery. On 6 November 1843 there was a fire at the north-west heading. Two days later the viewers and overmen pronounced the pit safe for work to resume. Men went down at 2 a.m., but many had to leave because of smoke and gas. They refused to go down again until the viewer had re-examined the workings. Whereupon the overman, cursing and swearing, called them "damned, lazy toads". Eventually, the viewers were called again, and re-affirmed their decision that the pit was safe for work. They said every man who refused to go down would be fined 2s. 6d. Some men went down, only to return because of the conditions they encountered. On 9 and 10 November the viewers once more declared the workings safe. A deputation of ten colliers met the viewers on 14 November and stated the men were prepared to work in any safe part of the pit. Later on, they called for their wages. They claimed that, just as the Bond stipulated how long the collier had to work each fortnight, it also stated how much the master guaranteed to pay him. They had said they were prepared to work anywhere that was safe to work—yet they had been denied their rightful wage. W. P. Roberts, for the men, put this case to the North Shields Court on 21 January 1844. He mentioned the importance of safety and proper ventilation; disregarding it had led to the great Wallsend disaster. Masters had no right, he claimed, to expect men to endanger their lives nor should they be allowed to violate the Bond with impunity. Nevertheless, Roberts' pleas fell on deaf ears. The case was dismissed.

"Mr. Roberts thanked them (i.e. the magistrates) and said he would get justice in any Court but North Shields. The men returned home in high spirits, although they had lost their trial, and resolved not to risk their lives until the pit was made safe. For they were sure, if they went to work under such circumstances and lost their lives,

[1] William Mitchell *The Question Answered: What do Pitmen Want?*

the agents would not be husband to the bereft widows, a father to the fatherless children, nor a comfort to the parents who had lost the affectionate sons, but, on the contrary, would have been ready to turn them out of doors after a few weeks."

This account ends a letter, signed "The Men of Seaton Delaval", which appeared in the *Advocate*.[1] Roberts himself also wrote about the affair, in his typically fiery and blustery way, while the dispute was still in its early stages:

"At a colliery not a hundred miles from Seaton Delaval, the masters are cursing and damning their men for not going to work. The pit it at this moment 'standing fire': it fired ten days ago: two men were seriously burnt—and yet the masters are not satisfied. We warn them that, unless they speedily change their conduct, we will 'shew them of', giving dates, and all their filthy conduct will be chronicled and immortalised. For the present we shall say no more, but the subject will not escape us."

The underlining is in the original manuscript, in Roberts' own handwriting. Two references to the Seaton Delaval coalowners being "religious men and subscribe to the chapel" were crossed out, apparently as an after-thought.[2]

⋆   ⋆   ⋆

W. P. Roberts threw everything he had got—his energy, invective, venom—into the struggle against the Bond. He spared neither himself nor his assistants. For example, soon after his appointment he was called to represent Lonsdale, a pitman who worked at Gameside pit, Durham. He was receiving a wage of only 14s. a fortnight instead of the 26s. guaranteed under the Bond. Mr. Marshall, appearing for the owners, contended the case was unproved. The Bond did not state that each individual should receive a minimum of 26s., but that this should be the average wage of all men at the colliery. Roberts retorted that, as a miner was legally compelled by the Bond to stay at the same colliery, if Mr. Marshall's contention was upheld, then the Bond would become, for some men, "a slave bond to the penalty of starvation". When the magistrates complained about the inflammatory nature of his speech, "Mr. Roberts replied he had done no more than his duty; and the inflammatory nature of the truth would not prevent him from uttering it." The magistrates found against the owner. In the same

[1] *Miners' Advocate*, 24 February and 10 March 1844.
[2] Pitmen's Strike Collection and *Miners' Journal*, 18 November 1843.

week, Roberts also defended nine miners, summoned for leaving work. He was able to seize upon a mistake in the wording of the Bond. "The coal-masters contended that this was a clerical error; Mr. Roberts, on the contrary, submitted that, in a prosecution under a penal statute, clerical errors were fatal." The case was dismissed. "Immediately on this result, a coal-master applied to Roberts for 'an amicable conversation to settle it.' 'No,' said Roberts. 'You first drag my men here as criminals, seeking to consign them to a felons' dungeon; and then, when foiled in your tyranny, talk of "settling" it. First learn to treat your workmen as honest men, and, if you must have criminals, seek for them amongst yourselves.'"[1]

Victory followed victory. Roberts stormed through Northumberland and Durham, winning cases, freeing men, gaining wages illegally withheld from them by the masters. Hitherto the law had been used against the colliers; now, for the first time, it was being made to work their way. A local paper conceded "he was more than a match for all the legal skill the owners could engage, though it had the favourable ear of a biased Court."[2]

The miners idolised Roberts. When he spoke, along with Feargus O'Connor and Beesley, at Sherriff Hill on 14 October 1843, "the men could be seen coming up to the Hill, headed by bands of music and carrying with them banners bearing different devices and mottoes. We counted sixty-seven flags and banners, but we could not ascertain the number of bands."[3] The assembled crowd, estimated at 20,000, heard Roberts recall his recent triumphs. The meeting, under his guidance, resolved "never to rest satisfied until they had broken down the tyranny of their masters and obtained justice for themselves and their families."[4]

But Roberts realised the size of the task. Not only were there laws with a bias against the working man, but the administrators of justice had their own homespun class prejudices:

"There are indeed men on the bench who are honest enough, and desirous of doing their duty. But all their tendencies and circumstances are against you. They listen to your opponents, not only often, but cheerfully—so they know more fully the case against you

[1] *Northern Star*, 16 September 1843.
[2] *Durham Chronicle*, 11 September 1843. Hylton Scott's article on "The Miners' Bond in Northumberland and Durham" makes the same point: "Except during the regime of W. P. Roberts . . . the colliers never made much use of their legal rights and the owners were clearly in a stronger position. (*Pro. of Soc. of Antiq. of Newcastle*, 1947).
[3] *Miners' Journal*, 21 October 1843.   [4] Ibid.

than in your favour. To you they listen too—but in a sort of temper of 'Prisoner at the Bar, you are entitled to make any statement you think fit, and the Court is bound to hear you; but mind, whatever you say', etc. In the one case you observe the hearty smile of goodwill; in the other the derisive sneer, though sometimes with a ghastly sort of kindliness in it. Then there is the knowledge of your over-whelming power when acting unitedly, and this begets naturally a corresponding desire to resist you at all hazards. And there are hundreds of other considerations all acting the same way—meetings, political councils, intermarriages, hopes from wills, etc. I do not say that all occupants of the bench are thus influenced, nor to the same extent; but it certainly is at the best an uphill game to contend in favour of a working man in a case which admits of any doubt against him. It never happened to me to meet a magistrate who considered that an agreement among masters not to employ any particular 'troublesome fellow' was an unlawful act; reverse the case, however, and it immediately becomes a formidable conspiracy which must be put down by the strong arms of the law."[1]

Acknowledging these gigantic obstacles to fighting for workers' rights in the Courts, Roberts adopted two tactics. First, he fought a war of attrition, contesting every case, even when there was no hope of winning. He wanted thereby to make it difficult to operate the Bond; from the owners' standpoint, not worth the candle. And, second, he saw that his only chance of succeeding in many instances was through some legal technicality, by which the case could be dismissed by a higher Court. Consequently, Roberts often indulged in what other-wise could be mistaken for comic opera antics to goad the Bench into making some mistake, a slip-up that would give him the legal loophole he required.

*　　　*　　　*

The Thornley case, an epic legal struggle over the Bond, exemplifies both points.[2] One of the largest collieries in Durham, Thornley had been one of the first to become unionised and was a stronghold of the Miners' Association. Consequently, it must have been exceedingly objectionable for the men to submit to a Bond which allowed the viewers to impose heavy fines and use weighing machines of doubtful accuracy. Eventually, the miners went on strike. In a public statement,

---

[1] *Flint Glass Makers' Magazine*, October 1851.
[2] Thornley trial material from special supplement to *Miners Advocate* (n.d.), R. Fynes op. cit., pp. 37–49 and various local papers.

issued by Joseph Hall (chairman) and Joseph Walker (secretary) for the Thornley men, they complained of being fined for unclean coal:

"It is utterly impossible to clean the coals and send them to the bank clean of splint, stones, or foul coals; besides the hewers have frequently to work with a safety lamp and breathing an atmosphere impregnated with noxious gases, calculated to stupify the physical and depress the mental system; and after working eight hours in this dreadful dungeon, in many instances, have come home in debt." [1]

For breaking their bond, warrants were issued against sixty-eight strikers. The case against three of them—Lawrence Smith, George Harewood, John Singlewood—opened at the Justice Room in the Durham County Court on 7 December 1843. Speaking for the owners, Mr. J. E. Marshall said the men were bound under the ordinary pit bond, and he would read the clauses bearing on the case. The men were under stringent terms and, if they suffered from them, they had themselves to blame, since they agreed to pay certain penalties for infraction of certain rules. He could not see what the defence could plead if the men had absented themselves from work; it was no excuse to say the agreement had been too strictly applied.

Immediately, Mr. Roberts applied to the bench to stop the case as the weighing machine had not been stamped in accordance with the provision of the Act. It made the Bond illegal. Mr. Marshall retorted that the machine had been used in previous bonds. The chairman rejected Roberts' submission.

Mr. Roberts: "I should like to have that taken down on the notes of the Court, as I shall most likely apply to the Court of Queen's Bench."

Mr. Heckles, resident viewer of Thornley, was then called for the prosecution:

"On the 13th November, I received a letter from the workmen, written and signed by James Bagley, as secretary to the workmen. The answer I gave was: I wondered why they didn't get someone who could write a letter plainer. I sent word to say that if the letter meant anything, they would have to send a deputation. On the evening of the following day, fifteen men called upon me and half of them spoke. The overman, according to instruction, deducted two shillings and sixpence fine for the day lost. [2] On the evening of the twenty third, a large body of workmen came up and asked why

[1] *Miners' Advocate*, 27 January 1844.
[2] On Saturday, 18 November the men had had a one-day strike, protesting against excessive fines. Mr. Roberts persuaded them to return to work.

the two shillings and sixpence was deducted? I told them they were asking the road they knew. (A voice in court: 'Just like you.') I offered on the Thursday, to let the men work on the pay Saturday to make it up."

Mr. Roberts objected to the evidence as none of the prisoners was present, but the chairman replied that Mr. Heckles' testimony would be accepted.

Then Mr. Heckles continued. He said that the incidence of fining increased after 12 November when they had adopted the practice of "laying out" each individual miners' stone, slate, foul coal, etc., in separate boxes. But some miners, who had not left "dirt" with the coal, were not fined at all. He agreed with Mr. Roberts that the weighing machine was not stamped. However, he thought sometimes it incorrectly favoured the men.

Chairman: "I am clearly of the opinion that the machine was incorrect against the masters and in favour of the men."

Cross-examined by Roberts, Mr. Heckles said:

"The Bond has been more accurately enforced since November 20th. I could not state the largest amount any one man has been fined in two days. The overman knows better. I don't doubt that one man may have been fined 22s. for two days. I do know that other men have been fined 8s., 7s., 6s., and 5s. a day since that time."

Replying to the chairman's question, Mr. Heckles said: "That is not the ordinary amount of fines. No workman would subject himself to such fines." Mr. Roberts interjected: "But the men have no other chance."

The prosecution concluded with factual evidence that the three accused were not at work after 23 November.

*   *   *

In his opening address for the defence, Mr. Roberts pleaded with the bench for mercy in this case. "He did not wish to be misunderstood. He did not speak of mercy in the ordinary sense of the term, because he believed the men guiltless—because he believed that their masters and Mr. Heckles ought now to be in the dock and those men now in that place ought to be standing as their accusers. But he asked for their merciful consideration because it was impossible to administer justice, fairly and honestly, unless they weighed all the circumstances of the case. These men were servants, most of them, unfortunately, hard bound ones. They were men who had much to contend with, who no doubt had much to learn, who had not received all the benefits, or any portion of them, of education; who had perhaps not received that portion of true religious instruction which the kindness of former ages gave the power to the clergy to administer, but which, he regretted to say, had not lately been extended to the poor as it ought to have been. Let the magistrates consider this—let them look to the advantages which attend the former, when the rich man was on one side and the poor man on the other, and he asked them to bring their most merciful consideration to the matter."

Mr. Roberts then contended that, whenever grievances arose, the pitmen were always anxious to reach a settlement. "But the men and the masters did not stand on a par. The utmost the men could do was to summon their masters for wages, where, perhaps, no jurisdiction could be found; but the masters could send the men to prison, however gross the fraud committed against them. It was reserved for this country to have a law to give the rich man the power of inflicting imprisonment whilst it did not give the same power to the poor man."

Then Roberts reminded the magistrates that, under the law, they could impose a fine, annul the contract, or imprison. In almost all cases, the magistrates inflicted the most severe penalty possible. "Was it always to be imprisonment—imprisonment—imprisonment, as if the men were all criminals and the masters all angels? The complaint in this case was against the masters and in favour of the men. The masters had proved themselves criminals in the eye of the law and, in fact, that if justice was done them, they would find themselves within the walls of the prison to which they were so eager to send their fellow men."

"And what was the case brought before them by Mr. Marshall? Why, it appeared that Mr. Heckles had for six months suspected that the weighing machine was wrong. True, he suspected it was wrong in favour of the men and against the masters, but when did they find a viewer who supposed anything wrong in favour of the men? Certainly not in Northumberland or Durham. By the wisdom of the law, all the benevolence was to be considered as existing on the one hand and all the fraud on the other. It would be for him to prove, in contradiction to what had been proved on the other side, that the law had been complied with by the men, so far as applying to the inspector went. He should be able to prove to them that application had been made for an inspector and that the application had been refused. Mr. Heckles said he did not know of the machine being stamped. He should show that it was not stamped, that it was incorrect, and incorrect too against the men. So it was in the case of every machine in the coal trade. Here he might say there is no case at all because the Act of Parliament referred to stated that no sale should be valid unless it was by the weighing of a machine properly stamped." Roberts contended that, as the provisions of the Act had not been complied with, the Bond was null and void; the masters could not use it against the men.

The Miners' Attorney then turned to his second line of argument: "The wages guaranteed by the Bond to the men had not been paid in the manner stated in the Bond; and, though he had heard of some very strange decisions, he had yet to hear that service was to be compelled from a man who had not been paid the wages he had previously earned." W. P. Roberts broadened the scope of this objection to make his third, and most profound, point—on the nature of the Bond itself: "Mr. Marshall had said that the law was that the men should be bound by their bond. He did not think that Mr. Marshall would say so in his sober senses for, if a man had entered into a bond, which it was morally impossible for him to fulfil, which would involve him in utter destitution, he must contend that though, under such a bond, a master had a right to come upon him for damages, yet it had no power to call on the magistrates to send the man to prison. They could not have more solemn evidence of the oppressiveness of the bond than that. Those men could voluntarily declare—so help them God—that they would not go to work till the men sent to prison had been released."

After a detailed examination of the heavy fines at Thornley, Roberts concluded his address: "He warned the masters that, in the exercise of their authority, they had proceeded too far. Not one of those men would go to work. He would tender them all as witnesses for the purpose of stating their injuries through the land—for the purpose of showing the masters exercised their authority in a mischievous manner; and he called upon them to discharge the Bond if he showed, as he was prepared to do, that it was impossible for an honest man to work under it."

Roberts then called his first witness, John Cookson, who said: "I don't think a man can get a living if the Bond is to be carried out in its strictness. If a quart of splint is to be fined for, I am sure a man cannot get a living. I will go to gaol before I will go to work under such a bond." Another miner, Thomas Dermot Moran said "I cannot earn a living if the Bond is carried out. I will rather go to gaol than work under the Bond. I was fined 27s. the last fortnight I was paid."

In a similar manner, Roberts called six witnesses, all of whom re-counted their fines, said they could not earn a living and would sooner go to gaol. Whereupon the chairman interrupted Mr. Roberts to ask if he had any evidence of a different complexion to bring forward?

"Mr. Roberts said he could not make out his case fully without bringing forward the evidence of every hewer who could not make a living. He should be happy to have an intimation from the Bench that he had already sufficiently proved the case; for, as it was a matter of opinion, he thought he ought to make his case as strong as he could. There were between 300 and 400 hewers, and he proposed to call every one of them in order, by the accumulation of evidence, to show the real state of the case."

After a heated discussion, during which the chairman declared that in this case large bodies of men had banded together in open defiance of the law, it was agreed to adjourn the case till the next day. It was hoped the parties would, in the meantime, arrive at an agreement.

These hopes, however, proved abortive. No agreement was reached, and so, next morning—Friday, 8 December—Roberts rose to continue his case. He began by alluding to the chairman's statement of the previous evening, when he had accused the prisoners of being "in open defiance of the law", and Roberts charged the bench with already pronouncing the prisoners guilty. One magistrate, Dr. Fenwick, replied that Mr. Roberts was conveniently deaf and behaving with the greatest insolence to the Bench. Another, Mr. Elliott, was surprised the pitmen were too blind to see what harm their advocate was doing. Continuing with his case, Roberts proceeded to call another ten witnesses, all of whom told the Court of the heavy fines, said it was impossible to earn a living under the Bond and declared they would rather go to prison than continue to work under the Bond.

After an adjournment till 13 December Roberts resumed his case, calling a further three witnesses. Then he applied to be allowed to produce steelyards in Court as evidence of fraudulent weighing of coal. He said he had known a case in which a horse was produced in court. But the chairman said the Court had already decided that the Act, relating to the weighing of coal, did not apply in this case. Roberts called another fifteen witnesses.

The following day another four miners strode into the witness box to give the now-familiar evidence. The fourth was asked by Roberts if he had heard anything to justify the imputation by the Bench that he (i.e. Roberts) had tried to widen the breach between masters and men.

The chairman objected to the question, as he was not aware of such an imputation being made. Roberts replied that it had been "by those who ought to be ashamed of themselves for doing so". Mr. Elliott said he believed Mr. Roberts was referring to an observation of his during the disorderly scene in Court last Friday. He was sorry and surprised to see a man, professing to have a liberal education, conducting himself as Mr. Roberts did and that was why the observation was made. He thought Mr. Roberts' conduct could only be styled indecent, and asked him for an apology.

Mr. Roberts: "Some people can only be lashed into justice, and I have applied the lash."

Mr. Elliott said this remark could not be taken as a personal insult but as an insult to the Bench. The magistrates retired, and then returned. Mr. Hays, clerk to the court, read the following resolution:

"The Bench is of the opinion that a gross contempt of Court has been committed by Mr. Roberts in the observations just addressed by him to the Bench, which, in a superior court of justice, would have led to immediate commitment, and the magistrates are willing to hope that another mode of proceeding which is open to the Court may be rendered unnecessary by a proper apology."

Mr. Roberts withdrew the expression and apologised. He then asked the Court if they were not satisfied that men could not earn a living under the Bond without him having to call all his witnesses. Eventually, the magistrates agreed that, as all the men's evidence would be the same, they would take it as if sworn.

Mr. Roberts then asked leave to give his own evidence. He described the sequence of events, stressing that only minor concessions would have had to be made to have kept the men at work. Mr. Marshall replied that, even if what Mr. Roberts said were true, the men had still committed a breach of the law. Anyway, they had no wrong of which to complain. He went on to read a declaration by the Company, stating it had no desire to victimise the men. If they returned to work, the same mode of fines would be adopted as at other collieries. Mr. Roberts expressed gratitude for the offer, but said the men would not return to work until their grievances were settled.

Giving the verdict, the chairman pronounced the prisoners guilty and sentenced them to six weeks' imprisonment. He refused Mr. Roberts' request for a deferred judgment and the prisoners were removed. Immediately after the trial, Mr. Roberts obtained a writ of habeas corpus. The prisoners were taken to the Court of the Queen's bench and, upon a formality, were acquitted.[1]

Mr. Roberts and the released prisoners returned from London to be greeted by scenes of ecstatic joy. People lined the route for miles, cheering the triumphal procession. At Thornley, the men were carried shoulder high round the village. As for Roberts himself, it remained the highlight of his career with the miners. Twenty years later, in a letter to the Leeds conference, he still recalled what happened: "Thousands, as I drove along came out to bless me; the homage was more than agreeable—it was intoxicative; and though I was in constant dread of violence, I was never so happy, and never should be so again."

*   *   *

After Thornley, Roberts intensified his struggle against legal injustice. As Engels says, he "carried on a crusade against the despotic Justices of the Peace and truck masters such as had never been known in England". Whenever a miner was sentenced by a magistrates court, Roberts obtained a writ of habeas corpus from the Court of Queen's bench, brought his client to London and always secured an acquittal. For example, soon after the Thornley victory, on 13 January 1844, Judge Williams, of Queen's bench, ordered three miners imprisoned by Bilston magistrates to be released. They had been jailed because they refused to work in a place that threatened to cave in and, in fact, actually did before they returned to work. In the same month, Roberts journeyed to Preston, where four miners were imprisoned, and secured their release before the sentence expired. Then, he went to Manchester. Seven colliers employed by Lancaster and Company at Patricroft colliery, Eccles, had been jailed because they had broken their contract by striking.[2] They had not given a month's notice. None of them earned more than 6d. a day and, when Mr. Maude (the magistrate) gave them time to reconsider whether they would return to work they remained obdurate. So they received a two-month sentence, which Roberts got the Court of Queen's bench to quash. In Prescott nine miners were in jail, accused of creating a disturbance at St. Helens; the mere arrival of Roberts secured their release. His services were then required in Yorkshire. After winning a legal battle in Wakefield, Roberts and "the liberated men were escorted to Barnsley with

[1] Court of Queen's bench: Before the judicial reform of 1873, it was one of the three high courts. It tried mainly political and criminal cases and heard appeals from the magistrates courts.
[2] *Manchester Guardian*, 24 January 1844.

banners flying and music playing". The colliers of Barnsley "came in thousands, with flags and music, to meet their advocate".[1]

Next to Chesterfield to condemn the conduct of the local magistrates, "who had sent four men to Derby jail without suffering them to speak for themselves".[2]

Roberts rushed around the country like a man possessed, freeing men in one coalfield after another. The Newcastle headquarters were inundated with requests like this from William Walker, secretary of the Derbyshire miners:

> "Mr. Roberts' services would have been of great use to us in this district if we could have him for a short time to have delivered the prisoners at Derby: in short, his very presence would have made the tyrants tremble. . . . . Sir, the very name of Roberts strikes terror to their very souls."[3]

In fact, this is no exaggeration. Engels echoed these sentiments: "The name Roberts began to be a terror to the mineowners. . . . One after another Roberts brought the disreputable mineowners before the Courts and compelled the reluctant Justices of the Peace to condemn them; such dread of this 'lightning' 'Attorney General' who seemed to be everywhere at once spread among them, that at Belper, for instance, upon Roberts' arrival, a truck firm published the following notice:

Pentrich Coal Mine

The Messrs. Haslam think it necessary, in order to prevent all mistakes, to announce that all persons employed in their colliery will receive their wages wholly in cash, and may expend them when and as they choose to do. If they purchase goods in the shops of Messrs. Haslam they will receive them as heretofore at wholesale prices, but they are not expected to make their purchases there, and work and wages will be continued as usual whether purchases are made in these shops or elsewhere."[4]

Triumphs such as these, as Engels acknowledged, "aroused jubilation throughout the English working class and brought the Union a mass of new members". On top of his legal work, W. P. Roberts found himself much in demand as a writer and speaker. He wrote much of the material that appeared in the Miners' Journal and, without actually holding a membership card, became the Miners' Association's most influential spokesman.

[1] F. Machin, The Yorkshire Miners.   [2] Derbyshire Courier, 6 April 1844.
[3] Miners' Magazine, March–April 1844.   [4] F. Engels, op. cit., p. 292.

But Roberts gargantuan efforts were time-consuming. In a letter to the union, explaining why pressure of work necessitated Beesley and himself relinquishing the editorship of the *Miners' Journal*, he gives an insight into his personal situation: "We are in the office frequently before eight and remain there till ten or twelve at night; and even Sunday, I regret to say, is also employed. I am writing this at ten on Sunday night and it is but a few hours since I took instructions to be at Bishop Auckland tomorrow at nine, starting at about four in the morning."[1] And this note in the *Miners' Magazine* tells its own doleful story:

"Chesterfield—The simple reason why Mr. Roberts did not stop there on the Thursday night was that he was fast asleep at the time —in fact, he did not wake till asked for his ticket at Derby. It sometimes occurs that Mr. Roberts passes four nights out of seven on the railroad and, so far from trying to keep awake, he is glad to get any rest he can."[1]

The same issue mentions the difficulty of correspondents whose letters to Roberts were likely to follow him around on his circular tours of Britain. Advising them to send letters either to his London or Newcastle offices, it says "he seldom stops more than a few hours at any one place except Newcastle. In cases of great importance it is best to send duplicates to both residences."

Roberts was young and energetic. While in the Northern coalfields he thought nothing of being up in the early hours in order to arrive at the pithead at 6 a.m., to talk to the morning shift before it went down. The men's confidence in him gradually grew until he received an adulation that the labour movement rarely gives to its leaders. This was especially true in Northumberland and Durham, where Roberts, in the miners' eyes, could do no wrong.

An indication of the high esteem in which he was held comes from many miners' songs. "The Colliery Union", a song written by Elizabeth Gair, a pitman's wife, contains the lines:

> "Success to your commander,
> And Roberts is his name,
> Since he has prov'd so loyal,
> We'll spread about his fame."

[1] Pitmen's Strike Collection.   [1] *Miners' Magazine*, June–July, 1844.

The song also mentions "young Beesley", "a man of wit possessed", and has the rousing chorus:

"So stick unto your Union,
And mind what Roberts say
If you be guided by his word,
You'll surely win the day."

Two ballads recount the story of the Thornley trial. One of them, entitled "Mr. Roberts, The Pitman's Friend", says:

"As their oppression was so great, they could not with it stand,
Which made them join in heart and voice, likewise in hand and hand,
And meetings rose in different parts their rights for to unfold,
Then O'Connor thought of Roberts and his name unto them told."

It also mentions that, after the Queen's Bench acquittal, Roberts took the released men to O'Connor for a celebration, and "he treated them far better than the noblest in the land". The twelfth, and last verse is:

"Now here's to Mr. Roberts, for he's the Pitman's friend,
He's worthy of his salary to make the tyrants bend,
Now may he live in unity and his men unto him cling
For to take all tyranny from them and out of them the sting."

The second song about Thornley has the chorus:

"Cheer up, my lads, for Roberts's bold;
And well defends our cause,
For such a drubbing he's gi'en them
With their own class-made laws."

But undoubtedly the most significant, both about the tradition of struggle in the coalfields and about Roberts' role at that time, is a very popular piece entitled "The Pitmen's Union". This had been the battle-hymn of the earlier Hepburn union of 1830-2, and the original version contained in the final verse the lines:

"Long, long, may Hepburn live;
Long may our Union last;"

A printed copy of this—evidently published in the 1830 to 1832 period—is in the Wigan Library Collection, and it shows how, even when the Hepburn union was smashed, some of his members wished to preserve its ideas and sentiments. But more important still is the fact that the name of Hepburn is crossed out and Roberts' name is inserted. The Collection contains two printed copies of this revised version. The colliers of the Northern Counties could not have paid him any greater compliment: Roberts had replaced Hepburn as the great miners' leader.

7

The Strike Question, 1843–1844

THE Association soon discovered, through bitter experience, that little progress could be made by appealing to the better nature of employers and the general public. The owners were as unwilling to sacrifice their profits as the customers were to pay a higher price for coal. Neither saw it as their responsibility to improve colliers' wages and conditions. So the Association was compelled to rely upon its own efforts, and quickly its discussions centred on the strike question.

At first, however, the tactic of restricting output was used. At the Newcastle conference of 6 May 1843, it was resolved to ask all hewers to limit their incomes to 3s. a day. Of course, this resolution was only applied in those areas where the Association had members. Nevertheless, Ben Embleton, addressing a mass meeting in July 1843, said it was already having beneficial results; they should continue restricting individual output until all miners were employed.

In an address to the Northumberland and Durham miners, John Hall disclosed the logic behind this tactic.[1] He based his case on the assumption that each hewer filled twelve tubs, each weighing six hundredweights, a day—in other words, three tons twelve hundredweights. The average number of workers per pit in the North-east was 114. So daily output would be 410 tons at each colliery. Trade was bad, and so miners could only expect to work eight days a fortnight. This meant that the estimated tonnage of an average pit for six months would be 42,640 tons, i.e. 410 × 8 × 13. If, however, only nine instead of twelve tubs were produced each day, then to produce the same output for the whole six months a further twenty-five days' work would be required. This extra work, Hall calculated, would mean that, in the 123 pits in the North-east coalfields, drivers would receive £2,152 10s. more, trappers £890 more, and offhanders £922 more. He continued:

"I would now ask whether is that money better in your pockets or your employers? Certainly in yours, because you have earned it by

---

[1] *Miners' Advocate*, 16 December 1843.

honest means. Would your masters care if they could persuade you to raise as much coal in eight days as you should send to the bank in 10? Not they; the more you send to the bank, the better for them, and the worse for yourselves. . . ."

Hall argued restriction would stop 2,000 from being dismissed at slack periods, being reduced to starvation-point, and then accepting whatever conditions the owners imposed at the next binding.

Opponents of the union regarded restrictionism as a sign of the miners' folly, a self-inflicted hardship. Commissioner Tremenheere bemoaned in his 1844 Report that:

"The young man, desirous of employing his strength and industry to accumulate a little money before marrying; the young man newly married, and anxious to lay up a little store against a pinching time when he is bringing up his children; the young and industrious and active father of a growing family, wishing to clothe and educate them properly; each of these is allowed to earn no more, though he could get through his quantity in six hours, than the old man who takes ten hours to do the same work."[1]

Tremenheere forecast this would ultimately result in disaster:

"They fancy that by thus regulating the 'output' of coal, they can regulate prices and wages; although general reasoning would be amply sufficient to demonstrate the impossibility of such a scheme. . . ."[2]

However, in his next Annual Report he has a somewhat different tale to tell:

"The combination of the colliers which, though directed against their masters and the public interests, must be ultimately far more disastrous to their own, still continues . . . the temporary success they have had in obtaining a higher rate of wages for a less amount of work, has given them increased confidence, and blinds all but the more intelligent among them to the severity of the reaction which they were preparing for themselves."[3]

Tremenheere goes on to cite two examples of this "temporary success". At Whitflat, Lanarkshire, between September 1843 and December 1844, a third was taken off the day's work and one-fifth added to the wages, "making the enormous difference of $53\frac{1}{4}$ per cent

---

[1] *Report of the Mining Commissioners, 1844*, p. 32.
[2] Ibid., *1845*, p. 7.
[3] Ibid.

against the master in the price he pays for working the coal."[1] At Monkland's eleven pits, providing coal for the iron and steel works, the men did eight hutches per day for 3s.; after April 1844, only 5½ hutches for 3s. 4d.—"in this case the addition is 36 per cent."

Despite improvements achieved by restrictions, the tactic had limitations. It depended upon all miners being able to sustain a self-imposed discipline. This became extremely difficult when non-unionists, who felt under no obligation to limit their wages, discovered that the Association's restriction policy enhanced their opportunities to increase their own incomes—by working long hours. Union members, therefore, had the galling experience of seeing their sacrifices profiting those whom they regarded as Judases to their class. Of course, these renegade miners need not be seen: they might work in far-distant coalfields, yet the coal they produced was transported to districts where it swamped the Association's efforts.

Difficulties also arose even when miners remained completely loyal to the union. For restriction could either be on hours worked or on wages. If it were on hours, then men in Northumberland and Durham, working under the Bond, could not comply. They were legally bound to work a stipulated number of hours, and prison sentences would be inflicted were they not to do so. On the other hand, were the restriction on wages, then it would have no effect in those areas where conditions were worst and exploitation the greatest. In Somerset, wages averaged only 1s. 10d. and in North Wales they were even worse. Yet owners in these areas would not be hit by a policy that restricted miners to earning 3s. a day; it would be the most generous coalowners, paying the highest wages, that would receive the hardest knocks.

For these reasons, the restriction policy was no solution. It was not an alternative to strike action; it merely posed the question of strike action in a more acute form. Indeed, some miners saw it merely as a temporary tactic: restriction on output would create a general shortage of coal that would make the ensuing strike more effective.

*   *   *

The first time the question of a general strike was discussed seriously was at the Newcastle conference on 1 September 1843. It was the first truly national conference, with 200 representatives from almost every coalfield. Delegates from Scotland, Lancashire and the Midlands spoke against strike action. They argued that, as total membership was only

[1] Ibid.

50,000, it would be ineffective. Some added, however, that at the present rate of recruitment the position would be transformed within the next six months and should be reviewed. Then W. P. Roberts, attending his first conference, endorsed this view and "was received with deafening cheers". Conference decided:

> "That, in the opinion of the delegates now present, a strike under existing circumstances would only be partial and inimical to the best interests of the Society; and that it would be injudicious to adopt such a measure until the country is properly organised."[1]

It was agreed that the general demand should be for 4s. for an eight-hour day. Colliers at each pit were required to make out a statement of their grievances, lay them before their employers and, if no redress was granted, to make a public statement of their case in the *Northern Star*. This procedure had two advantages. First, the initial approach by the union, at colliery level, would sound out employers' attitudes. And, second, statements of grievances from each colliery would constitute a vast accumulation of factual data. In the light of this greater knowledge, the next conference could decide, all the better, on what was to be done.

The next conference was held at Manchester, opening on 2 January 1844. Quickly, it got down to discussing a proposal to tighten the restriction policy: "That no man work on pay Saturdays, as it will be the means of keeping a great quantity of coals from the market." But, equally quickly, conference ran into difficulties, since conditions varied so greatly throughout the country. Some miners were paid on Fridays, not Saturdays. The Potteries' delegates said they worked little more than half a day on Saturdays and Mondays. There were only 1,000 tons of coal in reserve in this area; an immediate closure would be more effective. In contrast, South Staffordshire miners worked a full day—not a shortened day, as in most places—on pay day. Yet their delegates said they would abide by any decision conference reached. But in Yorkshire, miners only worked two or two-and-a-half days a week; they would, whatever conference said, be glad to work whenever they could.

Having reached this impasse on restricting working hours, conference turned to consider whether it was possible to restrict pay even further—from 3s. to 2s. 6d. In some parts of Lancashire this was already done; their delegates stoutly maintained others should follow

---

[1] *Northern Star*, 9 September 1843.

their lead. But W. Ballantine thought it would simply provoke the coalowners to replace them by unemployed workers. There were 1,500 men without work in his district, and so they had decided to maintain their existing arrangements. Thomas Weaver said that, where he came from—South Staffordshire—they got 3s. 6d. a day. However, employers would not permit restriction; therefore the miners had no option. John Berry, of Wigan, then suggested that, instead of working a full day, all should limit themselves to three-quarters of a day's work. But this would only be feasible if all were in the union, said Weaver.

With the matter still unresolved, conference returned to the issue next day. A Lancashire delegate said it was difficult to maintain 2s. 6d. if some were receiving 3s. Defending 3s., Chris Haswell, of Tyneside, claimed the market was not being glutted. Masters frequently sent ships away without coal. To restrict further would merely result in the owners bringing more men into the mining industry; each district should be left to decide for itself. His fellow countryman, T. Bell, disagreed with him: only three out of sixteen pits in the North received 3s. He worked eleven days a fortnight and was never paid more than 24s. Further disagreement came from executive member H. Berrill, who reminded conference that a policy of restriction, to be effective, needed to be universally applied.

There were insuperable obstacles to united action. Thomas Wakenshaw (chairman) reminded them that in Northumberland and Durham the Bond stipulated men should perform work at a specified price. If they failed to, they were fined 2s. 6d. It would be an absurd position for them to restrict themselves to a wage of 2s. 6d. a day and pay a daily fine of 2s. 6d. for so doing. William Dixon, spokesman for North Staffs, raised another problem. They received 3s. 6s. to 4s. a day. If the resolution were implemented, it would mean a reduction of 1s. 6d. for them. Yet, whatever wage they received, they would still be expected to do the same work; they were not paid by the job as in the North.

When it was put to the vote, 14,913 favoured restriction to 2s. 6d. and 12,784 to 3s. Staffordshire and Yorkshire abstained. That the policy could have a painful back-kick on the union's strength soon became apparent. The next resolution discussed was that subscriptions should be raised to 6d. a fortnight. Conference rejected it in view of the loss of income to members due to restriction.

★   ★   ★

Next, conference turned to the strike question. As the assembly was being held in Manchester, it could not help being made aware of the industrial strife throughout the whole of the South Lancashire coalfield. That day the Bolton and St. Helens miners had stopped work, and a resolution calling for a general strike was only reluctantly withdrawn. The discussion was opened by Westhead, of Lancashire, who told conference Lancashire was prepared to strike now. In fact, John Berry reminded them, many were already out. Twenty independent strikes had occurred throughout Lancashire; hundreds of men had been out for five months. Since the Association's last conference condemned partial strikes, these men had not received a penny from union funds. Disgruntled by this lack of support, they were determined to leave the union.[1]

Most delegates did not share Lancashire's strike enthusiasm. George Charlton feared "the masters would strike some of them off to Durham gaol"; a Staffordshire delegate said they were unprepared; and William Dixon talked of large quantities of coal cunningly hidden in manufacturers' yards for such an emergency. The views of W. P. Roberts, absent through illness, were relayed to conference by Beesley; he thought a general strike would be suicide; it was first necessary to strengthen the organisation.

This was the generally accepted opinion. It was decided to defer discussion until the next conference. Meanwhile, Beesley and Dixon were deputed to visit the St. Helens men on strike to explain the union's position.

Those wanting to avoid a head-on collision with the masters emphasised the need for negotiation. The last day of the conference was devoted to considering this topic. Heartened by the reception of a semi-official overture to two owners—Messrs. Crippen and Godfrey—Thomas Mycroft (Derbyshire) and Joseph Ramsay (Durham) said this pointed the way forward. Every effort should be made to reconcile masters and men. Endorsing this opinion, Berrill added it was important to put prudent men on the deputation. Then Henry Dennett, a leader of the 1831 Lancashire union, told conference of his experience as one of the delegation meeting Lancashire, Cheshire and Derbyshire owners at that time. "The result was that the masters were perfectly satisfied, and gave the men the wages they wanted." But when the men resumed work, they forgot the union and were lost.

[1] Membership of the union at St. Helens dropped from 1,000 in January 1844, to 219 in November 1844.

At this juncture John Berry jumped up. That morning he had heard the Earl of Balcarres' men had stopped work. They were determined to have their grievances redressed. It had been nothing but warfare between masters and men in Lancashire since the last union conference. He hoped a deputation from the Association would reach agreement with the owners, as it would save the union in some parts of the country. If an agreement were not reached, the Lancashire colliers confidently expected a strike.

The chairman, to give delegates an idea of the militant feeling in Lancashire, read a letter he had just received:

"Dear Brethren,
    This is to let you know that we, the miners of the Earl of Balcarres, have agreed at a great meeting that the present time is the most suitable for a strike, and are determined to have one, believing the corn is ripe at the present in our quarter; and if you be on our side, we shall be on your side when yours is ripe; and if not, remember that we are determined to withdraw, for it will totally break us up."

"After reading the letter, the chairman immediately tore it to pieces as a mark of disapprobation with its content."[1]

John Berry then said he "believed the delegates from Northumberland and Durham thought he had the bad feeling to urge a strike; but knowing the minds of the men, and their situation, he thought it was his duty to urge a strike at that meeting. ['It was,' shouted some Lancashire delegates.] And why? At the last conference word was sent to Wigan that he did not represent the men as he ought to do in Newcastle. ['Hear, hear'.] He knew before he came that a strike could not be accomplished, but, at the same time, he thought it his duty to deliver the opinions of those whom he represented."

The chairman assured Berry nobody blamed him for doing that.

In haste, conference resumed consideration of how to conduct negotiations with the owners. Mark Dent and Thomas Weaver moved that the Association's general secretary should enter into correspondence with the secretary of the coalowners for the purpose of adjusting differences. Immediately, Thomas Pratt stated he thought it impractical. His reason was not the crucial one—that the employers had no national organisation and hence there was nobody with whom to correspond—but that of local separatism. Seconded by William Richardson, he moved a resolution that each area negotiate separately.

[1] *Miners' Advocate*, 13 January 1844.

Martin Jude thought "a general wage for every man might be fixed in the first place; and then it might be left to the men of each colliery and each owner to agree upon the price of work so as to make the money up. He thought it better to appoint the deputation at once, and not discuss any more about it."

Conference, following Jude's impetuous advice and sharing his zeal for reconciliation, appointed a committee to negotiate with the masters. It had nowhere to go, nobody to see. It did nothing.

*   *   *

Manchester had been in inconclusive conference. On the three major questions—restrictions, strikes and negotiations—it had failed to arrive at any satisfactory conclusions. So, obviously, the debate continued. Three documents give a remarkable insight into opinions on the efficacy of the strike weapon. The first, a public appeal "To Employers, Agents and All Others connected with Collieries", was issued by the South Staffordshire committee of the Association on 8 January 1844. South Staffs was a stronghold of weakness. Colliers there were still smarting under the effects of the unsuccessful strike of the previous summer, and the union, led by moderates like Thomason, had risen from the ashes. Many thought the Association's continued existence in the Black Country depended on the coalowners being prepared to tolerate it. In turn, this depended on the Association's clear disavowal of strikes and wages demands. So the appeal said, "We seek no advance of wages: we unite not for the purpose of having a General Strike."

The union's national executive used the South Staffordshire appeal and drastically altered it as the basis for a document stating its own position.[1] Its amended version read:

"We only seek just and proper wages: we unite not for the purpose of having a General Strike, but, if we should be driven to it as a dernier resort, it will only be in self-defence and it should be remembered that the greater part of the strikes that have taken place have been to resist wage reductions, not to demand advances of wages. We unite to reduce the hours of labour, to call into employ the unemployed, and ultimately to make the product of our labour scarce in the market and thus give an advance of profit to the employers and better wages to the workmen."

[1] The original South Staffs document and the executive's document are contained in the Pitmen's Strike Collection. Various handwritten comments in the margin of the documents give a fascinating indication of how the discussion went on the executive.

The executive went on to remind owners: overproduction and competition had reduced profits as well as wages.

Wishing to reassure owners, South Staffs sought to show the futility of strikes:

"All former Associations were for the express purpose of seeking an advance of wages, in consequence of which serious strikes took place, injurious alike to the workmen and employer. To show we do not want to screen the evil of former Associations. . . ."

And then it enumerates the cost of former strikes: the Manchester spinners' cost £224,000 in 1810, £200,000 in 1826, and their more recent strike cost £174,000; Preston spinners lost £74,000 through strike action and the town lost £107,000, etc. The South Staffs statement continued:

"The strike of the colliers of Northumberland and Durham in 1831 and 1832 cost the enormous sum of £55,000, and did not better the conditions of colliers 50d. in a year! With facts like these before us: the pernicious and evil consequences of strikes, is it at all probable that we should (as is now stated by interested parties) wish for a strike? It is not."

All this anti-strike talk was erased from the executive's statement and replaced by:

"We have no secrets; all is done openly and to any of our meetings all are invited. Manufacturers! Traders! and Shopkeepers! You are deeply interested in our welfare. There have been unions in former times: in the year 1831, the pitmen of Northumberland and Durham gained an advance of wage equal to the reduction in the ten preceding years, amounting to the enormous sum of £300,000, at the same time reducing hours of labour from fourteen to twelve hours per day."

Wages were then £1 4s. 6d. a week, claimed the executive; now they were only 13s., and this had an adverse effect on trade.

A third view was expressed by W. P. Roberts. Unlike the moderates, he saw no possibility of a *détente* between masters and men. Capital and labour were locked in a deadly struggle. It was a war, and workers should fight it like a war, giving no quarter, making no concessions. Roberts remained confident of their ultimate victory. Whereas other miners' leaders, talking of "a fair wage", simply thought it meant more money, Roberts had an entirely different conception. He expounded a doctrine that many early 19th century radicals and Chartists accepted. He thought that work was the source of all wealth, and miners would only get "a fair wage" when they received the full fruits of their labours. In the first issue of the *Miners' Journal*, he put forward this view. He stated he was "convinced a working miner is of more value than all the Coal Pit Kings in Christendom. They shall now be taught, to the utmost of our humble abilities, that labour is more value than gold; and that without labour Mankind could not exist; and the splendid carriages in which are drawn the bodies of their owners; the magnificent palaces that are built on our green fields and in our fertile plains; the superb furniture with which they are adorned; the gardens and pleasure grounds by which they are surrounded, and in which are set steel traps and spring guns; the greenhouses and fish-ponds—have all been filched from the earnings of the working miners."

Since he equated profit-making with robbery, Roberts had no compunction about supporting strikes. He did not regard the general strike as a weapon to be used only in the last resort. It was a necessary and inevitable step in social emancipation. So Roberts sought to hasten the final confrontation that would lead to the workers' victory. His fiery oratory and prose made him the main spokesman of the militants, in marked contrast to the more conciliatory tones of Jude and the executive. Even when he was advocating the same tactic—for instance, opposing strikes at single pits—he couched his argument in more extreme terms and had different motives:

"During a partial strike, the particular colliery must be supported by those of the neighbourhood. Should this resource fail, the men on strike will be obliged to return to their labour, giving a triumph to the master, who (on the return of the hewers to their employment) immediately avails himself of it, by paying wages even less than those which occasioned the strike, increasing the fines, and adding to that disgusting insolence, which beyond all others—even beyond money grabbing—is the filthy characteristic of the genuine Coal King. On the other hand, should the experiment not immediately fail, it is a fearful 'pull' on the energies and resources of our neighbours, whose grievances are perhaps as great as our own; and who are rendered an easy prey to their owners by the exhaustion consequent on repeated drainings.

Again, it frequently occurs that the masters possess *several* collieries: a strike therefore at *one* merely leaves him to supply his trade from the *others*. He grins! evil devil that he is. More work is given to those who continue at their employ. The process which is starving a portion of his slaves, has no effect at all upon *him*, save enabling him to get rid of a stock that was fast mouldering away. He calculates that the strikers will now 'come to' and he calculates rightly; for he has nothing to 'come to' for. He grins again! His wife chuckles, pour soul, the 'partner of his bosom', and little Susan has a new pair of dancing shoes."

But, unlike Jude and company, the reason why Roberts did not want them to squander their powder on small strikes was that he eagerly awaited the big explosion, the great class battle that would lead, as Benbow believed, to the new apocalypse:

"There are many other reasons we might give against partial strikes. The last we shall give is, however, to our minds the greatest of all. Here it is: we are in favour of a strike, A GENERAL AND UNIVERSAL ONE: a general cessation of work in the pits in order that by a universal combination, the coal hewers may obtain a fair price for their labour. In our efforts we mean strictly to abide by the law and never to outstep it. For this, large sacrifices will be required from the pit-men; they must live hardly, both at the time and previously; they must buy a stock of eatables and drinkables to support them while their masters are awakening from their slumbers of luxury. We believe that this, if well and carefully managed, with provision, discretion and PLUCK, at the tight time, not a moment before, not a moment later, will do the whole thing *at once*. And why have a dozen sacrifices when one will do? Bear with everything, complain of nothing, lay all you can spare *and more*, and rely upon it that the time of your emancipation is not very distant; it may be nearer than the most sanguine of us expect. Let us then be *provided*. We deprecate partial strikes because they weaken us and thus postpone the hour of our social redemption."

Roberts' article appeared as an editorial in the *Miners' Journal*.[1] Doubtless, it caused shivers of fear down the spines of the moderates, who believed Roberts, unless checked, would wreck the Association by precipitous strike action. It probably provides the underlying reason for the personal campaign of vilification and abuse against Roberts carried on by pamphlet and at the crucial Glasgow conference. It may also be significant that, after the above-quoted editorial appeared, the Association discontinued the publication of the *Miners' Journal* with Roberts and Beesley in charge, and the *Miners' Advocate*, with William Daniels as editor, began to appear. The effect of this change was not lost on Tremenheere, the Mines Commissioner:

[1] Original manuscript in Pitmen's Strike Collection.

"The periodical first addressed to the members of the Union, called the Miners' Journal (October 1843), contained much intemperate language; the accusations of cruelty and oppression practised by the masters, and abuse of the men promoted to offices of trust; encouragement to use violence to those who refused to join the union; extracts from works calculated to give a false impression of the general conduct of the upper classes towards the lower; complaints relative to grievances; and recommendations to prepare for a general strike of all coal-miners in the kingdom. In the following December this journal was succeeded by a more temperate one called the *Miners' Advocate*, also published at Newcastle-on-Tyne. Some of the communications to this paper are in all respects unobjectionable, display excellent feeling and a sincere desire to promote the improvement of the colliers in every point of view."[1]

It may seem peculiar that the Association's official paper adopted a milder, more conciliatory attitude to the masters as a wave of militancy surged through the rank-and-file. The most outspoken advocates of strikes were the Northumberland and Durham miners. At the Manchester conference, in January 1844, men from these two counties urged moderation and were angry with the Lancashire miners for striking. Yet, at the Glasgow conference only three months later, the Northumberland and Durham miners had swung right over, become advocates of a general strike, and determined to strike themselves, whatever other coalfields might do.

How was this dramatic change accomplished? What was the role of Roberts? The North-east was his stomping ground. In the spring of 1844 he took a leading part in the mass agitation there. At the numerous large meetings W. P. Roberts' fiery oratory received ecstatic applause; executive members were usually conspicuous by their absence. He drew up an elaborate new Bond, to be placed before the owners when the old Bond expired on 5 April 1844. This new Bond, which stipulated the conditions under which miners would be prepared to work, was only to be an interim measure, lasting for six months, not the customary year. For the men (and their Attorney) saw the Bond as an evil thing to be smashed. The Bond—"if any there be"—would run from April 1844 to 5 October 1844, Roberts told the Northumberland and Durham colliers: "On the last named day ALL the pitmen of the kingdom must be freemen: it will be on a Saturday and all the pits of the kingdom must have a whole holiday."

[1] *Report of the Mining Commissioner, 1844*, p. 68.

In March 1844, W. P. Roberts, who had not written for the *Advocate*, started publishing his own paper—the *Miners' Magazine*—independent of executive control. It says in the first issue:

"The great thing I want to accomplish is to induce you to *think*—to talk, to argue—upon those matters which concern you; when once you really *do*, you are sure to think rightly."

W. P. Roberts goes on to advise men of the Two Counties to forswear drink so as to husband greater resources for the impending struggle. He always knew "the owners will not easily yield the power which wealth, union, community of interest and consolidation of thought have given them." But he comforted the colliers by reminding them, in his concluding sentence, of their collective resolve:

"The one great thing you have to be determined upon is TO BE FREE ON SATURDAY, THE FIFTH DAY OF OCTOBER, ONE THOUSAND EIGHT HUNDRED AND FORTY-FOUR!"

The Northumberland and Durham delegates arrived at the Glasgow conference on 25 March 1844 panting for action. They interrupted a discussion on the *Advocate* to ask for the strike question to be considered as they wished to send the conference decision home by the evening post. Delegates agreed. So Christopher Haswell moved their resolution calling for a general strike. An amendment was moved by Cloughan "that there be no strike, as it was not warranted by the present condition or future prosperity of the miners".

Quickly delegates aligned themselves on one side or the other. Derby and Notts favoured a strike, coal stocks were low. South Staffs thought it injurious and premature; a strike would increase miners' indebtedness and increase the power of truck shops. But David Swallow, now leading his native Yorkshiremen, stated that hitherto he had opposed a general strike; now, with the coal shortage caused by restriction, he thought it could be successful. A Leicestershire delegate, however, told him thousands of tons were stocked in Fife ready for shipment. Cloughan said 30,000 tons were also ready at Dundee and many hundreds of thousands of tons at Brommelaw. This did not dismay Ben Embleton though: English coalowners would not allow the Scots to capture the London market. If other colliers kept away, the Northumberland and Durham men would win.

Significantly, none of the districts that had recently indulged in industrial action favoured the resolution. Lancashire, so outspokenly in favour of strikes at the previous conference, seemed to have had their ardour dampened. One of their delegates—from Ashton-under-Lyne —said if conference agreed to a general strike they would be attending the funeral of the Association. Hunter, of Cumberland, said the district had been exhausted after its recent struggle, but they still would not damage Northumberland and Durham's chances. This view was echoed by Lanarkshire.

Martin Jude spoke strenuously against strikes; preferring reconciliation. W. P. Roberts, tongue in cheek, agreed with Jude, quizzically adding that in Northumberland and Durham it would not be a strike; only a renewal of agreement, an ending of an old and the beginning of a new contract.

The vote was:

For a general strike	23,357
Against	28,042
Majority against	4,685

But matters did not end there. Thwarted in their efforts to get a general strike, the Northumberland and Durham men sought conference's permission to go it alone. Next morning Christopher Haswell moved a resolution to this effect:

"that all the men of Northumberland and Durham, after using every other means and not gaining their end, be allowed to refuse work under the Masters' Agreement, which is to take place on April 6th; and that delegates from other parts of the Kingdom do hereby pledge ourselves to do all in our power to assist them in their struggle, and also to persuade men from coming in amongst them and, if possible, still further restrict their labour."[1]

The feelings of the men from the two counties were expressed by a Durham delegate: "If we cannot beat down the oppression of our cruel masters, they shall break our hearts." Another delegate said "it would be impossible to calm down the minds of the miners of Northumberland and Durham, especially as they had been told by lecturers of the Association that this was the time when the cessation of labour would take place and they would be allowed to enter into struggle against their tyrant masters. All they asked was non-interference of other counties and enforcement of the restriction system."

[1] *Newcastle Journal*, 6 April 1844.

A collision course had been decided upon in the two counties. Against this moderates fought a rearguard action in vain. Scott, of South Staffs, said the Bond should be placed before conference for everybody to judge. He understood the masters favoured monthly bonds, and he considered it a great improvement on the twelve-month system. "Mr. Jude said the delegates ought not to come to a vote to strike at any time as it was illegal and he would not be a party to it. Mr. Birrell agreed with Mr. Jude's remarks."[1] Nevertheless, conference agreed almost unanimously to pass the resolution.

Cloughan sought to circumscribe the ability of others to copy the independent militant example of the two counties. He moved that no strikes should be allowed in future until the men were properly organised, their case fairly examined, and consent of the majority of the union's members received. Conference agreed.

But after breaking for lunch, Swallow rose to object that Cloughan's motion had been passed while Yorkshire and Staffordshire delegates were out of the hall. He moved that Yorkshire receive the same privileges as had already been granted to Northumberland and Durham after the strike there had proved successful, but not otherwise. It was agreed. Then Mycroft asked that Derbyshire have the same. It was also agreed. Likewise Nottingham was granted the right to strike.

So the sluice-gates were opened to partial strikes. Martin Jude and the executive returned to Newcastle with misgivings. They had seen the union grow by 30,000 in three months, bringing the membership up to 80,000. In the same period twelve new lecturers had been appointed, bringing the total to forty-seven. Not a coalfield in the country was without its full-time organiser. Was this steady progress to be sacrificed? This was the fear of Jude and his colleagues.

[1] *Miners' Advocate*, 20 April 1844.

8

The Great Struggle in Northumberland and Durham, 1844

IN Northumberland and Durham no time could have been less opportune for a strike than 1844. Trade was suffering from a severe depression. The possibility of extracting major concessions from the owners remained remote. Sales had declined by 65,957 tons in 1843 compared with the previous year. Faced with a declining income, the masters did not want their pecuniary plight aggravated by higher labour costs. Naturally, they intended to resist the union's demands. A meeting of coalowners, held at Newcastle on 16 March decided not to grant any wage increase and formulated counter-proposals. Anticipating trouble when the Bond expired, they had prudently taken precautions, accumulating coal reserves wherever possible. They confronted the union united and determined not to yield.

The solidarity of owners in the two counties, which was in marked contrast to owners elsewhere in Britain, had firm historical roots. To a large extent, their prosperity had been based on united action. Since 1771, the owners met annually to determine the vend. This arranged the amount and quality of coal to be produced at each colliery. Any owner exceeding his vend was heavily fined. So there was a strict limitation on coal supplies; the market was never ruined by excess output; and the owners, thanks to the vend, enjoyed monopoly profits.

This idyllic situation—for the coalowners if not consumers—was gradually being undermined by the growth of railways. Until then, the North-east controlled London, the most important domestic market. In 1835, for example, London received 2,190,695 tons from the vend area, 27,394 tons from Yorkshire, 40,955 tons from Scotland and 35,420 tons from Wales.[1] From 1836 onwards the amount of coal brought to London by railways increased rapidly: 1836, 2300 tons; 1840, 22,000 tons; 1844, 72,000 tons. Other coalfields were breaking the vend's monopoly and drastically reducing profit margins. A

[1] M. Dunn, *Coal Trade of the North of England*, p. 229.

Northern coalowner bemoaned its effect on their London trade: "So great has been the competition that the prices obtained have gradually declined for several years until at length they have arrived at a status below any profit whatever."[1]

The advent of the railway had another damaging consequence. "New adventurers are encouraged to commence operations on account of some public railway."[1] A rash of collieries, using this rapid and cheap new form of transport, were opened. It meant owners had to enforce on each other even greater restrictions on output. These, however, were not enough. The trade was unable to avoid a crisis of overproduction, with the market glutted and prices plummeting.

Meanwhile, production costs rose. The surface-seams were being exhausted; the deeper, more difficult ones were having to be dug. As if to compound the owners' misery, the Government placed another obstacle to the selling of coal: an extra 5d. a ton on top of existing coal duty of 1s. 1d. a ton. Owners and merchants, led by Sir J. Duke, M.P., petitioned Parliament without avail.

Everybody in the north-east acknowledged the seriousness of the situation. The *Gateshead Observer* remarked that ship-masters and coal-buyers were looking elsewhere; "the trade, consequently, has been gradually leaving the immediate neighourhood of Newcastle". The *Miners' Advocate* rightly foresaw it would generate tremendous tensions in the coalowners' committee, "called the Newcastle Parliament, and it was often hinted that they had more power than Lords or Commons, for if the latter made the laws the former could evade them".[2] Yet, despite the committee's power, the influx of new owners into the industry and the smashing of the monopoly of London trade, were making it increasingly difficult to maintain the vend system. As the *Advocate* observed, "New speculators also so reduced the vend and the price of coals that, comparatively speaking, very small profits are now made, and there seems to be a disposition on the part of some of the owners to break up the vends altogether, and sell what they can."[3] The Coal Committee was fighting for its life: to stop low returns on capital dipping even lower, it had to defeat the miners' challenge.

*　　　*　　　*

The strike began in festive mood. In brilliant sunshine men from 130 collieries tramped to Black Fell near Gateshead with banners and flags

---

[1] Ibid., p. 213.　　[2] *Miners' Advocate*, 30 December 1843.
[3] Ibid.

flying, accompanied by numerous pit bands. A wagon, for use as a rostrum, was put at the bottom of the Fell, which was conveniently shaped like an amphitheatre. Estimates of the attendance ranged from 20,000 to 40,000. Mark Dent, chairman of the Durham miners, presided.[1] George Charlton, the first speaker, said, "We are an insulted, oppressed, and degraded body of men. If the masters had made anything like reasonable proposals, we would have accepted them; but they have brought forward a miserable proposition, an infamous bond, under which men have been working for a mere pittance; but we will do so no longer. We will stand together till we obtain our rights. . . . Had not tyranny caused thousands of their fellow-workmen to be hurried from life into eternity—to die of premature old age? And had not thousands more been victimised, worn down by unrequited toil and excessive oppression? He trusted they would shortly bid farewell to tyranny—yes, to tyranny of every kind." Then, he moved the crucial resolution to stop working until better remuneration had been obtained.

Robert Archer, seconding, declared, "The miners had been oppressed until they could stand it no longer, and now they were determined to throw off the shackles of slavery, and assert their freedom." When he sat down, Dent put the motion to the meeting. It was carried by unanimous acclamation.

John Tulip then rose. "It was anticipated by our employers that there would have been numbers of blacklegs," he said. "But they are deceived—every man has come forward and joined the union." Even the Dalton men, who the masters had expected to remain at work, had joined and were at the meeting. After this statement, greeted by thunderous applause, Tulip went on to declare, "I look at the battle as already won." And added "If any man has a right to be paid for his labour, it is the coal-hewer. He is the bee that makes the honey."

A motion, moved by Tulip, seconded by Jobling, affirmed that the bonds proposed by the masters were highly injurious to the miners' welfare, and the meeting pledged itself not to be bound so long as they remained in their present state. A complimentary resolution, moved by Edward Richardson and seconded by Thomas Pratt, declared that the bonds drawn up by W. P. Roberts were reasonable and just. Neverthe-

---

[1] Mark Dent, "one of the navvies or blacklegs that was set to work in defiance of the regular pitmen's last strike" (*Newcastle Journal*, 18 May 1844), was a clear indication of the impact the Miners' Association had, not only on the ordinary pitmen, but also on those who were unsympathetic to trade unionism in 1831-2.

less, despite taking this stand, the miners showed themselves prepared to negotiate:

"That the coalowners of this district, having refused to meet the deputation of the workmen to arrange the differences at the present existing between the miners and the coal owners, this meeting announces that such a deputation is still willing to wait on them, in order to settle matters, so as to prevent a continued cessation of labour, providing the said coalowners avow their intention to meet them for such purpose."

But from the way Joseph Beeston and William Daniels spoke in favour of this motion, neither appeared to believe this peace offer stood much chance of acceptance.

★ ★ ★

The workers displayed remarkable solidarity and determination. As Fynes observed, "the men seemed to have made up their minds 'to conquer or die' in the struggle, and they were supported in this resolution by their wives, who were equally determined." The whole industrial life of the two counties was paralysed. When Lord Londonderry heard of the strike he hastened home from Paris.[1] He was concerned with the strike, being Lord Lieutenant of Durham and consequently responsible for maintaining law and order, as well as being the largest coalowner in the county. He led the masters' struggle in a vigorously oppressive way.

Ships, leaving the Tyne with ballast, travelled to Scotland for coal. Local papers carried advertisements for patent firelighters which produced 144 fires for a shilling. "A tea kettle, etc., may be boiled in a few minutes, without annoyance of a constant fire—this rendering housekeepers, so far, independent of the pitmen's strike," it explained. And Monsieur Dillon, French consul at Newcastle, wrote to the Commissioner General at Le Havre to report that coal exports would be interrupted for four or five weeks. Everybody expected a long struggle.

On 6 April the owners wrote to the chairman of the Quarter Sessions expressing confidence in the authorities' ability to protect property. The magistrates swore in special constables. A Company of the 37th Regiment and two troops of the 8th Hussars were in readiness; many other troops in Ireland were on call. General Arbuthnot, commander of the Northern District, addressed the strikers. "He is stated

[1] Home Office 45/644.

to have recommended them to be peaceable, assuring them that in cases of violence the military would do their duty."[1]

Yet, this display of military might was largely unnecessary. The strikers themselves were determined to keep the peace. At their numerous meetings resolutions to this effect were invariably carried, with the added warning that anybody not so doing would be regarded as a traitor to the cause. Besides disliking violence, the union leaders realistically understood they would get the worst of any encounter with the military. Moreover, riots and civil disturbances would alienate the general public, precisely the people they wanted to convince of the justice of their case. Even papers hostile to the union commended the colliers' self-discipline and restraint:

> "It is as satisfactory as it is creditable to the sense of the men to know that nothing like a desire to violate the peace has been manifested to an extent likely to excite apprehension. Such disturbances as have occurred have been comparatively trivial in their character and seem to have originated in the ill-restrained zeal of the women and children rather than in any bad intentions on the part of the men. Rumours of mischief have been prolific as they have been groundless or exaggerated."[2]

There were a number of hoaxes. The military left Durham hurriedly because of reported riots at Lanchester and Craghead but "on reaching those places, affairs were found so quiet that interference or protection was unnecessary".

The *Newcastle Courant* admitted it would be "unjust to the great body of men not to state distinctly that their general demeanour is remarkably peaceable; hardships they appear to expect, but their determination to hold out stands unshaken. . . . In Northumberland, so far as we have heard, no breach of the peace whatever has occurred." Of the few minor disturbances in Durham, the *Newcastle Courant* comments "the women assumed as offensive a position as that taken by their husbands and, indeed, more reckless of consequences".[3]

The only serious incident occurred at Kelloe Colliery, Durham. A few blacklegs were loading wagons, watched by a large crowd, who started to boo loudly. Mr. Bryan, the overman, provided the blacklegs with pistols for self-protection. He shouted to the crowd that he would shoot anybody who went near them. Whereupon a stone struck him in the face, and he fired into the crowd, wounding William Hodgson

---

[1] *Newcastle Courant*, 19 April 1844.   [2] *Gateshead Observer*, 26 April 1844.
[3] *Newcastle Courant*, 19 April 1844.

severely. Incensed, the crowd rioted. Warrants were issued for ten of them but, by the time the military arrived, everybody had dispersed. Only five of the ten were eventually captured, taken to Durham, and charged with "conspiracy and riot, with the intention to raise wages".

*   *   *

The weeks passed by, industrial life lay paralysed, and the strike remained solid. The coalowners' special committee only began issuing detailed statements on the labour situation when the strike had reached its fifty-seventh day. Even then the trickle back to work was insignificant. Out of a total membership of more than 20,000, 215 men had left the union and returned to work—hardly sufficient to maintain output at the 126 collieries. So the masters started to look elsewhere. They did not follow the gratuitous advice given them by George Charlton at the great strike meeting. He had suggested, much to the amusement of his audience, a simple way employers could partly solve their labour problems: "I would like to see the owners, with their coats off, filling the wagons themselves." To such distinguished personages as Lord Londonderry, personal physical labour was as abhorrent as trade unionism. They sought another way of overcoming their difficulties—the mass importation of strangers from other districts into the mines. Owners sent their representatives to practically every part of the British Isles, searching for men to supplant the strikers.

The union attempted to counter this move by sending their own representatives to discourage workers from other areas coming to the North-east. Sometimes the owners had failed to inform the new men they would be used as blacklegs; union spokesmen had to inform them of the strike's existence. Other coalowners painted rosy pictures of conditions to tempt workers. The union issued many warning notices. A typical one—entitled "Appeal to the People of Carlisle"—said pitmen earned an average of 11s. a week during the previous year; "the masters will get rid of you when you have served their purpose".

One owner wrote to coal merchants in East Anglia asking them to try to get agricultural labourers for him. His letter, which was published as a handbill, said industrious men could earn from 3s. to 3s. 6d. and upwards of 4s. a day. Houses would be provided and they were encouraged to bring their families. "I have no doubt the men will bless the change, which will give them good wages for free industry," opined the owner. But the *Miners' Advocate* found this so amusing, so at variance with the reality of conditions prevailing at Jobling's mine, that they reprinted it for colliers' own enjoyment. Likewise when the owners of Scremston, Sharewood, Gathwick and Elmwood collieries issued a leaflet, asking for labourers, the strikers issued their reply. The leaflet promised the same terms as the previous year, which they said were 3s. 9d. for a ten-hour day, so long as they were not union members. But, said the strikers, these were not the conditions: "Be not deceived by the oily tongues and deceitful promises." They continued:

"As the bill (i.e., the employers' leaflet) says labourers must bring good characters from their last employers, we recommend all labourers before they engage at the above collieries, inquire about the character of the owners, agents, etc., from the men last in their employ."

Thirty-two Cornish men brought to Radcliffe colliery were engaged at 4s. a day. But, when they received their pay, it varied from 2s. 6d. to 3s. "The consequence of this," say Fynes, "was a strike for two days, during which time a great deal of abusive language, in broad Cornish, was used." Then, after fresh negotiations, they resumed work at the originally agreed rate. Unaccustomed to coal-mining, they only produced four tubs a day. After a month, the viewer reduced their wage to 4d. a tub and, disgruntled, all but four of them ran away. The owners offered a reward of £50 for their capture. The Newcastle police caught four, the North Shields police the remainder, but not before the overman, banksmen and police had had to chase them, riding and running over hedge and ditch, through standing corn, like a fox-hunt. However, all their exertions were in vain: a special Court at Alnwick on 25 July found in favour of the Cornishmen.

Notwithstanding minor victories like this, the strikers could see increasing numbers of strangers coming to work in the mines. Albeit very reduced, production at most pits was resumed and output was relentlessly rising. Granted some strangers went home, and others were poor workmen, ill-suited to pitwork. Yet, the sheer weight of numbers compensated for this.

In some instances, the union even paid the strangers to return home. But they pocketed the money and continued to work; the owners having paid them more. The Association issued many handbills. An "Appeal to Those now Employed in Northumberland and Durham" asked the strangers: "Are you aware of the evil you are doing, the misery you are creating, the hopes you are blasting?" A leaflet from the men of Cramlington vividly described their own plight:

"We would say when these scourges of humanity offer you the bribe, tell them you are not the base tools they imagine—tell them you will not eat the bread of shame not add one pang to the cravings of hunger—tell them they are worse than the wild barbarians of the woods, who have dragged the mother and new-born baby from the couch and thrust them into the midnight air, that you are above labouring for such inhuman monsters. Fellow men, think of 40,000 men standing three months, many turned into the highways, with only the covering of Heaven for a house, enduring all the privations of hunger and cold. Think of this, and ask yourself if all this is for nothing. Now we are ready to suffer all that famine can inflict, neither sword of the hireling nor the terrors of starvation shall make us submit to the tyrannical bonds now offered us."

*　　　*　　　*

The evictions from the colliery cottages, mentioned in the Cramlington leaflet, were necessary to provide accommodation for the strangers and their families. Richard Fynes, himself an eye-witness, described the pitiful scene:

"Wholesale turning to the door commenced in almost every colliery village; pregnant women, bedridden men, and even children in their cradles, were ruthlessly turned out. Age and sex were disregarded, no woman was too weak, no child too young, no grandma or grandsire too old; but all must go forth."[1]

A pregnant woman, already in labour, was evicted at one village. At West Moor, another woman was thrown out of her home and dragged along the railway for eighty yards until she fainted. And at Pelton Fell a blind woman, eight-eight years old, was turned out in the cold and the rain.

Lord Londonderry thought evictions necessary to teach a lesson to the "deluded and obstinate victims or designing men and crafty Attorneys". In a letter to "his" colliers, he admitted his efforts had so far been fruitless:

"I have been amongst you—I have reasoned—I have pointed out to you the misery, the destruction awaiting you, by your stupid and insane union. I gave you two weeks to consider whether you would return to your work before I proceeded to eject you from your

[1] Fynes, op. cit., p. 74.

houses. I returned to Pensher, and I found you dogged, obstinate and determined— indifferent to my really paternal advice and kind feelings to the old families of the Vane and Tempest pitmen, who have worked for successive ages in the mines. I was bound to act up to my word—bound by duty to my property, my family and my station. I superintended then many ejections—it had no avail."

However, this did not deter His Lordship from continuing his benevolent activities. He gave a week's notice that, unless the strike ended, more families would be thrown out of their homes:

"I will be on the spot myself; the civil and military power will be at hand to protect the good men and the strangers; and you may rely upon it the majesty of the law, and the rights of property, will be protected and prevail."

Genuinely believing he knew the men's own interests better then they did themselves, he ended his letter: "I am, your sincere friend, Vane Londonderry." He continued to display this same bonhomie by prosecuting an evicted collier—William Young—who had the impertinence to camp on his land.[1]

Evictions usually followed a set pattern. Policemen and sometimes troops, accompanied by the resident viewer, would enter a miner's house. Before touching the furniture, they would ask, "Will you go to work?" When being told "No!", orders were given. According to Thomas Burt, the men who actually did the eviction were "a regiment of ragged, ugly looking, ill-bred ill-mannered fellows, known locally as 'candy-men'."[2]

Furniture and belongings were carried out and put in near-by lanes. Families "stood with tears in their eyes and saw villainous wretches throwing to the door articles to which the memory of past years had given sanctity; but they had been taught by their leaders that if the peace was broken, they might bid farewell to their cherished union; and such was the power, eloquence, and advocacy of their leaders that the peace was not broken, even under such trying conditions"[3].

---

[1] In Lady Londonderry's biography of her forebears, she writes: "Both Frances Anne and her husband had a genuine affection for their pitmen whom from time to time they felt they were regretfully obliged to punish like wayward children." (p. 235).

[2] Thomas Burt: *An Autobiography*, p. 34.

[3] The pitmen's faith in Roberts is illustrated by a newspaper cutting, contained in the Pitmen's Strike Collection, marked 1 June 1844: "Among the pitmen in this neighbourhood are many of the religious sects termed Ranters and Latter-day Saints, and these men, it is stated, believe—poor, deluded creatures—that Mr. Roberts, the Pitmen's Attorney-General, is a second Moses sent for their deliverance."

W. P. Roberts made an eloquent plea for non-violence. He said the owners had resorted to mass evictions for two reasons: first in an attempt to coerce the strikers into submission and, second, to provoke disturbances. This would give them a justification to use the troops. The masters would be delighted to employ savage repression, slaughtering many and getting others transported.

Roberts continued, "You have trusted me as perhaps you never trusted a man before."[1] He then asked miners, when faced with eviction, to follow his advice: "Stay in the house, your families around, lock the door (as against an ordinary housebreaker), sit down or go to bed, firmly and quietly state your disinclination to leave the spot; and you may add (but only in joke, mind) that you have read in a book that 'an Englishman's home is his castle'. Beyond that, offer no resistance whatever. Let them *carry* you out."[2]

Whole villages sprung up by the road-side. Chests of drawers, desks and tables formed the walls; the roofs were supplied by canvas or bed-clothes. Sometimes sods of grass and earth were used. Yet, the strikers' morale stayed high. Fynes said "they seemed to enjoy themselves under their difficulties remarkably well. Here and there, fiddles might be heard; whilst the men grouped together, smoking, singing, or chatting about the great battle, but never wavering in their confidence or in their determination to fight the battle to the bitter end."[3]

Strikers received a small sum, probably 2s. 6d. a week, from the union. Obviously this was insufficient to buy food. They quickly exhausted their small savings, and then began the process of pawning and selling valuable personal possessions. Fynes says, "committees were formed to take goods away to pledge, and in hundreds of cases eight-day clocks, watches and other valuables, even to the wedding rings from the poor women's fingers, were yielded up in order that food might be bought for the starving creatures. In this strike there was a very remarkable communal feeling exhibited, for pitmen and their wives did not demand to have returned to them the whole of the value which the articles they had given up produced, but willingly allowed the food bought with the money to be meted out fairly and impartially as well to those who had not contributed towards its purchase as to those who had. Starving as they were, these poor ignorant and un-educated creatures were yet capable of teaching by example a fine

---

[1] Ibid.
[2] *Miners' Magazine*, June–July 1844 and also *Miners' Advocate*.
[3] R. Fynes, op. cit., p. 72.

moral lesson in humanity to those self-styled 'superiors', their recent employers."[1]

In some places, shopkeepers allowed miners to run up credit. At meetings traders were thanked for their sympathy and support, and pledges offered to pay for the goods once the dispute had ended. But there were limits to the amount of credit small shopkeepers could give. Moreover the coalowners, wanting to starve the men into sub-mission, were liable to take action against any who befriended them. A notorious instance of this was the proclamation of 20 July:

"Lord Londonderry again warns all the shopkeepers and tradesmen in his town of Seaham that if they still give credit to pitmen who hold off work and continue in the union, such men will be marked by his agents and overmen, and will never be employed in his collieries again, and the shopkeepers may be assured that they will never have any custom or dealings with them from Lord London-derry's large concerns that he can in any manner prevent.

Lord Londonderry further informs the traders and shopkeepers, that having by his measures increased very largely the last year's trade to Seaham, and if his credit is so improperly and so fatally given to his unreasonable pitmen, thereby prolonging the injurious strike, it is his firm determination to carry back all the outlay of his concerns even to Newcastle.

Because it is neither fair, just nor equitable that the resident traders in his own town should combine and assist the infatuated workmen and pitmen in prolonging their own miseries by continuing an insane strike, and an unjust and senseless warfare against their pro-prietors and masters."

While such proclamations aroused adverse comment in the national press, they served their intended end. Food supplies for the strikers were drying up. The miners were taunted by a master, "It's our long purses against your hungry guts." One paper reported, "Many of the men, it is said, are so reduced in strength from abstinence as to be unable to leave their beds." Yet, the strike continued. As one of their leaders, Mark Dent, told them: "There is nothing for us but this—there is no possibility of retracting. We must fight the battle out." Numerous meetings were held in villages, chapels and the open air. At these gatherings it was often said, "May God defend the poor oppressed against the rich oppressor." Some leaders, like William Richardson, were devoutly religious and led their audiences in prayer for the

[1] Op. cit., p. 93.

success of the strike. Others sought to bolster flagging spirits with songs specially written for the strike. "These were said to have been written," says a handwritten entry in the Bell Collection, "by travelling Methodist preachers and class leaders, or at least they got the blame for doing it. They were hawked about and sold at one penny each." The music sheets usually bore the name of the union's printer: "T. Dodd, 77, The Side, Newcastle, who has always on hand a large assortment of song."

But, however tuneful the Primitive Methodists and Ranters may have been, the bulk of religious opinion backed the masters. Granted there were exceptions. But these were more than outweighed by the many ministers who applauded the evictions and the decisions to deny the homeless refuge in the workhouse. The Rev. J. Burdon, of Castle Eden, published a leaflet against the strike; he suggested setting up an emigration fund as the answer, to lessen the surplus population. And a handbill which discussed whether Christians could be trade unionists claimed that unions were fundamentally anti-religious and ended with the comforting thought, "The Lord will provide".

*   *   *

The union leaders did not place their faith in the Lord making provision; right from the beginning of the strike, they saw it was necessary to mobilise as much support as possible. In the forefront of this campaign was Martin Jude who, though he opposed starting the strike, threw all his energies into the struggle once it had begun. Issuing a financial appeal to all districts, the executive clearly saw the dangers:

> "from what we can learn, the masters build themselves up so that, if they can succeed in breaking the Association here, it will go a great way towards its entire annihilation; therefore, it is that they seem more determined than they would have been."

Financial help from other districts would help to shorten the strike; better send the money now than later. "Every man must do his duty to save the Association," said the executive.

The strikers also appealed to the general public and fellow trade unionists. Meetings were held, first in the North-east, later in most industrial areas. Men with authorised collection boxes were dispatched to most towns. The strikers received many heartening gestures of sympathy. The inhabitants of Blackhill and Shotley Bridge provided a substantial meal of beef, mutton, ham, pies, etc., for 700 of the strikers and their families.

Many committees were formed to assist the miners by fellow trade unionists. They saw their own struggle as tied to the fate of the colliers. This is evident from a leaflet, published for the workers of Northumberland and Durham. After recalling their own reductions in wages, the leaflet continues:

"The case of the miners calls for the most strenuous support from everyone interested in the prosperity of the industrious classes, it being clear to the committee that, so far from this being a case between the Coal Owners and Miners alone, it is a question pregnant with the most important results to every man who has to earn his bread by the sweat of his brow, for should the masters succeed in their present unrighteous attempt upon the miners, the subjugation of every industrious section of the community will be fixed without remedy."

A mass strike meeting at Shadon Hill on 8 July passed a motion, thanking "the trades of London, Edinburgh, Manchester, Birmingham, Newcastle, the carpet weavers of Durham and Barnard Castle, and to the trades of the various towns; also to the miners generally of the United Kingdom, for support they have rendered during our present struggle, which we trust they will continue until our contest is brought to a successful close, and we pledge ourselves to assist them in return, should they ever be placed in like circumstances."

W. P. Roberts, while in London, had striven to gain support for the strike. From 4 June until the end of the dispute £429 10s. 0d. came from London. This was helpful, like other monies, but still inadequate to sustain the strike. A few weeks before the dispute began, the union had written to the masters asking for a negotiated settlement. Every letter went unanswered and, as the strike progressed, their tone became more plaintive. In July, John Clark (district secretary) ended his letter:

"Once more we appeal to you; can we obtain an interview? Tell us how, and by what means? From a consciousness that such an interview would be highly desirable, we entreat you to bestow on this, our address, your speedy and serious attention."

Instead of negotiations, the masters gave the union leaders abuse. They were depicted as avaricious and self-seeking, indifferent to the sufferings of the men. W. P. Roberts was singled out for special treatment. As the leader with the widest range of contacts in trade unions

¹ See chapter on the union and politics.

and other organisations likely to help, he devoted his energy and oratory to explaining the strike to people elsewhere. But the coal-owners and hostile newspapers branded him a coward, running away to attend lavish London banquets.

*   *   *

Perhaps surprisingly, the owners' repressive measures were criticised by the military. Lieutenant-Colonel Bradshaw disapproved of ejecting strikers from their cottages, "a custom rarely being resorted to", he contended, and "unprecedently so to the extent that was proposed". He was reluctant to use "the military force under such circumstances". He predicted confidentially that, if the masters would display kindness and good temper, making a few concessions on fines and wages, the whole of the pitmen would return to work. When Mr. R. S. Surtees, a local magistrate, provocatively rode a troop of the 6th Dragoons to a miners' meeting—causing "considerable excitement and alarm" according to Fynes—Colonel Bradshaw countermanded the order and had the troops withdrawn.[1]

Another officer, Major-General Brotherton, reported on his attendance at a magistrates' meeting, where four of the five J.P.s present were connected with the coal trade. In his opinion, "the coal-owners seem to rely solely upon the expedient of starving the colliers into submission on their own terms". He admitted "that the colliers are much more disposed to conciliation and accommodation than the owners". The masters "must, in many cases, be the gainers by the continuance of the strike". Eventually, he offered to mediate, only to be rebuffed by the owners.

When General Sir T. Arbuthnot heard about it, he expressed regret: "There is cause to conclude that the masters, from interested motives, are not likely to extend themselves, to put an end to the present strike, as soon as could be wished."

But how could there be conciliation when the masters were deter-mined to get unconditional surrender, an abject capitulation that would mean the end of Roberts and the union?

In the sixteenth week, with the influx of strangers growing, wide-spread rumours of a resumption of work alarmed pitmen. These tales were fanned by newspapers, leaflets and ministers. So the union tried to scotch them. John Clark published a reply, "Viewers v. Pitmen, or

[1] R. Fynes, op. cit., pp. 76–7. H.O. 45. O.S. 650, 1844.

Falsehood *v.* Truth", in which he says, "Viewers have been at considerable trouble to circulate reports that certain collieries have got bound and begun work on the master's terms. This is to give notice that such is *not* the case at any of the collieries reported." The leaflet goes on to instance examples of blacklegs returning home and ends by asking them to disbelieve flyposters from the masters. Also as reassurance, a massive meeting was held on 1 August. A procession four miles long, with seventy-two banners, wound its way to Newcastle Town Moor. The *Tyne Mercury* estimated 25,000 to 30,000 were present, "considerably larger than the last we attended at Shadon Hill, which was estimated at 20,000". The *Newcastle Journal*, said, "The tone of the resolutions and speeches was one of determined adherence to the strike". The men raised a large board with the inscription:

> "Stand firm to your union
> Brave sons of the mine,
> And we'll conquer the tyrants
> Of Tees, Wear and Tyne."

Many talked of pledging their last few remaining articles so that they could continue to hold out. They thought, optimistically, that the autumn demand for coal would make the masters seek agreement. This hope was passionately expressed by James Hardy. After mentioning that all the union's attempts to reach an amicable arrangement had been met with insult and contempt, he moved a resolution again imploring the masters to negotiate a settlement.

Among the other speakers was Robert Archer, weakened and very ill, who spoke of pledging themselves to repay all the debts they had incurred once the strike was over. Then Thomas Pratt mentioned the cruelty of evictions:

"Henry Barrass, in his 80th year, with his wife in her 75th, (had been) turned out. The old man had worked on the collieries belonging to the Marquis of Londonderry for 30 years. He thought he might say to the world, 'Hear this, you feeling part of mankind, and be astonished.' Ought not this old man to have his house and fire free, with reasonable pension to live on? Two days ago the foundation stone of a monument was laid on Pensher Hill to the late Earl of Durham, in the presence of 30,000 persons, the cost, exclusive of the stone which was given by the Marquis of Londonderry, being £3,000. If the Marquis thought this noble deed should be recorded in history, let it also be recorded that Barrass was a working man, and had worked in his pits for 30 years, and that he was then in his 80th year, houseless."

Thomas Pratt raised himself to his full height and shouted at the top of his voice: "The day of retribution will come!"

*   *   *

Be that as it may, the Marquis of Londonderry's ruthlessness had a decisive impact. His policy, copied by the other Durham coalowners, played an important role in breaking the strike. The hardship and suffering there made the men of the Durham collieries the first to capitulate. Rumours of Durham miners returning to work reached alarming proportions. So, to bolster their buckling confidence, the men held a further meeting at Newcastle Town Moor on 13 August. The strike had now lasted eighteen weeks, and a resolution was passed calling upon those who had returned to work to rejoin the union. A further motion, moved by Haswell, pledged the meeting "to stand by the Association and to continue united until we obtain our rights". At the request of the Northumberland men, the same resolutions were put to a meeting at Durham the following day. Despite the large attendance at this demonstration—10,000 on Durham sands compared with 1,200 at Newcastle—the drift back to work at the Wear collieries continued. It turned into a raging torrent when some of the collieries refused to take back old hands. Panic-stricken Durham men started crossing the Tyne, looking for work in Northumberland, where the strikers still retained considerable solidarity.

The Northumberland men were still not disposed to submit. An enthusiastic meeting of strikers from twenty-seven Tyne collieries was held on Scaffold Hill, and resolved to fight to the last. Two men were to be deputed from each pit to go among the men of the Wear and Tees, asking for their support and appealing to them to stay away from the Tyne. But this move came too late: the surge of Durham men into Northumberland was too powerful to be halted.

Reappraising the situation, the union leaders decided that no other course was open to them but to end the strike. They instructed the men at each colliery to hold a meeting at which this resolution was put:

"Seeing the present state of things and being compelled to retreat from the field through the overbearing cruelty of our employers, the suffering and misery of our families, and the treachery of those who have been their tools during the strike, we, at the present time, deem it advisable to make the best terms with our employers we can."

On 17 August 1844, Robert Gill, from the Coal Trade Office in Newcastle, sent a laconic message to all coalowners:

"Sir,
    The Special Committee have the satisfaction to inform the trade that the whole collieries of these districts, with very unimportant exceptions, have engaged all the workmen they require, these engagements having been formed on the terms and conditions offered by the coalowners previous to April 5th last."

The strike was at an end.

*   *   *

Weekly returns, issued by Robert Gill,
of the Coal Trade Office, Newcastle.

	Hewers at work	No. Left Union	Chaldrons Produced
1 June	1,386	215	1,955
7 June	1,975	430	2,718
15 June	2,656	474	3,565
22 June	3,235	651	4,603
29 June	3,639	766	5,117
6 July	3,975	889	5,541
13 July	4,334	1,073	5,984
20 July	4,832	1,370	6,591
27 July	5,040	1,467	6,963
3 August	5,528	2,009	7,630
10 August	6,160	2,508	8,310

In April 1844 the following were the
figures for employment in this district

Tyne	15,556
Blyth	1,031
Wear	13,172
Tees	4,211
Total	33,970

Number of Collieries in the North-East

District	1800	1830	1836	1844
Tyne	29	37	47	70
Wear	8	18	9	28
Tees	0	0	0	22
Hartley & Blyth	4	4	4	6
TOTAL	41	59	76	126[1]

[1] *Source:* M. Dunn, op. cit., p. 203.

K

9

The Resumption of Work

THE return to work followed a set procedure. At each pit colliers sought to preserve their unity by approaching the management collectively. At some places they were greeted with tolerance. Viewers expressed the hope that all rancour between masters and men would vanish and there would be no more disputes. But at others, viewers clearly indicated their intention to pick and choose: no militants would be re-employed. In some instances, the victimisation was even extended to the relatives of prominent unionists. The Haswell family was an example of this. Christopher Haswell, junior, well known for his part in the strike, wandered around the two counties vainly looking for work. Eventually, the men of Seghill decided to employ him themselves in the powder store, handing out candles and powder. But when the owner heard he compelled the men to dismiss him and, for good measure, also sacked Haswell's father and brothers, who worked at the same mine. Try as they would, all the Haswells found it impossible to find employment. The name Haswell ranked high in the masters' black book. Nevertheless, the old man of the family refused to discard it. "I was named Christopher Haswell when I came into the world," he said, "and will be Christopher Haswell till I go out of it." His son Christopher, like many leading unionists, was forced to leave the North-east. Some went to other coalfields, others went abroad. As for young Christopher, he journeyed to Scotland, where his union work was unknown to the masters. Only years later, when passions had cooled in the North-east, did he dare to return. Eventually, the Haswells gained employment at Charlaw colliery at Seghill. But it was only after suffering years of deprivations.

In spite of such personal tragedies, complacently regarded as an inevitable concomitant of class struggles of that period, the Miners' Association thought it had emerged unscathed from the fray. The men's loyalty to the union appeared to be unimpaired. After meeting the master about the resumption of work, the men at each pit returned to their meeting-room and unanimously passed resolutions pledging their continued faith in the Association.

In this atmosphere, the great strike looked, at worst, like a temporary setback. Confidently, the union expected to be able not only to retain all existing members but also to recruit many of the new men who had come to the area as blacklegs. John Hall issued an announcement in August to every pitman: they would be given a month's grace, after which it would cost them 10s. to join the union.

The *Miners' Advocate*, of 24 August 1844, exuded the same optimism. It expected the union's strength to grow and in a later issue claimed, "There are now upwards of 100,000 men in the Union and we are increasing from day to day."[1] The editor, William Daniels, persisted in maintaining that neither side had won and objected to the press saying the men had gone back on the employers' terms.

Yet, in the autumn of 1844, grim reality punctured the union's rosy illusions. Nobody was left in doubt who the final victors were. The masters pushed the men into a greater servitude than ever before. Many strikers failed to get their jobs back; strangers continued to occupy what had previously been the miners' houses and many families had to remain in their road-side encampments; and the great surplus of labour gave owners an opportunity to apply the Bond with unparalleled ferocity. It was these conditions prevailing after the strike—not the strike itself—that smashed the union in Northumberland and Durham.

Soon colliers were complaining bitterly. A typical letter described the deterioration:

"What were the threepence per quart fines for splint or foul of last year compared with the sixpence for splint or foul this year? At Sacriston and Charlaw collieries such is the case . . . one man at Charlaw was minus eightpence per score on his last fortnight's earnings for laid-out."[2]

At the Wakefield conference in November, Edward Richardson admitted that wages had been reduced and the colliers of the two counties subjected to fines and forfeitures worse than before.

The substitution of a monthly for the yearly Bond helped owners to impose a stricter discipline. Mr. Liddell, manager of Gosforth collieries, explained to the Mining Commissioner: "The monthly hiring, by enabling us to get rid of bad characters as soon as they show themselves, will be some security to us."[3]

[1] *Miners' Advocate*, 21 September 1844.   [2] Ibid. 9 October 1844
[3] *Report of the Mining Commissioners, 1846*, p. 26.

The monthly Bond could be used with deadly effect because of the labour surplus. Large numbers of strangers stayed on after the strike; their resolve to remain in Northumberland and Durham did incalculable damage to the union. It meant owners could pick and choose, and weed out any miners who showed the least inclination to be pro-union.

The immense surplus of colliers can be judged from Mr. Liddell's testimony:

"We were obliged to discharge after the 'strike' fully two-thirds of our whole number, of whom we have taken back about one-fourth since. Many of the rest were anxious to be taken back but we declined. There were few families among them that did not get into debt at the 'strike' to the amount of from five pounds to twelve pounds . . . some are not out of debt now after two years."[1]

For well over a decade, cut-throat competition for work was a major factor in maintaining labour conditions at a low level and strangling all attempts to form trade unions. Quickly, miners were made to understand the owners would not readily forgive or forget those who took part in the 1844 strike. Mr. W. Bailey, an underviewer at Hetton, Ellmore and Appleton collieries, clearly expressed this viewpoint:

"Out of the one hundred new hewers about forty or fifty remain, and also about ten other men employed about the collieries. We have still a fifth of our whole number employed who are new hands, brought in at that time and who are competing with the old colliers for employment. We are now dividing the work amongst them and giving employment to many more than we need, in order to keep them from the parish. We shall very likely have to discharge many before long, and they will be those who engaged in the strike."[2]

A severe depression in the coal trade aggravated the situation. As already mentioned, the North-east coalfields were going through a bad time. The construction of railways increased competition from other coalfields in markets that, up till then, had been the sole preserve of Northumberland and Durham. At the same time, fresh capital was pouring in to the North-east, and the opening of twenty new collieries only worsened the position. It was a crisis of over-production.[3] There

[1] *Report of the Mining Commissioners, 1846*, p. 26.
[2] Ibid., p. 24.
[3] Between 1835 and 1845 productive capacity in Northumberland and Durham had increased from 5,440,000 tons to 10,300,000 tons (P. Sweezy, op. cit., p. 110).

would, in any case, have been extensive unemployment; the presence of large numbers of strangers merely served to magnify the miners' misery.

Nor could the men gain any satisfaction from the break-up of the masters' powerful organisation, which was another consequence of the strike. As long as the owners met to determine "the vend"—the amount of coal to be produced and the price at which it was to be sold—it helped to cosset the coal trade from the worst effects of competition. With "the vend" no longer in existence, the bottom fell out of the market. Prices and profits plummeted. One Durham owner, Joseph Pease, told the House of Commons that prices in the London market were so low they did not even cover freightage. He had given away 10,000 tons to mend roads. Their own incomes falling, owners angrily sought to reduce labour costs. They expected colliers to work longer and harder for less money. The numerous men hanging around the pit banks, eager for work, made it easy for the owners to make further exactions. So, paradoxically, the collapse of the coalowners' organisation merely exacerbated the plight of the Miners' Association.

For many years the masters ruefully recalled the disintegration of "the vend". It was a traumatic experience, "an event which threatened to bring destruction upon all the trade."[1] It had been "the greatest capitalist combination of the first half of the nineteenth century (which) passed out of existence after an almost uninterrupted sway of seventy-three years".[2]

This calamity was not unexpected. For some time "the vend" had been subjected to intense internal strain. Owners of rich mines, with many natural advantages, chafed about restricting output, and hence profits, to allow the less fortunate a share of the market. Moreover, bickering broke out constantly over what prices should be charged for the various grades of coal. Dissension grew worse as competition from other coalfields increased. Owners in the North-east countered this by increasingly severe limitations of their output, an attempt to prevent the market being glutted. By 1843, they were only producing 43 per cent of the quantity of coal envisaged as "the vend". After the strike, some collieries resumed production sooner than others. Consequently, when the Coal Trade Committee came to examine the position, they discovered a great variety of performance. Some collieries had

[1] Select Committee on the Cause of the Present Dearness and Scarcity of Coal, 1873 p. 297.
[2] D. J. Williams, *Capitalist Combination in the Coal Industry*, p. 54.

exceeded the amount prescribed for 1844 ("overs") while others had produced far less ("shorts"):

	Overs	Shorts
Tyne	108,680 tons	216,837 tons
Wear	76,056 tons	163,946 tons
Tees	15,227 tons	95,190 tons

In accordance with the rules of "the vend", those producing "overs" should pay a fine to the Coal Trade Committee, which, in turn, was supposed to hand it on to those owners who had produced less than the amount stated. The penalties for the "overs" came to the astronomical figure of £49,790, of which £10,000 was due from three owners. Being in strained financial circumstances, both from the strike and trade depression, these owners were reluctant to part with their money. To gain compliance, the Committee agreed to scale down the grand total to £29,874, but the owners failed to rise to the bait. The fines were never paid. "The vend" was at an end.

★   ★   ★

Whatever disagreements arose among employers, they were as mild as a children's tea-party compared to the ferocious internecine strife that broke out among the workers. The first source of trouble, the large numbers of strangers in the district, led to a serious flare up even before the strike had ended. On 15 August, two Welshmen, who had worked at Seaton Delaval during the strike, got involved in a fight with two Northumbrian men at the Hastings Arms Inn. Within half an hour, it developed into a pitched battle. Thousands of English, Welsh and Irish fought one another with pick-shafts, garden-railings and any-thing else to hand. More men, from neighbouring districts, rushed in to join the fight. Amid a hail of stones and bottles, Mr. Atkinson, the colliery underviewer, tried to restore order. But when a pick-head went right through his dog, standing at his feet, he rushed off to a near-by farm where troops were billeted. The soldiers refused to act until the Riot Act had been read, so a messenger was quickly sent to South Shields for a magistrate. Meanwhile, at Seaton Delaval, the Welsh and Irish were beginning to retreat. They escaped over the railway down behind the hedges, and into the houses they occupied. On both sides, many had been injured, some seriously. It was only the imminent arrival of troops that prevented the English from pursuing their adversaries, destroying them and their homes. During the next week large numbers of combatants were arrested. Usually, the police came at night. Men were awoken, handcuffed and taken to the colliery farm, from whence they were moved to Shields' magistrates court. As Fynes commented, "the impartiality of the law" was maintained: only Northumberland miners were arrested and punished for their part in the disturbance.

Rioting was followed by less dramatic, more enduring signs of hatred and disgust. Everything possible was done to discomfort the strangers. They were defrauded of their earnings by stealing the "tokens" from the side of their tubs. Stones were thrown among the coal they had hewn and many, heavily fined, failed to make any money after working all day. Clothing was regularly stolen from their working places and, especially at Cramlington, Delaval and Seghill, strangers' working gear, picks and drills were thrown down old workings. The most dangerous practice was to hang a rope across the main roadway of the mine at neck-height. It was customary for the putters, having pushed a heavily-laden tub out of the pit, to rush down at great speed for the next load. Any stranger doing this job was liable to receive a nasty jolt, as the miners' ballad grimly warns:

> "Oh don't go down the Seghill Mine;
> Across the mainway's hung a line
> To catch the throat and break the spine
> Of the dirty, blackleg miner.
>
> So join the Union while you may;
> Don't wait until your dying day
> For that may not be far away,
> You dirty, blackleg miner."

Despite these manifestations of militancy—which were themselves indicative of the union leaders' loss of authority—the real picture was bleak. Subscriptions now came from only a third of the pits. The income of the Northumberland and Durham union fell from the low figure of £84 16s. 7d. from 20 July to 7 September to £27 5s. 4½d. from 8 September to 12 October. Rumours spread, and were believed, imputing dishonourable motives to the leaders of the late strike and accusing them of misappropriating the funds collected for the unemployed. This disenchantment was clearly expressed by the following chorus:

"Hokee, pokee, wankee fum,
Roberts and Beesley, England's scum,
The curse of all, the fear of some,
This rogue of a pitman's attorney."

From the strike's defeat most miners drew the lesson that strikes and unions were futile; co-operation between masters and men had to be the new approach:

"Also, O Lord! give men to see
That strikes and kick ups winna dee
But best when men an' maisters 'gree
Upon each place
To bargain for his sell, be free,
Each knows his case.
So farewell Union and farewell Roberts
And farewell Beesley and all sick loberts."

*   *   *

The *Miners' Advocate* continued to report meetings addressed by William Daniels, Ben Embleton, Robert Henderson, James Fawcett and others. Almost all of these took place north of the Tyne, and it was from that area that F. Smith, an agent of the Association, claimed the union was in good health. "It has appeared of late, in many of the public newspapers, that the Union in the North is completely done away with," Smith wrote in his letter to the *Advcoate*.[1] He then went on to rebut the charge, claiming full activity was being maintained at Seghill, East and West Cramlington, Seaton Delaval, Cowpen, Bedlington and Radcliffe.

The implications of some of the official union statements at the Wakefield conference, of November 1844, were less brave and comforting. A long and serious discussion took place there on "whether those lecturers who are in arrears of wages have the same made up".[2] The decision was, yes; but apparently funds were never available to implement it. Then, at the end of the conference, delegates found it necessary to pledge "greater reciprocity of action . . . mutual goodwill and affection for each other . . . to allay all bickerings and contentions among members".[3]

Reviewing the deliberations of the Wakefield conference, the

---

[1] *Miners' Advocate*, 19 October 1844.   [2] Ibid.   [3] Ibid.

Miners' Advocate opined: "We are convinced that the enemies of labour dread much more deliberative meetings of this kind than they do noisy public meetings, however numerously attended."[1] This remark, by the editor, may be taken as recognition of the fact that the union no longer saw any possibility of holding "numerously attended" meetings in Northumberland and Durham. The article then went on to proclaim "the vaunted boast of the masters that 'the Union is dead' is mere expression without reality, a chimera of the brain, where the wish is father to the thought." He saw the salvation of the Association in the new tactics adopted by the Wakefield conference. First, greater importance was to be attached to political activity: "a new light has beamed upon the miners . . . they are determined to lay their grievances before the public, and to apply to Parliament for redress." And, second, a change of union attitude from class conflict to conciliation:

"It gave us great pleasure to observe the improved healthy feeling which pervaded the Conference especially as regards the baleful tendency and consequences of strikes. We have always been opposed to sectional strikes or sectional unions, being convinced that strikes do not answer the purpose intended in one case out of ten hundred —that they create acrimony and ill-will between master and man (a state of things which ought by no means to exist)—that they cause disunion and discord among the men, and generally end in placing those engaged therein in a worse position than they were in prior to the strike, to say nothing if the wages lost, the suffering and misery endured. These among a thousand reasons have convinced us long ago that strikes were wrong."

Doubtless, William Daniels wrote every word of this with the recent disaster in the North-east coalfields very much in his mind. It was a painful experience that merely served to confirm the already convinced union leadership (Jude, Hall, Birrell, etc.) of the inadvisability of strikes. But this was far from being a universally accepted conclusion. As we shall see in the next chapter, almost every coalfield in Britain was locked in conflict at some time during 1844. In some counties the miners' union was smashed; in others it emerged strengthened, with higher wages and a greater membership. So it was unlikely the position of Jude and company would go unchallenged for long. In Lancashire, for instance, a buoyant market for coal gave colliers a glorious opportunity to press their wage claims by militant action. So they went on strike—and disregarded the leaders in Newcastle.

[1] *Miners' Advocate*, November 1844.

There were other reasons why the national leadership's authority was waning. It consisted almost entirely of men from Northumberland and Durham. This was partly because, due to the training of Tommy Hepburn, a capable and resourceful nucleus had emerged in the North-east, greater in ability than the local leaders elsewhere. Their predominance can also be attributed to the large number of union members which, until the autumn of 1844, made the Two Counties the strongest single unit within the Association. But after the great strike, Jude and company, with their local support dwindling to nothingness, found themselves unable to carry out traditional trade union functions, namely, to protect members' wages and conditions.

The smashing of the union's North-eastern stronghold severely weakened the degree of centralism. Its membership lay largely in places strongly permeated with localist sentiment, which was probably tinged with envy of the Northern Counties' monopoly of power during the previous eighteen months. It became, therefore, progressively more difficult to persuade districts to remit the monies due to the General Board at Newcastle, which might squander it on hopeless attempts to revive the corpse of the union in the North-east.

The Wakefield conference attempted to cope with this problem by defining anew the relationship that should exist between the General Board and the County Association. In some matters conference simply recognised the granite-firmness of localism, and gave its blessing to existing arrangements. In other matters, where central control was considered vital, it sought to reassert the authority of the executive. It was resolved that each district be allowed to pay its own lecturers, merely remitting the surplus to the central board, and be given discretionary power to admit new members. At the same time an effort was made to tighten up on payments to the central funds. All districts were ordered to be one payment in advance, and to retrieve the Association's funds a levy of one halfpenny a week per member was to be paid until the next conference.

Economic difficulties also bedevilled the debate on making the *Miners' Advocate* a stamped paper. Being unstamped, the law forbade it to print news happening within the previous month. This was a grave handicap. An editorial, published in the *Advocate* on 9 March 1844, had outlined the advantages accruing from being stamped: the paper would become a better means of defence, able to answer immediately the charges being made against the Association with increasing frequency in the press; transport costs would be reduced, as the paper would then qualify to be sent by post; and, finally, extra sales and advertising revenue was likely to result, bringing a profit to the union. The Glasgow conference in March 1844, had accepted this view. By 48,295 votes to 6,976, it agreed to make the *Miners' Advocate* a stamped paper. But this decision was never carried out. The only possible explanation appears to be that the Association found it financially impossible to raise the £600 surety, required by law.[1] During the great strike, the *Advocate* was fined for printing news that was not a month old, and so, when the Wakefield conference met in November, it was confronted with an urgent problem. Yet, lack of money prevented a solution being found, and the matter was left over till the next conference. Before the next conference arrived, however, the *Miners' Advocate* ceased publication. In February 1845 the Association had no paper.

The failure of the *Miners' Advocate* exemplified the failure of the central organisation. The journal had been far too dependent on Northumberland and Durham. Edited and published in Newcastle-on-Tyne, it had always concentrated its attention on the Northern Counties. As a consequence, most of its circulation was there. This coverage never corresponded to the actual balance of strength within the Association. Like the general board, its dependence on a single area was its undoing. With the debacle in the North-east, the *Miners' Advocate* lost its circulation and the general board its reliable source of revenue. From having a circulation at its peak of 11,000, it dropped to 5,500 in the autumn of 1844.

*   *   *

Centrifugal tendencies had been strengthened. Advocates of separate unions and partial strikes had been encouraged by some successes, especially in Yorkshire and Lancashire, that had been achieved despite disapproval from the union leadership. It proved the limbs could manage very well without the head. Even where local initiative proved inadequate—for instance, the success of some Lancashire strikes was endangered by blackleg labour—the members still did not see the need for tighter national unity. Instead, there was likely to be only a greater feeling of bitterness and animosity against their fellow miners living in the coalfields from which the blacklegs had come.

---

[1] The failure of the *Miners' Advocate* to become a stamped paper is another indication that grandiose talk of the union having large financial reserves is without foundation.

Ironically, as unity among miners became less tangible, many of them hankered after unity on a much wider and less practical basis. They wished to achieve solidarity throughout the working class as a whole, not simply a section of it. This idea had arisen, to a large extent, out of the Northumberland and Durham strike. On the one hand, some colliers in other coalfields had been unhelpful. The Cumberland, miners had even refused to employ their destitute brothers as musicians at their gala. They had come from Durham, hoping to make money as strolling players, but only the Whitehaven carpenters befriended them and took an interest in the strike. In Yorkshire, men from the Northern Counties, collecting for their strike fund, became involved in a violent quarrel with Yorkshire colliers, who were themselves on strike and regarded the Northerners as interlopers and poachers. In contrast, many other sections of the working class, especially in the large cities, made extremely welcome contributions to the strike fund. Naturally, it led many colliers to ask themselves: had they not got more in common with the weavers, engineers, masons and the like who helped them than they had, say, with the Cumberland miners? Moreover, if all workers were in the same union, then it would be impossible for the masters to find blacklegs anywhere. These points were succinctly expressed by Robert Forbes in the *Miners' Advocate* correspondence columns:

"As capital can alone successfully invade labour through a division in its ranks, it is clear that nothing short of all labour united can effectually defend it. . . . Then let labour be united, let all trade combine, and they would be like the Roman phalanx, invincible."

Editorial comment favoured the proposal. The subject was placed on the agenda of the Wakefield conference, where it received qualified approval. Nevertheless, conference resolved to leave the matter over to the next conference. In the meantime, it hoped other trades would discuss the proposal, and publish their views in the *Northern Star* and other working-class newspapers.

Out of the discussions, the National Association of United Trades for the Protection of Labour emerged in March of 1845. It had the same type of loose structure as the Miners' Association. So, instead of the two organisations being complementary, they were competitors. Those who had striven for greater unity had merely made disunity greater. From 1845 onwards, miners were to have their own divisions widened by a further aggravation: their differing attitudes to the National Association.

Not surprisingly, the great strike of 1844 marked the high-water mark of the Miners' Association—its greatest membership and internal cohesion. From then on, fragmentation became the dominant tendency.

10

Other Coalfields in 1844

DEFEAT in the North-east coalfields, the union's stronghold, was an important turning-point in the history of the Miners' Association. It represented a clear indication that official union strategy, as practised until then, had collapsed. Right from the Association's inception it had been generally accepted that combat should be avoided so long as the adversary remained stronger. The union had based all its calculations —its opposition to partial strikes, its failure to be lured by provocations —on the belief that only when its might was greater should it engage the enemy. Until then, like the Roman general Fabius, it hoped to win victories by refusing to fight.

This view, however commendable, was at variance with reality, since in many coalfields to join a trade union was a hostile act, a decision bound to enrage the masters. When it was followed by a restriction of output—the implementation of the union's Manchester and Glasgow conference decisions—then all coalowners' blood pressure rose. They were liable, in blinding temper, to do whatever they could to smash the union. But the union still believed it could organise workers, get them to limit output, and perhaps even make plans for a general strike, while the owners simply counted the pieces of coal and took no moves against them.

In fact, however much the Association might deprecate partial strikes, they remained inevitable in an age when the right of workers to unite was still bitterly opposed. This became obvious when the Association tried to organise Cumberland, the kingdom where Lord Lonsdale was absolute monarch. Conditions there had always been bad. In 1842, one of His Lordship's supervisors had his arm broken in two places when he came to inspect coal-baskets and pronounce them under-weight. "We have heard of two men who had seven and twenty baskets stopped in one week—or, in other words, they had 13s. 6d. of their earnings stopped for faults—if faults at all—of the most trivial nature." This was common in the Earl of Lonsdale's pits, continued the *Whitehaven Herald*: "We are satisfied the miners have

many grievances to complain of, we fear that there is little chance of
their prevailing against such fearful odds."[1] In such a position, colliers
would be immensely strengthened by a union. They saw this; so did
Lord Lonsdale. As a result, the Association's attempt to organise
Cumbrian miners encountered stiff opposition. Despite repeated
conference decisions about the need to avoid partial strikes, it found
itself locked in a ferocious fight to establish men's rights to join a
union.[2] Cumbrian colliers, acutely conscious of wage reductions of
between a half and two-thirds during the past ten years, stood firmly
behind the attempt.

The Association did what it could to support the men's struggle.
It sent P. M. Brophy there as a lecturer. An Irish immigrant himself,
he realised that the owners would strive to crush the strike, as they
had done all previous ones, by importing labour from Ireland. At his
instigation a letter, with 336 signatures, was sent to the people of
Dublin, appealing for assistance. A quick response came from the
Irish Suffrage Union, which distributed a leaflet advising men not to go
to Cumberland and blackleg, and also sent a reply to Whitehaven,
extolling Brophy's personal qualities. In Dublin, he had been
persecuted, losing his job, wife and child.[3]

Notwithstanding Brophy's efforts, and the ensuing international
goodwill, Lord Lonsdale and Company were able to secure fresh
hands. Many Cumbrian miners found their pits working again—and
they were not. Again, the Association tried to help. All members in
Northumberland and Durham paid a 6d. levy, Lancashire colliers a 3d.
levy, and David Swallow even attempted to get newly-recruited men
in North Staffordshire to make a contribution. But the dispute ended
with 278 men still out of work.[4] Moreover, two prominent strikers,
Garatty and Doran, were imprisoned in spite of W. P. Roberts'
exertions on their behalf.

For the Cumbrian miners, the struggle had been distinctly
unsuccessful. They slumped back into resigned indifference, resentful
of organised labour. Mindful of the threefold assistance it had given—
providing a lecturer, finance and legal aid—the Association thought
the Cumbrian colliers guilty of base ingratitude. In September 1844, it
wrote them angrily denouncing "the steps you have taken in the last
twelve months in opposition to your brethren in every other part of
Britain".[5] A twelve-hour day was common, union orders were

[1] *Whitehaven Herald*, 20 April 1842.
[2] *Northern Star*, 16 September 1843.   [3] Ibid., 30 September 1843.
[4] Ibid., 14 October 1843.   [5] *Miners' Advocate*, September 1844.

disregarded, and even the dispatch to Cumberland of John Auty, a highly experienced organiser, led to no improvement. With the exception of a little activity around Workington, the Miners' Association had ceased to exist in the county by the autumn of 1844.

*   *   *

Events in Derbyshire followed a similar pattern. The union was slow to gain a foothold there; when it did, matters rapidly reached a climax. In October 1843, colliers at Clay Cross wrote to the *Northern Star* asking to be put in contact with the Miners' Association. The Manchester conference, in January 1844, was told there were only 169 members in Derbyshire-Nottinghamshire. The following month Thomas Mycroft, of Bishop Auckland, and another lecturer of the Association arrived in Chesterfield, "endeavouring to unsettle the minds of the colliers".[1] Within a week, the *Derbyshire Courier* reported they were "succeeding to an alarming extent". Those who had already joined were using "all possible means to entice others".[2] By 25 March, when the Glasgow conference began, numbers had swollen to 3,265 of an estimated 4,000 colliers working in the coalfield. Evidently in a happy mood, William Walker, the union's district secretary, wrote to the *Miners' Magazine*, saying restriction of output had commenced and stocks at wharves were almost exhausted: "the masters are in trouble and the men rejoice."[3]

In contrast to this provocative statement, Derbyshire members of the Miners' Association printed a circular that disclaimed any intention to strike, preferring an "amicable adjustment of differences". Colliery owners and agents remained unconvinced. They decided not to employ any union members. This swift retaliatory move took the local Association by surprise. Its whole existence was being brought into question. Naturally, it looked to the Newcastle headquarters for help, but the executive was preoccupied with the struggle in Northumberland and Durham. Strike pay, which had been promised the Derbyshire miners, never arrived; the union's resources were already over-committed.

Some colliers quickly capitulated. Others returned to work only after the owners had given a small wage increase, a concession made in return for the men's undertaking to quit the union. A few miners remained out until June. Then, a series of riots, the result of mounting

---

[1] *Derbyshire Courier*, 17 February 1844.   [2] Ibid., 24 February 1844.
[3] *Miners' Magazine*, March–April 1844.

hunger and bitterness, led to arrests, repression, and the end of the strike.[1] But the defeat in Derbyshire was not as catastrophic as in Cumberland. Although the union had lost considerable strength, it still continued to function. On 18 November 1844, 300 miners attended a meeting at the Queen's Hotel, Ilkeston, to revive the union, and accounts of its activities subsequently appeared.[2]

*   *   *

In North Staffordshire, unlike Derbyshire, the coalowners did not make a determined attempt to crush the union. Perhaps they wished to avoid a repetition of the orgy of violence that had occurred during the general strike two years previously. For some had still not made good their losses. Lord Granville's pits at Shelton had employed 300 men in 1842, but two furnaces had been blown up and not replaced. Now only 100 men were employed.[3] Yet, in December 1843, the Shelton miners, many of them not in the union, struck and won a wage increase.[4] Doubtless with events like these in mind, the North Staffs Coal Trade met in December 1843 and, after a long discussion, decided to tolerate the existence of the Miners' Association in the coalfield.[5]

According to Tremenheere, North Staffordshire masters were "well-known for kindness and consideration. . . . The conduct of nearly all the masters towards their men in relation to wages and employment appears to have been marked with liberality and fairness."[6] Grievances like those complained of in other areas "never existed here, except to a very limited extent". Yet the atmosphere of bonhomie and contentment was rudely shattered by a six-week strike, from 14 March to 20 April, throughout the whole Potteries. Mr. Bower, the Cheadle colliery-owner, symbolises the drastic change. Six months previously, in a spirit of goodwill, he had attended a union meeting, announced a pay rise and given free drinks to the men. Now he was calling for special protection because strikers had threatened to destroy his colliery machinery.[7]

The local district committee of the union, by trying to apply national policy on restriction, had wrought this transformation. In early March

---

[1] See J. E. Williams, *The Derbyshire Miners*, pp. 89–99, for a detailed account of the 1844 strike in Derbyshire.
[2] *Northern Star*, 23 November 1844.
[3] *The Potters' Examiner*, 18 December 1844.
[4] *The Inspector of Mines Report*, 1845, p. 66.
[5] *Staffordshire Advertiser*, 23 December 1843.
[6] *The Inspector of Mines Report*, 1845, p. 58.
[7] *Staffordshire Advertiser*, 20 April 1844.

L

it had written to the masters, proposing that both sides co-operate rather than compete. At the same time, it stated the men's claim for an eight-hour day; many were working ten or twelve. It also wanted a wage increase: "By the paucity of our income we have been deprived of the means of mental cultivation. Our degradation has been a byword to other classes." The statement, reprinted in *The Potters' Examiner*, was couched in a mild, courteous tone. In contrast, another declaration, made after the masters had rejected the claim, boldly proclaimed: "Labour was the first institution of property. Therefore it is the source of all wealth. Capital is worthless without the application of labour."[1]

The union's demand was for 3s. a day for eight hours' work. Many smaller owners met the men's claim. It was the larger owners, with greater resources, who were adamant and, in many instances, succeeded in beating the strike. So colliers in the Potteries were returning to work while the Northumberland-Durham strike was in its first phase. Financially and organisationally weakened, the North Staffordshire miners were in no position to assist their brothers in the North-east, as the Glasgow conference had asked.

★   ★   ★

The Association's next national conference, held at the Temperance Hall, Burslem, 15–19 July 1844, had to appraise the industrial conflicts that had broken out during the past three months. Things had not developed as planned. The union, at its conferences, had always condemned partial strikes. Yet they had taken place in coalfield after coalfield, from Scotland through to Lancashire, Yorkshire, Derbyshire and Staffordshire. All over the country, the union's strength was being sapped precisely at a time it was needed to sustain the North-east.

The Burslem conference did not question general strategy, although it was becoming increasingly obvious that the union's policy on restriction was leading to partial strikes or being used as a means for making wage claims. Instead the conference busied itself with practical measures to help Northumberland and Durham. In order that the North-east would not have to find his salary, W. P. Roberts was made general legal adviser to the whole Association. Each member was to contribute a half-penny to the maintenance of the legal department, whose books would be audited at each conference. Then, at the instigation of the Bury district, the union established a general fund.

[1] *The Potters' Examiner*, 30 March 1844.

In the first instance, this was to help the men in the North-east, but later it was "for the purpose of supporting all miners when on strike".

As a result of the industrial disputes, many miners were unemployed or victimised. The Burslem conference decided to investigate the feasibility of starting a relief fund "for the purpose of supporting those on the tramp, as it is found to be attended with great inconvenience to those situated, not knowing where to apply". And another resolution, directly related to the recent strikes, was an appeal to the Welsh miners. For it had been from Wales, with its poor conditions and scanty union organisation, that most of the blacklegs had been recruited. Conference adjured the Welsh:

"to remain in their own locality, as the very act of coming into those districts where men are out on strike tends to protract such strikes and engender feelings of hostility where bitter feeling should not exist. They are also recommended to join our Association, and the hand of fellowship will be given to them and their interests will be considered as our own."[1]

Besides the actual deliberations, an important function of the Burslem conference was to hold an intensive campaign in North Staffordshire in an attempt to restore the local union organisation to health. Public meetings were held in towns and villages throughout the Potteries, with W. P. Roberts as the main speaker.[2] On the fifth and final evening, local colliers met at Longton to reorganise their lodges. Just as the initial impulse had come from outside—the work of Swallow, consolidated by Dixon and Lomas—so the reconstruction was largely prompted from without. As there were 4,000 miners in in North Staffordshire, nearly 1,000 of whom were permanently unemployed, it is hardly surprising the union remained weak and in a poor bargaining position.[3]

*   *   *

In another coalfield the colliers ran into trouble. "The Yorkshire miners apparently believed that the strike in the North would be short-lived and that they would then be able to draw on the generosity of other districts."[4] But instead, when they were involved in the most

[1] See *Miners' Advocate*, July 1844, for account of the Burslem conference.
[2] Public meetings held included Longton, Hanley on Monday; Longton, Hanley, Smallthorne on Tuesday; Knutton, Alsagers Bank on Wednesday; Longton, Tunstall on on Thursday. The speakers were: W. P. Roberts, W. Dixon, J. Lomax, H. Birrell, J. Taylor, B. Watson, C. Parkinson, T. Weaver.
[3] Figures from *The Inspector of Mines Report*, 1845, p. 59.
[4] F. Machin, *The Yorkshire Miners*, p. 62.

protracted struggle of any coalfield—some men were out for more than three months—they found Northumberland and Durham miners entering Yorkshire to collect for their own strike funds. Thrown back on their own meagre resources, in some districts strike pay was as low as 7d. per family.

This was because the union had been slow to develop in Yorkshire, and consequently had few resources. It was only when David Swallow returned there, in January 1844, that the Association became properly organised. Six months before, when a delegate meeting was held at Adwalton, only thirteen centres bothered to send representatives. But Swallow quickly organised fifty-three centres, with fortnightly district meetings at Halifax, Dewsbury, Wakefield, and Barnsley. He denounced the violations of the Truck Act, a common occurrence in Yorkshire, and illustrated his point by "exhibiting a piece of hard stuff which, when struck upon, sounded like a piece of board". This he explained, had been supplied as bacon from a master's tommy-shop. Swallow went on to cite other grievances, such as stoppages and poor wages.[1]

Yorkshire owners could not fail to be aware of the rising tide of discontent. Mr. Cooper, of Worsbro' colliery, dismissed six men "whom they had reason to believe were ringleaders in spreading dissatisfaction among others". A large owner, Earl Fitzwilliam, took a similar stand. He told his miners "that all those who joined the Colliers Union were to leave their work and houses". Later, his Agent wrote him: "Your Lordship's well-timed letter . . . has had a most beneficial effect. All the men disclaim any connection with the Union, and express their determination not to countenance it in any way."[2] A few miners refused and either left their work or were locked out. At Stainborough colliery five men were prosecuted for breach of contract, the three magistrates on the Bench being all coalowners.

After the Glasgow conference, a garbled version of its instructions was given to Yorkshire miners. Their delegates told them conference recommended that proposals be placed before the masters, that they be given a week to consider, and then, if the masters' answer was unsatisfactory, notice to cease work was to be given. Delegate meetings at Adwalton, Wakefield, Barnsley and Sheffield endorsed this policy. Publicly announcing it, David Swallow proposed that "uninterested persons", chosen by both parties, should consider the claim. If the

[1] *Sheffield Independent*, 30 March 1844.
[2] Wentworth Muniments. Letter from his Agent to Earl Fitzwilliam, 5 March 1844.

employers refused, then the strike would start a month hence.[1]

On 22 April the employers met at Wakefield. They refused arbitration or to raise wages. They regarded the miners' union's demands as "an unjust and uncalled for interference with the rights of masters and men, and under that conviction, the parties now refuse to employ any miner who is a member of the Union". Moreover, any miner not producing the normal quantity of coal "shall be taken to be a member of the union and shall be forthwith dismissed".[2] Earl Fitzwilliam even required his men to sign a loyalty oath, a declaration that they would dissociate themselves from the union.

In West and South Yorkshire work ceased on 12 May. In some pits, men had been eager for the fray. The previous month they had cut their output and earnings to 6d. a day. The owners had consequently been faced with the alternatives of either prosecuting the men in Court, underemploying their machinery, or dismissing men. It was this last course of action they usually adopted.[3]

As in North Staffordshire, some of the small owners, especially in West and South Yorkshire, conceded the men's demands. In these collieries, the union made a weekly levy of 5s. a man and 2s. 6d. a boy for the strike funds. But those owners who held out were distinguished by their ingenuity in finding blacklegs. "Navigators, shoe-makers, watch-sellers and all they could pick up" were used as knobsticks. The *Wakefield Journal* reported "in some pits tailors, shoemakers and men who followed other trades are now working as colliers".[4] Finding blacklegs could be expensive, as agents of Messrs. Smithson and Company of Haigh Moor Colliery, Wakefield, discovered. In St. Helens they provided fifteen potential knobsticks with £5 15s. worth of ale, plus another 5s. for "one more sup" next morning. With numbers reduced to nine after these festivities, first-class rail travel to Wakefield and good lodgings there cost a further £6. Next morning they were taken to Haigh Moor to work:

"But such a thing as that had never entered the heads of the Lancashire lads. They were 'quite willing to have a sup of drink with them' or 'to accommodate them by having a ride in a first-class carriage at their expense', or 'they would, rather than differ, eat their bread, cheese and beef', but to go to work in the coal pits at Haigh Moor, whoever heard of such a thing? So if there was nothing

---

[1] *Wakefield Journal*, 12 April, 1844.
[2] Wentworth Muniments, letter from Agent to Fitzwilliam, 22 April 1844.
[3] *Sheffield Journal*, 11 June 1844.
[4] *Wakefield Journal*, 11 June 1844.

more to do in the shape of first-class trains, or treating, or drinking, they must bid them good-morning, and make their way back to St. Helens, as well as they could."[1]

Lord Londonderry and the Countess of Durham gave their advice, from personal experience, on who made the best blacklegs. The Irish had been imported into Durham and "though at first rather inefficient hands, are now tolerable workmen".[2]

Other tactics of Lord Londonderry were employed. Union leaders were singled out for special attention; a determined effort was made to starve strikers into submission; and mass evictions were used. Often furniture was deliberately handled roughly and broken. Many families "were now lying on the cold ground without any covering".[3]

Such treatment aroused widespread sympathy for the miners among the general public. The *Leeds Times* commented: "Every week the cause of the collier is exciting more sympathy amongst the public and the subscriptions, which at first were trifling, have now swollen to a large amount".[4] Fellow trade unionists were particularly active in rallying support. In Sheffield, "members of the Table Knife Forgers drew a wagon containing 600 loaves of bread through the streets, being preceded by a band of music and followed by a large crowd. The White Metal Smiths organised a procession to deliver a wagon-load of bread. They also carried a bag of money and then came a great number of cabs and hackney coaches containing members of the trade. On another occasion, the women in the employ of the Hair Seating Manufacturers proceeded in procession to the Robin Hood Inn and presented the Committee with eleven pounds-odd which was the amount of an advance which they last week received from their employers."[5] A Committee of Associated Trades, specially formed to assist the miners, predicted it would be able to sustain the strikers.

But the flow of blacklegs into Yorkshire continued uninterrupted. The first serious disturbance occurred at the Soap House pit, the largest in the Sheffield area, following evictions and the introduction of Derbyshire blacklegs. They were being housed in "temporary barracks" in the pityard. A crowd scaled the walls, forced the doors, broke every window and belaboured the blacklegs. The military were called in, but arrived too late. On 19 July before Mr. Justice Cresswell, three men were charged with riot and sentenced to fifteen years' transportation.

---

[1] *Miners' Advocate*, 24 August 1844.   [2] *Sheffield Independent*, 3 August 1844.
[3] *Northern Star*, 11 May, 1844.   [4] *Leeds Times*, 13 July 1844.
[5] F. Machin, op. cit., p. 59.

Another incident was at the Deep pit, Sheffield on 25 August. Strikers blew up the engine-boiler to prevent the resumption of work. But the gunpowder exploded prematurely, and one man was killed. Because of the fear of other outbreaks, the authorities stationed troops at the collieries.

The drift back to work began in South Yorkshire in early August and was all over in that district by October. Donations to the strike fund started to dwindle during September. But in some parts of West Yorkshire the men stayed out until November—twenty-four weeks.

On the whole, Swallow was optimistic about the outcome. Soon after the strike began, he had said the men "had thrown off the yoke. It would be their own fault if they put it on again." After the strike ended, he argued it had been no defeat for the men. In many instances, owners were compelled to reduce hours of work. The sheer tenacity and militancy of the miners would make the owners more cautious in future.

In the post-strike period, many Yorkshire owners came to accept the hold of the Miners' Association over their men. It was especially true of the small collieries around Leeds. For example, the Commissioners were informed at Mr. Maud's Churwell colliery: "All the men are in the Union. They restrict their labour; but are earning from eighteen to twenty-four shillings a week." Likewise at Gelder Road colliery: "The men struck last year and were out thirteen weeks; they gained their point."[1] In the Bradford district, as well, the union remained strong and restriction continued. But the picture was confused. Most of the large pits had succeeded in disposing of all union members.

It was these disparities, the intermingling of union and non-union pits, that sapped the strength of the Association in Yorkshire during the winter of 1844-5. With working conditions and the state of the union varying so widely from pit to pit, it became increasingly difficult for the Association to maintain cohesion. Then, as in the North-east coalfields, there was the labour surplus, the presence of blacklegs, ever ready to depress standards. So the strike had a delayed-action effect: just as in Northumberland and Durham, the Yorkshire miners emerged from the fray with their organisation in a reasonable condition; it was only as the long-term effects became apparent that the union started to spiral into oblivion. The *Miners' Advocate*, of June 1845, referred to the intense internal difficulties of the Yorkshire

[1] *The Inspector of Mines Report*, 1845, p. 30.

Committee: "Unless shame or a sense of duty can bring them into action again . . . the consequence will be destruction to us as a society in Yorkshire."

A general delegate meeting was held at the Punch Bowl, Beeston, 5 July 1845. After that, the Miners' Association appears to have become extinct in Yorkshire.

*   *   *

In contradistinction to Yorkshire, the Association was never strong in Wales. More seriously, for the English colliers, the union never succeeded in plugging the hole, the flood of Welsh miners ever prepared to pour into England and swamp any strike. At the Manchester conference, in January 1844, there were no representatives from South Wales. In North Wales union support at that time consisted of 534 members in Flintshire and 400 Denbighshire miners, roughly half the total number of miners in the coalfield. Conference considered conditions in North Wales worse than elsewhere. For twelve to fourteen hours workmen received 1s. 6d. to 2s. per day; only one colliery in Ruabon was without a tommy shop. So conference decided to waive payment of union dues by the Denbighshire colliers.

In his book *The Industrial Revolution in North Wales* Mr. A. H. Dodd confirms this opinion: "From about 1830 to 1850 wages in North Wales' coal mines were at best not much more than three-quarters, and at worst barely half those paid in England and Scotland."[1] The Miners' Association was unable to do much to alter it. After an ill-timed strike, all union organisation was smashed. In January 1846, John Auty, visiting the area endeavouring to get some re-groupment, discovered that men had to hew fifty-three hundredweights of coal before they received payment for a ton.

In the spring of 1844 the union sent two lecturers to South Wales. George Williams, who had had some success organising North Wales, toured the smaller collieries in the South, accompanied by William Taylor, a Chartist lecturer. Initially, he made head-way: headquarters were established at Merthyr, where thrice-weekly meetings were held. But the masters decided to stamp out the union. They employed their own spies to keep the union's activities under surveillance, while the Chief Constable of Glamorganshire duly noted, in April, the efforts "to entice both the colliers and miners to join an association

---

[1] A. H. Dodd, *The Industrial Revolution in North Wales*, pp. 343–4.

styled the Miners' Union [*sic*] of Great Britain."[1] Then the owners struck a blow: at pit after pit men were dismissed for belonging to the union. "It is monstrous," wrote George Williams, "to see coal masters binding their men to such conditions. He that refuses is sure to be starved out. There is so much tyranny prevailing in this part."[2]

The Miners' Association appears to have been wiped out in Wales. Periodically, local unions did emerge there, with which the Association nationally tried to make arrangements; but throughout the Association's whole life Wales remained the worst organised area with the worst conditions. That is why it was such a fruitful field for strike-breakers.

*   *   *

The Scottish miners rarely, if ever, were used as blacklegs. This was because in all the Scottish coalfields, to varying degrees, trade unions existed.

Viewed as a whole, Scotland could be regarded as an area of exceptional vitality at the end of 1844. But that it was one of the main areas in which the union survived only served to weaken the central control of the national Association. The considerable triumphs of the Scottish miners, made without any assistance from the union executive, tended to strengthen rebellious and separatist tendencies. Many could not see they derived any benefit from belonging to an organisation of miners throughout Great Britain; whatever advances they won—and they were considerable—were won through their own exertions. By January 1845 wages throughout Scotland rose to an average of 3s. 4d.—an increase of 4d. in a month. The same month the Scottish national delegate meeting had, as its first item of the agenda, disaffiliation from the Miners' Association. After a long discussion, the resolution was defeated. Although hesitant, the Scots remained in the Association and were, next to Lancashire, the strongest section of the union.

*   *   *

The year 1844 began in Lancashire with a spate of strikes. As John Berry told the Manchester conference, there had been nothing but warfare between masters and men and, on the whole, the men had won—at least, gained considerable wage increases. That being so,

---

[1] Glamorgan Quarter Sessions Records. Chief Constable's Report, 18 April 1844, quoted E. W. Evans, *Miners of South Wales*, pp. 68–9.
[2] *Miners' Magazine*, March–April 1844.

their delegates made it clear to the Manchester conference that they regarded their own efforts—there were nineteen separate strikes in the vicinity of St. Helens at the beginning of 1844—merely as a prelude to a general strike. Though conference rejected this proposal, the Lancashire men continued to conduct partial strikes whenever they thought them likely to be to their advantage. The conference's condemnation of them made not a whit of difference.

At St. Helens, the miners refused a 9d. per day wage offer.[1] After a month's strike, they changed their minds. But so did the employers: now they wanted the increase linked to the introduction of a yearly Bond and the renunciation of the union. Next week, a party of Welsh colliers arrived, and were met by 1,000 strikers "who assailed them with stones, brick-bats, and other missiles, severely hurting several of the police".[2] Arrests were made but the police were compelled to let all but three of the prisoners go. Eventually order was restored when troops, under Colonel Wemyss, arrived.

All over Lancashire the miners were coming out. The Earl of Balcarres' men and others in the Wigan district stopped. Likewise at Bolton. Colliers at Poynton, Worth and Norbury also came out. As coal stocks were low, this stopped some of the textile mills in the Stockport area. At Patricroft colliery, Eccles, the men were supposed to give a month's notice. When the owners, Messrs. Lancaster and Company, realised that a strike was pending they reduced miner's earnings to as little as 6d. a day. Then the 120 workers struck. Seven of them were arrested for breach of contract. Mr. Maude, the magistrate, told them, he would not send them to prison if they would return to work. They remained obdurate, and received a two months' sentence.[3] But W. P. Roberts, who also succeeded in gaining release for St. Helens and Wigan strikers, applied to the Court of Queen's Bench for a writ of Habeas Corpus and the men were freed.

By March 1844, the strike wave had ended. The union emerged intact. In St. Helens the employers placarded the town, stating that before the recent advance of 1s. the men had received an average of between 3s. 1d. and 3s. 9d. The Miners' Advocate challenged this statement; significantly it had nothing to say about the large wage increase.[4] Such large advances were, however, being won in violation of official union policy, which condemned partial strikes. Sometimes the union even sent its representatives along to remonstrate with the

---

[1] Manchester Guardian, 10 January 1844.
[3] Ibid., 24 January 1844.
[2] The Times, 1 March 1844.
[4] Miners' Advocate, 6 April 1844.

men and strike pay was refused. This led to some disenchantment, and men dropped out of the union. But it was still very strong in the autumn of 1844, when it resumed its offensive.

So strong was the Lancashire union it sometimes obtained reinstatement of dismissed union members and even applied the "closed shop" principle. In November a successful strike, plus W. P. Roberts' legal exertions, compelled a Wigan owner to re-employ an engineer dismissed for joining the Association. In December a strike began at Kirkless colliery. After it had been in progress for seventeen weeks, the *Manchester Guardian* explained: "The only grievance ever alleged against the proprietors of these works is the employment of one man who refused to subscribe to the Miners' Association."

The *Manchester Guardian*'s repeated references to the union, its constant attacks on it, themselves constitute a grudging recognition of its power. In December 1844, the *Guardian* published what purported to be a balance sheet of the Lancashire union for the six-week period 21 October to 30 November. In that time, the income amounted to £1,244 19s. 8½d., of which the General Fund spent £593 and the Legal Fund £511. The county was organised into 172 lodges contained in 22 districts. According to the report, the dues paid were very much higher than the 6d. entrance fee and 1d. a week prescribed in the national rules. It cost £1 for a man and 10s. for a boy to join, with a weekly subscription of 1s. 8½d. An additional 3d. a fortnight was levied. The *Guardian* believed this was intended for ale, as meetings were usually held in public houses. Since the Lancashire union began, its total income had been £8,150. Its monthly income averaged £741.

The authenticity of the balance sheet is debatable. When checked against the union's membership returns, which were usually accurate, certain facts emerge. Both agree Lancashire was divided into twenty-two districts. The county membership claimed on 18 November was 6,486. If they were paying almost 2s. a week, and recruitment was a little more than 100 a month, then this could be reconciled with the union's monthly income averaging £741. The *Guardian* report stated that the lecturer's weekly wage was about £1 3s. No other source ever puts it so high though admittedly, if repayment of the 5s. in the pound donated to the North-east strike fund was being made, as the Wakefield conference stipulated, then £1 3s. was, at that time, a reasonable figure. The *Guardian* proceeds to name seven lecturers who were working in the county. But only three of those named were actually

¹ *Manchester Guardian*, 18 December 1844.

lecturers.[1] So, if the balance sheet is genuine, the union must have been in the inconceivable position of not knowing who was in its employ and paying wages to the wrong persons! Again, the *Guardian* gives Roberts' salary as £400 for the six weeks. On this basis, his annual salary would be somewhere around £3,500, and if that were the case, it is extremely unlikely that opponents of the union would have failed to make much of it. The probability is that the *Guardian*'s balance sheet was a forgery, based on a certain amount of research. To dismiss it, however, does not mean that we deny that the Lancashire union was then extremely prosperous.

In the same month the *Manchester Guardian* made another attack on the union. It opposed the men's demand for a 2*d*. in the shilling wage increase, complaining that miners were already earning 4*s*. for an eight-hour day and that the demand for an advance was tantamount to asking the owners to increase the price of coal and join the colliers in exploiting the public. Finally, the *Guardian* asked the miners what they would think if the owners followed their example, forming an association with the object of paying the least possible wages.

Replying for the Miners' Association, William Grocott and William Dixon did not deny the wage rate quoted by the *Guardian*.[2] They merely reminded readers of deductions for candles, powder and tools, as well as fines for "short-measure" and "not clear". These effectively reduced miners' wages to 15*s*. 6*d*. a week. If the proposed wage increase were granted, it would have a trifling effect on the public. Their letter ended by arguing that, as the *Guardian* knew full well, the owners did have an association. It had been the practice, since 1841, to give "quittance" papers to men when they were dismissed, stating the reason for dismissal. As any prospective employer wanted to see a man's "quittance" papers before he employed him, it resulted in prominent unionists being victimised.

Grocott and Dixon were definitely wrong on their last point. While Lancashire owners had generally acquired the habit of issuing "quittance" papers, this did not indicate the existence of an employers' association in the county. Many attempts to found one were made, but they all ran up against the same obstacle in the individualism of the employers.

The Lancashire coalowners, weakened by disunity, usually responded

[1] The *Manchester Guardian* gives Holgate, Dennett, Price, Bowen, Welsby, Dixon as the Lancashire lecturers. The Wakefield conference, however, had appointed Dennett, Holgate, Price, Parkinson, Alfred, Harris and Embleton.
[2] *Manchester Guardian* 18 December 1844.

to the colliers' demands for more pay by making concessions. They would then pass on their increased production costs to the public.[1] This was no more than following the logic of the Miners' Association's own policy. Its spokesmen had argued that restrictions, and the consequent reductions in supply, were beneficial to masters as to men. In fact, at times, the Association exhibited a strong desire to do a deal with the masters. It hoped to see the colliers and coalowners combined in a struggle to force the rest of the community to pay a higher price for coal. An expanding market, such as existed in Lancashire, was ideally suited to this unnatural harmony.

In some instances, the miners complained, the owners took advantage of wage claims to raise the price of coal by more than was needed and consequently to increase profit margins. The men's leaders resented the blame for price increases falling on them. They hastened to point out how the Dukinfield employers had increased the selling price by 4d. a tub to give the miners an advance of a half-penny a tub. Messrs. Daglish, Blundell and other Pemberton proprietors were accused of having raised coal prices 1s. 8d. a ton when miners only asked for 2½d. a ton.

But, whatever the cause of higher prices for coal, the *Manchester Guardian* fulminated against them. As the leading apostle of free trade and competition, it protested in the name of manufacturing industry against the repeated increases in the price of coal, especially as an element of collusion probably existed between masters and men.

*   *   *

The state of the union at the end of 1844 was thus one of immense contrasts. Some sections were successful, others shattered. Some were prosperous, other penurious. The great diversity was produced by the different stages of development and the different tactics pursued. It also reflected the wide variety of industrial and social conditions that existed in the various coalfields.[2] But, most important of all, it showed that a national market for coal did not exist in Britain at that time. Each coalfield produced for its own separate market. Consequently, each reacted to its own particular supply and demand conditions. Northumberland and Durham were the only coalfields affected seriously by the coal export tax. Yet, while they were feeling the

[1] Minutes of a Coalowners' Association for the Wigan district, September 1843 to December 1843, contain repeated references to expulsions for refusing to obey its resolution.

[2] See Chapter 3.

pinch, Lancashire found its own market, within its county boundaries, rapidly expanding through the growth of industry.

The Miners' Association had set itself an impossible task. In trying to formulate and apply a common strategy in all coalfields it overlooked the particular, local factors that were often the most significant. Not until a national market for coal had come into being, with the result that changes in one coalfield directly affected another, were the necessary pre-conditions for a unified and national union created.

II

The Collapse of the Newcastle Leadership

THE national leadership refused to accept the fact that Northumberland and Durham were irrevocably lost. From its Newcastle headquarters, it waited anxiously for the first signs of revival. In the eyes of Jude, the strong union tradition in the North-east coalfields made a comeback certain. The increasing severity of the masters' exactions was sure to arouse a protest. For the well-being of the Miners' Association as a whole, it was a necessity: the North-east, with 34,000 of the country's 196,000 pitmen, was needed for stability. So the Association still continued to give the area special attention. Although its staff of lecturers had been reduced to twenty by early 1845, it still spared four —Watson, Hammond, Holliday and Wilde—for the North-east. Their efforts could have been better used salvaging some of the shattered organisation elsewhere.

Till the North-east revived, the executive saw its task as essentially a holding operation. It had to prevent, if possible, other sections becoming involved in the type of open confrontation with the masters that had been so disastrous in Northumberland and Durham. Therefore, the union had to forswear the strike weapon. In its place, it should rely upon peaceful persuasion. It had to appeal to Parliament and the British people. One of their spokesmen had a comforting thought: "Truth, justice, reason, scripture and public opinion are all on our side, and these are more than all that can possibly be against us."[1]

This attitude, a reflection of the weakness in the North-east, was unsympathetically received in Lancashire and Scotland, where more positive action could be taken. A letter from Tranent, in the Lothians, echoes this view:

"The time has now come when the grievances of the miners are somewhat known by all classes throughout Great Britain, from Sir Robert Peel to the humblest of the community, and, I ask you,

[1] *Miners' Advocate*, July 1845.

brother miners, has the knowledge of this great fact brought sympathy from those who are in duty bound to sympathise with us, or a redress of one single grievance from those who have the absolute power to redress the whole? No! Instead of this the reverse is experienced. . . . Nothing yet has been done for us, nor will anything be done to benefit us, unless done by ourselves."[1]

Lancashire and Scotland did not heed the executive. They continued to strike whenever they thought fit, while the executive watched apprehensively.

The Newcastle leaders were far from being alone in their expectations for the Tyne, Wear and Tees. Certainly the coalowners and their allies did not regard their victory as final. They, too, thought the union would rise from the ashes of the Great Strike. So, to forestall any re-emergence of the union, a group of Durham Tory magistrates proposed that the rural police should be strengthened. The *Weekly Dispatch*, which carried the story, said Lord Londonderry, as Lord Lieutenant of the County, and Sir James Graham, the Home Secretary, warmly applauded the move. But, despite this influential backing, a majority of Durham's J.P.s rejected the proposal. Graham felt called upon to administer a stern rebuke, expressing regret at so irresponsible a refusal. A second meeting was called, and again the proposal was defeated—this time 25 votes to 10. Deploring this second refusal, the Home Secretary argued that "the same emergency (the strike) attended by the same bad consequences may sooner or later be expected to occur again".[2] Although no explanation was given for the Durham magistrates' reluctance to engage more policemen, the reason was almost certainly the extra expense.

The strike itself, followed by the rapid drop in coal prices, had brought many owners to the verge of ruin and depressed the whole economic life of the county. Many coal masters saw their only salvation in re-creating some kind of "vend". Numerous ideas were mooted until opinion tended to solidify behind one, very drastic, proposal: to amalgamate all Durham collieries and form one big company. A number of prospectuses were circulated; meetings considered the proposal; committees were even appointed to estimate the value of collieries. Owners of smaller mines enthusiastically supported the idea. Some owners of large collieries also favoured the plan. As one advocate put it, "a combination would enable the owners

---

[1] *Miners' Advocate*, July 1845.   [2] Ibid., November 1844.

to deal with the purchaser was well as with the workmen."[1] But the scheme never came to fruition, largely because a few owners of the largest collieries refused to co-operate.

Lord Londonderry, who was described as "a great giant in the county at the time", poured scorn on the suggestion, and others followed suit.[2] Perhaps he was partly motivated by a desire to retain his aristocratic independence. Of the landed aristocracy in Durham only the Lambtons and the Londonderrys actually operated their own collieries. Other landed families had withdrawn from coal mining, as they thought it too risky. The mines, were operated by colliery lessees, colliery viewers and adventurers.[3]

But Lord Londonderry also had sound economic reasons for opposing the amalgamation. It was obvious that a combination to regulate output and prices was no longer practical. The growth of means of communication meant it would be impossible for any coalfield, by combination, to secure monopoly profits. It would have to compete with other coalfields for markets. Whereas most Durham owners, quite rightly, feared this competition, Lord Londonderry's powerful financial position gave him greater strength. He had more to lose from close association with his fellow Durham owners, whose arrangements would doubtless impede his expansion, than from owners elsewhere.

Besides his collieries, Lord Londonderry gained a steady income from ownership of land, houses and shops. Throughout the 1840s, his profits from Seaham harbour averaged £5,000 a year and "showed that the risk that Londonderry took in building the harbour was well worthwhile".[4] So, while other Durham owners were retrenching, he was able to accumulate capital and sink fresh mines.

A curious incident occurred when some of His Lordship's lady guests went to observe progress being made at the new Seaton pit:

"In one of the buckets, at the particular request of the ladies, two workmen ascended resembling drowned rats more than mortals. On their appearing out of the abyss, they were politely requested to run about and show themselves, which they as politely refused to do."[5]

[1] Select Committee on the Cause of the Present Dearness and Scarcity of Coal, 1873 p. 297.
[2] Select Committee on the Cause, etc., 1873, p. 296.
[3] F. M. L. Thompson, *English Landed Society in the 19th Century*, pp. 264–5. Also the Buddle Collection, North of England Mining Engineers' Library.
[4] Lady Londonderry, *Frances Anne*, p. 228.
[5] Lady Londonderry, *Frances Anne*, p. 229.

M

In April 1845 there appeared to be a serious chance of the union reviving. The largest gathering of Tees miners since the strike assembled at Cockton Hill. After hearing Daniels speak, they passed a resolution to stand by the Miners' Association, as "the union alone can save us". It was also resolved to ask all owners for a wage increase since the export tax had recently been repealed. The press reported this event with misgivings. The *Tyne Mercury* published an appeal to coalowners and pitmen.[1] It did not want to see a repetition of last year's strike. Both sides had to show greater tolerance and understanding. Hitherto the masters had been too obdurate and unbending. They only made concessions under duress, which was the worst possible way, since it gave "the men an exalted idea of their own power". The *Tyne Mercury* said the men "seem to imagine that, as by their last strike they obtained whatever they desired, they have only to make a like demand now to obtain still further concessions". It advocated that the union should disband.

Replying to the *Tyne Mercury*, the Northumberland and Durham colliers made the frankest admission yet on the outcome of the strike. It was untrue, they said, that there had been mutual concessions. When they returned to work, they expected the terms of the Bond offered in April 1844, which had been the same as the previous year's Bond. How cruelly they had been deceived! But with the fresh Bond, in April 1845, things became even worse. The men had not obtained "whatever they desired" at the last strike, nor did they "now seek to obtain further concessions". In fact it was the men who had made all the concessions:

"There is not one Colliery unbound where the same terms have been offered as were given last year! So far, indeed, from the men seeking higher terms, the Owners have insisted on a reduction—some a shilling, some of eightpence, some of sixpence, some of fourpence, and some of twopence per score, and the men, whenever they could obtain a hearing of their Owners, have offered to bind on half the above reduction being made, but the viewers in this, as in all other instances, have insisted on the full amount of the proposed reduction.

"But a change still more important and more ruinous to the men has been proposed on the part of the owners. At the last binding it was settled men should forfeit threepence for every quart of foul coal, splint or stone found in a corf when brought to the bank, but now it is proposed that they should forfeit the corf. . . . Think, now, on the hardship of this!"

The miners' leaflet continued by saying this new arrangement would mean that men, after working for eight or ten hours unconscious of committing any offence, would come to the bank and discover the fines imposed on them were greater than their day's wages. "The oppression of the Israelites, who were compelled to make bricks from straw, was light compared to this," it concluded.

Martin Jude, in a letter to the *Newcastle Chronicle*, of 10 May 1845, listed the collieries where reductions in wages, ranging from 12 to 33 per cent, had taken place. Somewhat unconvincingly, he argued against the cuts on the grounds the "state of the trade had never been more healthy than now, as is evidenced by the market price of coals and the moderate rate of freights".

Few, if any, organised protests came from miners. Yet the *Miners' Advocate* remained undaunted. It looked to the union's national conference, opening at Newcastle on 7 July 1845, to reorganise the two counties. "In this cause talent, perseverance and patience will do much," wrote the editor, "for while there is hope we will never despair." Recruitment demonstrations held during the Burslem and Wakefield conferences achieved some success, and similar attempts were planned at Newcastle. But meetings at Scaffold Hill, Sheriff Hill and Botany Bay were attended by less than fifty men.[1] The press commented derisively: "The pitmen of this district have been holding various meetings during the week, at all of which the delegates who attended recommended that preparations should be made for another strike. The discarded attorney-general, Roberts, is still lurking about the neighbourhood, but he is short of means and powerless for mischief."[2]

Repeatedly the press made the totally false charge that the union favoured another strike. It probably enhanced the Association's unpopularity. Yet, the basic reason for lack of support was the extreme persecution anybody remotely connected with the union had to undergo. On 6 July Hammond, speaking at Wreckington, said owners were dismissing men, not merely for being members, but even for going to union meetings.

Finally, an official admission of the real state of affairs was made. The executive committee reported to the Newcastle conference that

---

[1] *Newcastle Journal*, 12 July 1845.   [2] *Tyne Mercury*, 25 July 1845.

the vast majority of the Northumberland and Durham miners had left the union.

*   *   *

With its influence waning in the North-east coalfields, the executive struggled on throughout 1845. It needed to find some other solid basis for support. It also realised that the Association's well-being—indeed, its very existence—depended on it gaining a steady, regular income. Some sections of the union were not without funds—Lancashire and Scotland were fairly well off—but they were loth to contribute to the executive. Newcastle, to them, appeared far away, and their own needs more pressing. The national leadership was ailing through lack of finance.

Undoubtedly, the executive raised this issue at the national conference held at Rhosymedre, Denbighshire, starting 15 April 1845. This could be termed a mystery conference. It is very difficult to say who attended. The Scottish colliers made it clear they thought North Wales too far and had no intention of going. But a month or so later, they sent delegates to the Consolidated Trades conference in London. So their complaint about the distance of Rhosymedre appears to have been merely an excuse, a sign of their lukewarm affiliation to the national union. But, besides Scotland, the Association's other big stronghold—Lancashire—apparently failed to send delegates. William Grocott, the county secretary, was speaking in Lancashire at the time the conference was held and W. P. Roberts was defending three workmen at Hyde in Cheshire. The *Northern Star* carried no account of proceedings at Rhosymedre nor did Welsh papers carry any reports of recruiting rallies, usually conducted in conjunction with national conferences.

A conference, however, did take place. One of its decisions was to resume publication of the *Miners' Advocate*. It reappeared in May 1845. In smaller format, the paper still espoused the same principles and was published from Newcastle. Another decision was that all dues be sent to the national secretary rather than the county secretary. It may be that, with the two main opponents to this move absent, its supporters thought they had scored a tactical success. Yet it was a hollow victory: Scotland and Lancashire seem simply to have ignored the resolution.

John Hall pleaded in vain for all districts to obey the Rhosymedre instruction. He said it was the "only means of bringing the Miners' union to what it should be". Indeed, his efforts to gain compliance

probably heightened tension between the executive and Scotland.
In its report to the Newcastle conference in July, the executive
reported that parts of Scotland, as well as North and South Staffordshire, were neglecting to pay subscriptions to headquarters. This was
galling since good progress in recruiting fresh members continued to
be made in Scotland County Associations, and the National Union,
with a deficit of £57 6s. 11d., badly needed the money. The financial
difficulties were alluded to in a conference report appearing in the
Newcastle Journal.[1] After mentioning that the assembly was being
held at the Swan Inn, Martin Jude's establishment, it continued:

> "the first subject for discussion was furnished by Mr. Jude himself
> who refused to 'score the pints', or fill the pewter, till satisfied as to
> the mode of payment, there being, it was stated, 'a long score' stand-
> ing on the old account. An arrangement was finally effected by a
> cheque on the consolidated fund. When this difficulty had been got
> rid of, the delegates proceeded to develop their plan for another
> strike of the pitmen of Northumberland and Durham. The delegates
> have since been continuing their sittings at Martin Jude's, where
> they will of course remain till the 'consolidated fund' evaporates in
> the evanescent fumes of 'beer and bacca'."

Jude commented, more in sorrow than in anger: "As the poor
gentleman has to please his masters to obtain a little bread for his wife
and family, it is impossible for him to refrain from following the
occupation he was hired for, viz., that of throwing cold water on any
movements of the working classes to better their conditions." As a
result of press misrepresentation, the Association debarred reporters
from the Newcastle and all subsequent national conferences. It adopted
the procedure of circulating branches with agendas, resolutions and
reports. Since none of these documents are extant, information about
later gatherings is rather scanty.

The next conference was at the Queen's Head Inn, Ilkeston, 6 to 9
January 1846. In its report on the half-year, the executive committee
referred to "a considerable increase in numbers".[2] These were mainly
in Staffordshire, Derbyshire and Nottingham. Notwithstanding, the
union's deficit had risen almost £20, to £76 0s. 7d. The difference
could be "attributed to falling off of several districts in Scotland,
principally brought about by the insincerity of professing friends in
that quarter". Certain Scottish leaders were advocating a sectional

---

[1] *Newcastle Journal*, 12 July 1845.   [2] *Miners' Advocate*, February 1846.

union, continued the executive's report, for the "gratification of personal feeling and individual caprice".

Personal friction between Scottish and English miners must have played a part in causing the split. But the important factors lay much deeper. The Scottish unions, on the whole, were powerful and rich. Their dues, when dispatched to Newcastle, were used to help sick union organisations in English coalfields. The Scots, therefore, put money in and had little, or nothing, to show for it. Naturally, many thought they would be stronger without their English brethren. Moreover, what was probably the most important function the Miners' Association was performing at that time for its component sections benefited Scotland very little. The executive described this function when referring to the advantage of having a nationwide network of lecturers:

> "when the tyranny and oppression of the masters compels a locality to cease work, the speedy communication thus established prevents, to a considerable extent, those masters from procuring hands to supplant their fellow-men, by false pretences, as to the cause of requiring hands."

It often proved effective. Even where men did not belong to the union, lecturers were usually able to dissuade them from going to another coalfield to blackleg against their fellow colliers. For blacklegging was not a popular occupation: prudence led men to avoid trouble in other areas if only because they had enough trouble in their own. But, also, the union could appeal to men's sense of solidarity, their goodwill, their indebtedness to miners in other districts. Thus, just before the Ilkeston conference the Lancashire miners were involved in dispute and the masters tried to bring labour from the North-east. The executive issued a handbill, "To the Miners of Northumberland and Durham", listing the Lancashire collieries in dispute and continuing:

> "it would be INGRATITUDE OF THE BLACKEST DYE to go and supplant them under the present circumstances. The Lancashire miners have nobly and bravely stood by and supported the Association up to the present time and they did support you during the late strike more than all the other miners in the country."[1]

This appeal was almost entirely successful. The men from the Two

---

[1] *Miners' Advocate*, December 1845.

Counties might no longer have been union members; this did not mean they were willing to become blacklegs.

Undoubtedly, the "strikebreakers prevention service", as it might be termed, played a useful role in English coalfields. However, it did not bring the same benefit to Scotland. No English colliers could be induced to journey to Scotland. Hence the Scottish unions never needed to contact the Newcastle headquarters to stop an influx of labour. Any blackleg labour used in a Scottish dispute would be Scottish, and it would be possible to counter it without contacting Newcastle.

The executive told the Ilkeston conference that, "with the exception of the division in Scotland, the prospects of the Association are brighter than hitherto". This was unfounded optimism. The blow inflicted by Scottish defections was crippling. It drained the union of finance and support. It was the final punch which knocked out the Newcastle leadership. For some time, the Newcastle leadership had been unsteady. A sign of its weakness was its failure to implement conference decisions. The *Miners' Advocate* had not been made a stamped paper; W. P. Roberts had not become the Attorney-General of all British miners; and neither the relief fund nor the strike fund had been set up, as the Burslem conference instructed. The executives' failure to comply with conference decisions was not because it was unwilling but because it was unable. Insufficient funds limited its scope. Localism and separatism were growing forces. The mere fact that colliers did not feel the same urgency to meet each other, and had six-monthly instead of three-monthly national conferences, meant they were attaching less importance to central control and direction. The executive's inability to prevent the Scottish miners from quitting further reduced its prestige. Funds became even less and, in February 1846, the *Miners' Advocate* stopped publication a second time. This was the end for the Newcastle leadership.

The centre of gravity moved to Lancashire, where union fortunes were high. It was decided to resume publication of the *Miners' Advocate*. As there were special postal concessions in the Isle of Man, William Daniels, who was still editor, was told to make arrangements for printing the journal in Douglas, John Hall, the general secretary, moved headquarters from Newcastle to Preston, where regular boat services made for easy contact with the Isle of Man. Then, by November 1846, William Meadowcroft, the Lancashire county treasurer, replaced Martin Jude as national treasurer. The following year Lancashire's predominance was made complete when William Grocott, the county secretary, replaced John Hall as general secretary. Just as in 1844 all the principal office-holders were Newcastle men, so in 1847 they were all from Lancashire.

12

The Emergence of the Lancashire Union

FROM spring 1844 onwards Lancashire colliers, unlike their brothers elsewhere, enjoyed almost uninterrupted progress. Through combined action they regulated the supply of labour, regularly gaining wage advances. The Lancashire miners' prosperity, the strength of their union, the size of its coffers, were a source of awe and astonishment to friend and foe alike. The Lancashire union frequently achieved its objectives without strike action, but when it did strike its opponents felt its formidable strength.

The Lancashire union's basic structure differed from Northumberland and Durham. There the mining village and the colliery were synonymous. When the pit ceased to produce, economic activity ceased altogether. Accordingly, the colliers looked first to their pit, then to their county organisation. Representation reflected this fact: the delegates of the Northern Counties were listed by colliery. In contrast, the Lancashire miners lived in highly diversified industrial areas, where industrial conflicts necessarily affected the rest of the community. Consequently, some kind of co-operation or consultation with weavers and other trades was essential. The Lancashire miner regarded himself as an inhabitant of a town, not merely the employee of a pit. It was, very often, a matter of indifference which particular colliery employed him. Until recent times, a perpetual problem of union organisation in Lancashire has been that a miner joined the lodge nearest his home, or the one to which his friends belonged, whether he worked at a particular pit or not. The strength of the town or district organisation reduced that of the county. In the 1840s it made Lancashire unable to provide the type of leadership given by Northumberland and Durham. Indeed, Lancashire never sought to impose centralised control. Instead, it wanted a loose, federal structure, a national replica of what existed within the county.

Lancashire's form of organisation had certain advantages. Whereas centralisation meant that one heavy blow could shake the whole set-up, in Lancashire the union could be obliterated in a district and

elsewhere continue to function unimpaired. The diffusion and intermingling of the union membership made it difficult for owners to
apply the practice of playing one pit's colliers off against another. On
the other hand, by skilful use of partial strikes, the union was able to
exploit the disunity among employers. An owner would find his pit
paralysed by a stoppage while his competitors maintained production.

Strikes in the county followed this pattern. The Bolton or Wigan
colliers would come out, often supported by combinations of other
trades in the town as well as by their fellow miners elsewhere in
Lancashire. It was a type of guerilla warfare specially suited to the
times. Ample support was given to those on strike. They received
strike-pay, food, rent and even had their fines paid for them. Yet the
Association kept its funds safe. The large numbers of miners in other
parts of the county, still at work, paid levies. It was a traditional tactic
of Lancashire workers. The Webbs say John Doherty initiated it in the
cotton spinners' strike of 1830.[1] The Lancashire mining industry, with
its numerous tiny pits, was peculiarly vulnerable to this tactic. Small
owners, with little capital to fall back on, could not afford to have their
pits idle for long periods. Their resources were less than the union's,
and, as a result, they had to come to terms.

The Association, realising this, played on the owners' weaknesses.
When a strike occurred, the union sought to establish friendly relations
with other employers. Thus it avoided the war on all fronts which
had been so disastrous in the Northern Counties. As a consequence the
Lancashire executive consistently preached the need for industrial
harmony while, at the same time, it indulged in grim struggles with
individual employers. The same ambivalent love-hate attitude was
manifest by the masters. Wage cuts, evictions, the mass import of
blacklegs—this was but one side of the coin. On the other, owners
went out of their way to reach agreement with the men. When the
union held galas (as it frequently did) owners would send peace
offerings of meat and ale.

The owners' policy of appeasement, in marked contrast to the
Northern Counties, in part resulted from their own weakness, a failure
to build a powerful employers' organisation like "the vend". This, in
turn, arose from the intense rivalry, the competition of hundreds of
small coal-producers fighting for the same market. An analysis of the
Wigan Coalfield in 1851 showed that 58 per cent of all collieries had

---

[1] S. and B. Webb, op. cit., pp. 119 and 122.

an output of less than one hundred tons a day.[1] In Leigh, in the same year, there were seventeen pits, the largest of which employed fifty-two men and produced 208 tons.[2] And this was the pattern throughout the county: most pits employed less than twenty-five men. It was very different from the Northern Counties, where collieries like Cramlington had 766 men and Thornley 560 men. Yet, the trend towards the concentration of capital existed in Lancashire as well.

Large owners saw that amalgamation was necessary for the economic working of shallow seams and imperative for deeper ones. Lord Crawford describes how his ancestor, the Earl of Balcarres, strove to lessen competition. He bought up small workings, even when he had no immediate intention of developing them; he undercut his small competitors by selling coal at a more moderate price: and he extensively used his right to transport coal by canal without paying certain duties.[3] In this way, the Earl of Balcarres and others fostered the tendency to large-scale production. By 1851, the Wigan coalfield had nine collieries with outputs above 300 tons daily, accounting for more than a third of the district's total production; six collieries, drawing more than 450 tons daily, accounted for a quarter. These big companies could not be bent so easily to follow the union's wishes. Often they were prepared for disputes of long duration and, with greater contacts, were more inclined to import blackleg labour.

Although 1845 was a good year for the union, when it gained increases in most places, it was marked by a serious setback. In March 1845, a strike broke out in the Duckinfield-Ashton area.[4] The men had the usual grievances: excessive fines for dirt and non-payment of allowances for working on "faults", "steps" and "hitches". The employers took steps to intimidate miners and replace them. Bailiffs were sent to the miners' homes for the rent, which was paid out of Associations funds. Denied the pretext of non-payment of rent, the owners still carried out their eviction plans, supplanting their former workmen by blacklegs from Derbyshire. A public meeting of all trades at Stalybridge pledged its full support for the strikers, and a joint committee of spinners and miners was set up at Ashton to co-ordinate support. In May the masters felt in a strong enough position to offer a settlement on their own terms. The men were to return to work at the

---

[1] A. J. Taylor, "The Wigan Coalfield in 1851". *Trans. of the Lancashire and Cheshire His. Soc.*, p. 118.
[2] A. Lunn, *The Historical Past of a Lancashire Borough*, p. 269.
[3] Earl of Crawford, *Haigh Cannel*, Manchester Statistical Society, 1933, pp. 17-19.
[4] *Northern Star*, 29 March 1845.

same prices as when they struck. But a Bond was to be introduced, which would compel workers to give three, six or twelve months' notice of termination of employment while the masters reserved the right to discharge at fourteen days' notice. The strikers rejected the proposal and struggled on with little prospect of obtaining work. The Association erected booths at Liverpool and Newton-le-Willows Races to appeal for money to help the displaced men.[1]

The failure at Dukinfield was seen by the union as part of a general tendency. Its Travelling Committee, whose task was to assess the situation in the county, recommended more stringent restriction. The owners wanted to create surplus labour or coal stocks as a weapon to reduce wages. Their attempt to do so failed. The union successfully resisted attempts at Bellfield colliery, Rochdale, for example, to introduce an eleven-day fortnight and then it went on to the offensive itself. By using restriction as a prelude, a means of running down stocks, it weakened the employers' position. In successive districts— Oldham, St. Helens, Rochdale—the owners conceded advances, ranging from 8d. to a 1s. But, as the winter wore on, the general state of the economy began to deteriorate. With it, the demand for coal and the price of coal dropped. The owners began to dig in their heels and appeared less inclined to capitulate before union pressure.

By January 1846, the turn had come of the Bolton miners to pursue their claim. They had written to Lord Bradford and other owners, asking for an increase. Their plea was rejected, so the men struck. Nobody denied that miners were enjoying greater prosperity than hitherto; the men's quarrel was that their wages had not increased commensurate with the owners' increases in coal-prices. The *Bolton Free Press* thought this complaint unreasonable. It contrasted the collier's comparative wealth with the handloom weaver's penury, toiling for fourteen to sixteen hours for 10s. Anyway, the miners should be grateful, it argued, for the advances already obtained: "Since the improvement in trade, from the end of the year 1842, the colliers have demanded, and have obtained, several advances in their wages: so that now they can earn four shillings for eight hours' labour; while, four years ago, they had to work twelve or fourteen for fourteen or fifteen shillings a week."[2]

The strike began in a spirit of good-humoured optimism. At a mass meeting, held outside The Grapes, Ringley, colliers from Bolton, Bury and Radcliffe cheered the arrival of W. P. Roberts. They cheered

<hr>

[1] *Northern Star*, 28 June 1845.   [2] *Bolton Free Press*, 31 January 1846.

again when he reminded them that in two years they had received five wage increases, amounting to a rise of 2s. 6d. a day. He thought the strike was as good as won.[1]

Other speakers, as well as Roberts, referred to the miners' recently-won prosperity. William Welsby pointed the moral:

"Now the principles of the union had become spread, the children got more buttercakes to eat and clogs on their feet. The union had done it, and should they forsake it and turn their back upon it? No!"[2]

He suggested that colliers' wives, by making a Lysistrata-like sacrifice, could give a lead:

"Both men and women were interested in the union cause and he believed that in many places women were better than men as to upholding the principles of the union; and they might depend on it, if the women got on their side the men would. If the women would resolve on 'lying by themselves', they might depend on it the husbands could thus be made into union men (Laughter)."

Welsby's speech was followed by one from William Holgate, who was known as "the biter from Yorkshire".[3] The *Bolton Chronicle* reported, "Holgate larded his discourses with a number of blasphemies, which appeared a sort of condiment to the taste of his hearers, each oath being received with a burst of laughter." He told the meeting of an encounter he had with an overlooker:

"An overlooker at Billinge said he was employed to get the greatest amount of work for the least amount of wages. He (Holgate) said *his* business was to get them the greatest amount of wages for the least amount of work, and he asked the miners of Billinge which position they preferred."

Holgate said in Lancashire there were 8,000 colliers who, when their numbers were added to those of drawers and waggoners, brought the total labour-force to 16,000. Colliers, on average, produced two tons of coal a day. The price had risen 2s. 6d. a ton. Hence Lancashire owners were receiving £10,000 extra. Yet they increased colliers' wages only 2d. a ton.

[1] *Bolton Chronicle*, 31 January 1846. The paper report also said, "Mr. W. P. Roberts was as bitter as his more ignorant accomplices."

[2] *Bolton Free Press*, 31 January 1848.

[3] William Holgate, of Colne, was visiting Bolton *en route* for Cumberland, for which the Ilkeston conference had appointed him lecturer. He was a Chartist, and had addressed the mass meeting of 15,000 on Pendle Hill during the 1842 general strike, when Beesley was arrested for advocating the use of force (*Manchester Guardian*, 14 June 1842).

Holgate's figure can be queried. Dickinson, the mines inspector, said output per collier in Lancashire averaged four tons.[1] Moreover, Holgate's figure is difficult to reconcile with another statement made at the strike meeting. William Welsby said colliers received 10d. a ton whereas owners got 5s. 10d. profit. If Holgate were correct, and colliers hewed only two tons, then this would mean average earnings stood at the ridiculously low figure of 1s. 8d., an assertion borne out by none of the evidence. The higher estimate would result in profits exceeding the extra £10,000 calculated by Holgate—that is, if coal prices had risen as much as he said. *The Bolton Chronicle* said they had dropped by 2s. 3d. in London.[2]

From the morass of conflicting data, it appears likely that prices, having risen considerably, were beginning to dip. Many newspapers contained reports of growing recession. Nevertheless, nobody denied the union's assertion that prices were still, despite the drop, higher than when the men received their last rise. The questions remained: How much higher? And, should the men receive an increase?

To begin with, the strike followed the customary pattern. Many owners conceded the men's demands. They included the D'Arcy Lever Company, James Hardcastle's and Robinson's collieries at Bury, and Garbett's at Horwich Moor. But then, towards the end of February, the masters' resistance began to harden. "Numbers of strangers continue to take up the employment made vacant by the dispute," reported the *Bolton Free Press*. "One or two have a full complement of hands."[3] A fortnight later, the same paper observed "There seems to be an inclination on the part of many of the old hands to return to work." This happened at Fletcher's (Atherton) and Knowles (Ringley). At the same time, Welshmen with their families came to work for the Earl of Bradford.

Union spokesmen lost their confidence. Henry Dennett spoke bitterly about Wilberforce and others "who seem to have forgotten that, while they were looking after the interests of the slaves abroad, there were black slaves at home". Strike meetings, attempts to rally flagging enthusiasm, were badly attended. Few were at the Antelope Inn, Little Hulton, to hear W. P. Roberts and George Ramsay; most had already returned to work. Apparently, the union had by now silently scaled down its demands: Roberts told the audience they were only asking for 4d. He continued by reminding them wages had

---

[1] Quoted A. J. Taylor, "The Wigan Coalfield in 1851", p. 119.
[2] *Bolton Chronicle*, 31 January 1846.   [3] *Bolton Free Press*, 28 February 1846.

doubled during the union's existence and ended with the consoling prediction that the strike could only last another three weeks.[1]

Faced with the steady influx of strangers, miners still on strike resorted in desperation to acts of sabotage. At Hind's colliery, Bury, strikers cut the winding rope to prevent a resumption of work. At Spotland colliery, Rochdale, they damaged the engine. At Messrs. Knowles' pits, Little Lever, an angry crowd assembled to express disgust at the blacklegs. Four were charged with inciting people to commit breaches of the peace. The prosecution alleged it was "nothing less than a riotous assemblage" that "wished to deter parties from working who were willing to work".[2] But the accused were found not guilty. A spate of cases for assault came before the Courts. The most serious case happened at Rochdale, where David Howarth, who had worked at the Meadowcroft pit, bit off the nose of a blackleg named Pollard. John Dugdale, a friend of Pollard, went the following night to the Elephant and Castle public house to remonstrate with Howarth. An argument developed during which Dugdale swore at Howarth and struck him in the face. Whereupon Howarth picked up a poker from the fireplace and hit him on the head. Dugdale received a three-inch-cut—and his assailant was sent to the Liverpool Assizes.[3]

Throughout the dispute, W. P. Roberts regularly appeared in Court defending strikers. The men had unbounded faith in his ability: "If a warrant were taken out against a man, he said, 'Oh, never mind, Uncle Bobby will defend me', and even if sent to prison, 'Uncle Bobby will get me out again'." William Dixon, who made these remarks while chairing the initial Ringley strike meeting, said he thought that "if it were not for the legal talents of Mr. Roberts, there was not a prison in Lancashire but would be full of colliers".[4]

W. P. Roberts' prodigious efforts, however, were not always crowned with success. As the dispute dragged on, owners became more insistent that prison, not fines, should be the sentence. For they realised that fines inflicted no personal hardship when they were simply paid out of union funds. A prosecutor told the Bolton Quarter Sessions in April, "In other cases fines have been inflicted, but I do not consider that a punishment since it was paid by the union."[5] That the Association could maintain this policy after eight weeks' strike was indicative of its wealth.

[1] *Bolton Chronicle*, 14 March 1846. [2] *Bolton Free Press*, 28 March 1846.
[3] *Bolton Chronicle*, 7 February 1846. [4] Ibid. , 31 January, 1846.
[5] *Bolton Free Press*, 4 April 1846.

Yet, despite its resources and solidarity, the union found the problem of blacklegs insoluble. By late April, the *Bolton Chronicle* reported owners had imported an abundance of hands from Wales: "The mines are now almost supplied with workmen and, as the summer approaches, the demand for coal is sure to be less."[1] It considered the miners would either have to give in or seek work elsewhere. Many of them, in fact, were going elsewhere. The strike was nominally still continuing in June, but the battle was in reality over.

No clear-cut victory had been gained by either side, although the masters had, on the whole, gained the better of the encounter. While some employers re-engaged their old colliers at terms more favourable to the men, others filled their pits with strangers. Where the latter had happened, the old hands were forced to wander around seeking a fresh job or to return to the same pit months later when the dispute was forgotten. In the early phase, events had gone well for the union. As in previous strikes, many masters were anxious to resume production and capitulated to the men's demands. It had been possible, later on, to get the majority of workers back to work, yet on increasingly unfavourable terms. What had alarmed the union was that, for the first time, they had been confronted with the mass importation of blacklegs. And, at the end, 1,400 strikers found themselves without work.

The struggle had taken place against the backcloth of general industrial unrest throughout the area. The carders at Bolton went on strike. So did the weavers of Messrs. Hargreaves, Bolton, who summoned eight operatives for leaving work without giving notice. At Smethhursts', Chorley, 369 weavers remained out till their union's funds were so low they received only 1s. 5d. per head and were all near starvation. Then, the Bolton joiners stopped work. At Wigan weavers' wages were reduced by 6d. and they struck. To add to the picture of general disorder, the *Bolton Chronicle* ominously reported, "There is a sort of civil commotion in the bed-quilt trade . . . bordering on a turn-out."[2]

After the dust of battle settled, the Miners' Association discovered that its organisation had been virtually wiped out in the Bolton area.[3] The only pits in which the organisation was healthy appear to have been those where there was little or no dispute in 1846. One of these

---

[1] *Bolton Chronicle*, 18 April 1846.   [2] Ibid., 11 April 1846.
[3] Even a year later, in May 1847, a union lecturer was expressing the pious hope that "Bolton shall again gain that proud and leading position which it assumed before the late strike." (*Miners' Advocate*, May 1847).

belonged to W. P. Hulton, a large coalowner who had fought hard in 1843 to stop the union gaining a foothold in the Bolton area, but eventually decided that the most judicious course of action was to arrive at a *détente* with the Association. As a result, he was unaffected by the stoppage—his colliers remained at work when others struck— and, in January 1847, he showed his gratitude by providing a dinner for union members. William Daniels, editor of the *Miners' Advocate* chaired the proceedings. Toasts were drunk to "The Queen", to "The Union" and then to "William Hulton, Esq. and Son, God Bless Them!"[1]

The *Northern Star* commented, "The workmen in this case appear to be quite content with their employer, and the employer perfectly satisfied with the conduct of the men—both striving to promote the welfare of the other. This is as it ought to be."[2]

In other areas, news of the Bolton strike setback had little effect. W. P. Roberts addressed a mass meeting on Shevington Moor, near Wigan, and stressed the need to remain united. David Swallow, at a mass meeting at Hindley Green, claimed "They were not dying or dead: the Association was in as flourishing a state as ever."[3] If collieries in the Bolton area are excluded, Swallow's remark is correct. The union's membership and strength remained intact. By early 1847, it still possessed 160 lodges and successfully fought at Chorley to maintain the closed shop principle. Union members only returned to work after the management had paid the non-unionist's membership arrears for him.

Yet a problem remained, and loomed larger as links with other coalfields slackened—the problem of blacklegs. As effective action against them became increasingly difficult, the Association indulged in invective and issuing dark threats. Cornish lead miners were informed that two or three of their number who came to Lancashire "have nearly been killed with the buzzard falling on them". The *Miners' Advocate* also showed its hatred and contempt for strike-breakers in the following poem:[4]

THE NOBSTICK (alias B. . . . . .)
Since Adam, at first, on this earth was created,
Of manners and men a great deal is related;
But Nature has never yet finished a job
So mean in itself as that creature—the Nob!

[1] Ibid., February 1847. [2] *Northern Star*, 9 January 1847.
[3] *Bolton Chronicle*, 18 July 1846. [4] *Miners' Advocate*, December, 1784.

N

By NOB we mean everything that is knavish;
By NOB we include everything that is slavish;
In NOB we can find everything that is vile—
A treacherous, unworthy monster of Guile.

Chorus

Then shun with abhorrence Nobsticks who annoy us,
And cold be the heart that would try to destroy us;
The thief who goes boldly to plunder and rob.
Is better by far than the dastardly NOB!

How mean is the wretch who respects not his neighbour
Who steals from his brother the rights of his labour!
When tyrants oppress us by all that they can
We doubt of a NOB, but we fear not a man;
For man is still noble, unflinching in trial—
As true in his course as the sun on the dial;
But a nob is a villain, a cheat and a knave,
Unworthy of aught—save an infamous grave.

13

Dissension within the Union

UNLIKE Northumberland and Durham, Lancashire never sought to establish a centralised policy. The events of 1844 had shown this to be an impossibility. But, in any case, the Lancashire union's tactic, which it pursued with considerable success, did not depend on united action. Rather, it involved a series of skirmishes—partial strikes—without a head-on confrontation. It is not surprising, therefore, that Lancashire saw the national role of the Association in a different light to Jude. It regarded the union as having a threefold function: to provide protection against the importing of blacklegs from other areas; to give miners throughout Britain an opportunity to discuss mutual problems; and to foster co-operation in a campaign to get Parliament to pass beneficial legislation. Such tasks did not require regular conferences. In fact, it appears that in the summer of 1846, with Lancashire pre-occupied with consolidating lodges after the Bolton strike, no conference was held. The half-yearly rule was forgotten.

The next conference was held at the Legs of Man, Wigan, starting on 12 January 1847. William Grocott appealed, on behalf of the Lancashire men, to colliers elsewhere to appoint delegates:

"Men of Lancashire would feel proud to see each county represented by men duly elected for the purpose. But, as it is not likely the whole of the mining districts can accomplish an object so desirable under present circumstances, written communications, containing suggestions as to the best mode of arousing the miners from the apathetic indifference so lamentably prevalent, and inducing them to co-operate with their brethren in Lancashire, will meet with the most respectful attention of the Conference."[1]

Grocott added that "the brave men of Lancashire" would, if necessary, "fight the battle alone", but they had the "right to expect the assistance and co-operation of the whole of the mining districts".

This plaintive appeal seems to have evoked little response. Only

[1] *Northern Star*, 2 January 1847.

twenty-four delegates attended. All the evidence suggests they came overwhelmingly from Lancashire. When conference tackled its main item of business—a campaign for mining legislation—it appointed a committee of five to take a petition to Parliament and lobby Members. Of the five, Martin Jude was the only non-Lancastrian. Another indication of growing enfeeblement was the shrinking number of lecturers appointed; Dennett, Price and Swallow for Lancashire; Scott, Welsby, Holgate and Duro for Northumberland and Durham. While the national union could only afford to appoint seven lecturers, it is significant that the following month the Wigan lodges appointed twelve lecturers for their own local purposes.[1] Apparently the strength in one's own district was considered more important than developing it nationally.

In other coalfields miners' organisations continued to exist, albeit in a less flourishing state than hitherto; but they did not feel the same need for close contact with each other. Commissioner Tremenheere, in his mines inspector's report for 1847, was far from confident the threat of trade unions had been overcome. He dwelt at length on "the combinations amongst the colliers into which their want of intelligence is so often betraying them". He mentioned Lanarkshire, Ayrshire, Lancashire and Staffordshire as the remaining strongholds, with upwards of 30,000 members, "to which are to be added those in union in Wales and in other mining districts. . . . In Northumberland and Durham, the combination has, for the time, run its injurious course, and is, for the present, exhausted; but efforts are at present being made for its revival."

The union's efforts in the North-east were, as usual, a failure. Besides a labour surplus, economic conditions were unpropitious. Owners met in Newcastle to discuss "the very inadequate remuneration generally derived from capital in the collieries of the district over the past two-and-a-half years".[2] The Coal Trade Committee commented: "The abolition of the 'vends' has been the means of reducing prices, in many instances, below a remunerating return, and many of the smaller collieries have suffered greatly in consequence." Nevertheless, the large owners, like Lord Londonderry, were not feeling the draught. It was for them a period of unparalleled prosperity and expansion. Between 1840 and 1848, production in the North-east coalfields rose from 5,587,841 tons to 7,250,000 tons, an increase of 30 per cent. At

---

[1] *Miners' Advocate*, March 1847.
[2] *Newcastle Journal*, 25 September 1847.

the same time, the stock of capital mounted to £24 million, an addition of £9 million.[1]

The union gained comfort from neither of these developments. On the one hand, the small owners, with their backs to the wall, fighting for economic survival, naturally resisted all demands that would increase labour costs. And on the other hand, the large owners, with their immense economic might, could easily crush the first signs of workers' organisation, relying upon the large pool of surplus labour.

The intensity of the persecution of militants can be judged by the case of the old stalwart, Ben Embleton. He had worked for the Association as a lecturer in practically every coalfield until the Wigan conference, through economic difficulties, failed to re-engage him. After that, he returned to the North-east, where he sought work in vain. On 12 July 1847, Embleton wrote a pitiful begging letter, which the *Miners' Advocate* published. After reminding them, "I have been fighting in the union field thirty-seven years, and have grown old in your service", Embleton recalled some of his past triumphs and continued:

"Brethren, I appeal to you. Shall I, who have fought so long in the good cause, be visited with starvation? Shall I be obliged to seek the shelter of an infamous poor law Bastille, wherein to lay down my old body to die? Shall I be driven to the hard necessity of ending my life on parish pay? For the sake of the Union principles, I have borne reproach, I am become a stranger unto my brethren, and an alien unto my mother's children for the zeal of the union has eaten me up, and the reproaches of them that reproach the Union are fallen upon me! May every friend of humanity in the Miners' Association give me a helping hand to help me out of the deep waters of want and not suffer the flood of poverty to swallow me up."

The untenable position of the union was clearly illustrated by a newspaper debate between Jude and Thomas Pringle, junior, a master, on the advisability of combinations. Jude argued that, from 1810 to 1820, hours had been increased from fourteen to sixteen and pay reduced from 4s. 6d. to 2s. 8d. Further reductions took place from 1820 to 1830. But in 1831, "the memorable strike took place, which ended so advantageously for the workmen that they got back full 25 per cent of their previous reductions". That Jude had to delve so far into history before he could cite an instance of how trade unionism had benefited colliers in the North-east showed the weakness of his case. Most men

[1] *Durham Gazette*, 30 March 1849.

were all too painfully aware of a more recent strike, when they had made colossal sacrifices and gained nothing to show for them. The only victory the union could claim from the 1844 struggle was the highly dubious one of smashing "the vends": Mark Dent boasted they had destroyed "the Golden Chain that held the Coal Kings together".[1]

★   ★   ★

To add to the Association's difficulties, a quarrel developed with the *Northern Star*. It appears to have begun during the Bolton strike of 1846. For, throughout that strike, the *Northern Star* failed to inform its readers of developments. When a reader wrote enquiring why this was so, the editor simply replied that the Lancashire leaders had not supplied him with news. He considered this an insult and base ingratitude; the paper had always helped the miners in the past. Martin Jude, in an endeavour to smooth over differences, replied that reports had not been sent to the *Star* because the publicity might attract blacklegs. It was not a case of "burking" the paper. But Jude's excuse lacks conviction. News of the Bolton strike had been extensively published in other papers, and it is doubtful whether any blackleg, who did not already know about it, would have found out through reading the *Star*. But, in any case, Jude's point was incorrect since the *Star* printed the Bolton appeal for strike funds in its columns, as well as occasional acknowledgements of contributions.

But the Bolton strike was merely the tip of an iceberg in a sea of trouble. The *Northern Star* continued not publishing news about the colliers during the summer and autumn of 1846. Then, in November, an editorial appeared:

> "It is now some time since we published the doings of the colliery leaders and lecturers, which were neither to our taste nor calculated to serve the best interests of those by whom they are paid, and upon whose confidence and industry they live; and we were only checked in the further exposure of much more that came to our knowledge by what we must characterise as the weakness of Mr. Roberts, who assured us of the devotion and kindliness of those who hoped to smother our voice in the colliery districts."[2]

In spite of rebuffs, the paper expressed its abiding interest in the colliers' cause and their "indomitable union": "We have jealously watched the formation of their society from its infancy to its giant growth."

———

[1] *Miners' Advocate*, May 1847   [2] *Northern Star*, 14 November 1846.

A letter in the same issue from "A Chartist Collier" gives a further insight into the dispute. He claimed the union's leaders were "trying to overcome the popular voice by the most disgraceful tricks and insinuations". They obtained their living only by exploiting grievances and now, although they had had numerous legal triumphs, they planned to sack Roberts. "I know Roberts has announced his intention to resign," the letter continues, "but I beg him to change his mind till the colliers have a chance to speak".

The following week William Grocott replied, describing the letter as a "tissue of malignant falsehoods and slanderous libels" and asked for the name of the writer. Grocott also sent a copy of a resolution passed by the Lancashire delegate meeting, which affirmed its utmost confidence in the union's leaders and attacked the *Star*'s editorial "for interfering in the affairs of the Miners' Association".[1] After publishing the resolution, the editor appended his own comment. The *Northern Star* had been thanked many times by the union for its "interference"; now there came the demand for non-interference. The paper said it had the utmost confidence in Grocott, but cryptically added, "One scabby sheep infects a whole flock." Those with complaints should say so openly, not speak slyly in public houses.

The quarrel between the Miners' Association and the *Northern Star*, expressed in statements fraught with hidden meaning, went much deeper than a clash of personalities. Its genesis lay in the union's gradually worsening relations with the National Association, an organisation the *Star* staunchly backed.

When the National Association was formed in the spring of 1845, harmony prevailed between the two Associations. Miners' delegates from Lancashire and Scotland attended the inaugural conference, while the North-eastern colliers, unable to send delegates because of financial difficulties, nevertheless sent their good wishes. T. S. Duncombe, who was elected president of the National Association, responded with the same cordiality. He said no strike had been more justified than that of the Northumberland and Durham colliers. To cement the friendship, conference appointed W. P. Roberts to its nine-man executive.

There can be no doubt that in Lancashire the formation of this broad, loose federation of workers belonging to all trades corresponded to local conceptions. In the county they had, for a long time, been careful to foster co-operation with other trades. During the strikes joint committees were sometimes formed. When, in 1845, W. P.

[1] Ibid., 21 November 1846.

Roberts established his headquarters in Manchester he became a symbol of this unity of the working class. At a dinner held in his honour at Bolton, Grocott went out of his way to remind those present that Roberts' services were used by all trades, not merely the miners. Two months later, in May 1845, workers showed how well they understood this: striking weavers and mechanics from Bury joined a procession of colliers to welcome Roberts from Bolton station.

The same spirit pervaded Scotland in a more intense form. William Cloughan, of Holytown, whole-heartedly supported the National Association. He believed that when the industrious portion of the community were banded together then "oppression would turn pale, sink back, and expire". He therefore gave greater allegiance to the National Association than to the Miners' Association. In adopting this attitude, which found growing support in Scotland, Cloughan was making the two organisations into competitors, not collaborators.

As we have seen, the Scottish miners were doubtful about their membership of the Miners' Association in February 1845. A Scottish National delegate meeting had considered a resolution to disaffiliate, but had left the matter over till their next meeting. Meanwhile, they had shown how lukewarm was their support for the miners' union by not sending delegates to the Rhosymedre conference but to the National Association conference in London. In May 1845 Cloughan complained that Lanarkshire miners had been restricting their labour for the past fifteen months and had been forced to fight a three-month strike to maintain their right to do so, but they had received no support from England due to apathy and the Northumberland-Durham strike. In July 1846 the executive reported to the Newcastle conference that "an altercation of a local nature in Lanarkshire has destroyed our hopes there for the present". It went on to refer to ensuing unpleasantness and recommended that conference appoint two extra lecturers for Lanarkshire. This proved to be without avail. The executive informed the Ilkeston conference of further defections in Scotland. It attributed the growing financial difficulties to a "falling off of several districts in Scotland, principally brought about by the insincerity of professing friends in that quarter".[1]

An attempt at reconciliation occurred. The Scottish and English miners met at Berwick. John Berry, who attended the National Association's inaugural conference, made great efforts to heal the breach. But, regardless, the two organisations continued to drift apart.

[1] *Miners' Advocate*, February 1846.

A Scottish National Delegate meeting at Falkirk on 17 September 1846, heard a speech from Jacobs, an organiser of the National Association. He spoke about the problems of workers generally and then set forth the advantages for the colliers of joining the National Association. The Scottish miners decided to join and the meeting ended with three cheers for the National Association.[1] So the split had become final and irrevocable. Significantly, the *Northern Star*'s editorial outburst against the miners' union came soon afterwards.

The flames of inter-union rivalry were fanned by organisational and policy differences. The National Association approximated, in a loose form, to a general union whereas the Miners' Association was industrial. The latter had greater solidarity, finance and militancy. Hence it was more strike-prone, less likely to rely on conciliation to settle disputes with masters. The National Association frowned on the frequency with which the colliers resorted to violence during strikes and the way the union condoned this by paying their fines. The Miners' Association, however, saw in this only a grudging acknowledgement that its rival lacked funds. It stiffened the resolve to keep intact the Miners' Association as a separate entity and not to weaken it by uniting with less well-organised workers.

At the centre of this quarrel stood W. P. Roberts. If he could be made to renounce his connections with the Miners' Association, the union would suffer a severe blow. He was nationally known as its leading spokesman. The *Northern Star* tried to entice him away from this primary allegiance:

> "We have frequently thought, and still think, that Mr. Roberts' exclusive engagement to the colliers, though highly beneficial to that trade, is nevertheless a great national loss."[2]

Yet, this remark of the *Northern Star*'s was untrue. Roberts frequently appeared for workers in other industries who fell foul of the law. Indeed, a few months after the *Star*'s comment, he fought one of his most arduous cases. He defended twenty-six engineers charged with conspiracy and illegal combination. The indictment contained 4,914 counts and reached the mammoth length of fifty-seven yards! The union spent £1,800 on the trial, and Roberts secured the release of seventeen of the accused. With commitments of this magnitude, Roberts can hardly be accused of working exclusively for the colliers.

Nevertheless, this kind of remark was calculated to worry the Miners'

---

[1] *Northern Star*, 26 September 1846.   [2] Ibid., 26 September 1846.

Association. Its rival had secured the allegiance of disaffected Scottish miners, had even tried poaching in Northumberland and Durham. Who was to say it would not steal Roberts from them?

The last national conference of the miners took place at the King's Head Inn, St. Helens, on 10 August 1847.[1] Like the previous conference, it was national only in name. It elected an executive committee consisting of the Lancashire Travelling Committee plus the Secretary and Treasurer, completing and consolidating the identification of the Miners' Association with the Lancashire Union. It was resolved at St. Helens that the *Miners' Advocate* should henceforward be published fortnightly, yet another conference decision which was never implemented though it was reaffirmed at a General Delegate Meeting, held at Shevington in January 1848.

That this was the last of the conferences is indicated by the decisions taken at Shevington, where it was further decided that the union should disentangle itself from the fluctuating fortunes of the paper:

"That the proprietorship of the *Miners' Advocate* be turned over to Mr. W. Daniells; that he be sole proprietor and that he take all risk and responsibility on himself, but that we do all we can to encourage him and to obtain a good circulation for him: and that the *Advocate* be still the recognised organ of the Miners' Association."[2]

The reasons for this decision were not found "politic or prudent" to state. One thing, however, is certain; whatever the future of the *Miners' Advocate*, the body making decisions such as these had previously been the full conference of the Association and not a general delegate meeting of the Lancashire miners.

[1] A. J. Taylor, op. cit., states in error that the last of the conferences of the Miners' Association was the one held in Wigan, January 1847.
[2] *Miners' Advocate*, January 1848.

14

Accidents and Inquests

"Now look at the dangers we all undergo,
While we work for our bread in the caverns below:
The rope may soon break and the falling stone kill,
And the waters burst forth and the pit quickly fill.
Then the gas may ignite in the mine when we're under,
Then flashes the lightning and roars the dread thunder:
Then choke-damp unsparing flies hot through the mine,
Then happens the horrors of Tees, Wear and Tyne!"

THIS account of the hazards undergone by miners is part of a poem
written by William Johnson, a pitman who worked at Framwellgate
Moor. Entitled "The Miners' Grievances", its purpose was to explain
the miners' case to the general public and enlist their support. It ended
with an appeal for funds for the great strike in the North-east coalfields,
which was then taking place. It also stated the men's demands on safety
matters:

"No longer we'll work in the mine without air,
Ventilation we'll have and we'll make it our care;
Two shafts they may sink for down and up cast
To prevent the strong hydrogen making the blast."

Even with these precautions, Johnson acknowledged that some
deaths would still occur. He stated the miners' claim that accident
victims should receive free burial, the owners defraying costs, and that
their widows should receive an adequate pension. At that time most
owners made a five shillings a week allowance to the widows of men
killed in the pit.

Many songs and poems were written about mining disasters. The
1840s was a period when, with deeper mining operations, a series of
terrible disasters took place. They aroused intense feelings of shock and
horror. The explosion, a new and dreaded phenomenon, would wipe
out virtually all the male population of a village. Coal-mining

communities, living in constant fear that they might be the next to suffer, had in their mind's eye a vivid picture of what it would mean:

> "O, sudden and sad is the miner's doom;
> See the clouds which up the shaft now come!
> The alarm is given—'she's fired!' they cry:
> To the shaft, to the shaft, all quickly fly."[1]

What it was like at the pit-head was described by William Hammond:

> "And now begins the tragic scene.
> Wives, mothers, sisters, sweethearts scream,
> And when to the bank and the corpses come,
> To claim their own, behold they run.
> The corpse is seen—but none can claim
> Nor yet the mangled body name!
> They take some buttons from the clothes,
> And ask if one these buttons knows.
> Examined well, they're pass'd around,
> And then the hapless owner's found.
> A mother cries they are my son's,
> To clasp the corpse in haste she runs."

After being restrained from grasping her dead son, the mother is taken, aided by neighbours, to her home. The corpse is also taken home where

> "The lifeless form the females clean.
> The clothes they strip, wash hands and face,
> Still no known features can they trace."

Meanwhile, back at the pit the recovery of bodies continues:

> "There coffin upon coffin pil'd,
> Some for father, some for child."

In writing this poem, "The Explosion", Hammond's intention was not merely to depict the horror; he wished to expose the farce of the coroner's inquest. In those days inquests were a formality, a means of exonerating the colliery owner and management from all blame. A typical coroner was likely to say, in summing up:

---

[1] From "The Miner's Doom" by Henderson Fawcett of South Wingate.

"The case I have examined through.
The overman and viewers, too;
And all the witnesses declare
The gas was small, but strong the air."

After making a few fatalistic remarks about accidents being inevitable in coal-mines, the coroner turns to the jury:

"So, gentlemen, it is up to you
To pass a sentence just and true;
You've heard the witnesses declare
How each engaged used every care,
So choose a foreman and withdraw,
Be in accordance with the law,
And if you think there's one to blame,
You have full power that man to name!"

The jury then retires and, having been out for an hour, returns to pronounce its verdict:

"Well, Sir, this is a serious case,
Each witness'd word has had its place,
And well we've searched for pro and con,
But blame we find attached to none.
And here we are convinced at last
That accident produced the blast!
No human prudence can foresee
The workings of our destiny."

These comments in Hammond's poem merely echoed the views, expressed with complacent resignation, at numerous inquests. For instance, in 1838 Stephen Reed, the coroner, said that the Wallsend disaster "was one of those lamentable accidents which were so common to coal pits and which no human foresight could prevent. . . . The fate of Providence had gone forth, and one hundred human beings were launched into eternity."

★   ★   ★

The unsatisfactory character of inquests, as then conducted, became increasingly apparent. So long as the colliers were without a legal spokesman, capable of battling against a hostile Court, little could be done by them to alter things. But the presence of W. P. Roberts gave them a spokesman, and the Haswell disaster gave them an opportunity. It occurred on 28 September 1844, and ninety-five lives were lost. A number of other disasters had preceded it, awakening public disquiet about the carnage in the collieries.

W. P. Roberts, assisted by Clough and Jude, wished to establish that the colliery had been badly ventilated and that an accumulation of foul air had produced the conditions in which the explosion took place. He claimed that the management "having charge of the colliery, could have exercised control, and by doing so have prevented the calamity".[1]

In trying to advance his case that there had been criminal negligence, Roberts soon found insuperable obstacles placed in his way. His first clash with the coroner came over his submission that an independent investigation of colliery conditions should be conducted by an impartial expert, Mr. Matthias Dunn. For the owners, Mr. Marshall told the Court they had personal objections to Mr. Dunn performing this task. Roberts countered by arguing that, in the circumstances, personal objections should be discounted. "Justice would not be done," declared Roberts, "the ends of fair enquiry even would not be answered if the owners refused to allow Mr. Dunn to examine the pit."

The coroner said he could not allow such objections as those of Mr. Roberts to be made.

Then, Roberts sought a two-day adjournment. He wished to contact Her Majesty's Government so that it might appoint observers to attend the inquest. Again, the coroner refused.

Their second clash came over witnesses. Roberts argued it was totally wrong that Mr. Forster, the colliery's head viewer, should be allowed to prevent a witness from giving evidence because of a personal objection. "Apply this doctrine to the Old Bailey, and how many cells in Newgate will be occupied?" he asked. Notwithstanding Roberts' protests and his submission "that other witnesses should be examined who were in readiness and who, he believed, would give an entirely different version as to the cause of the explosion", the coroner remained unmoved. All the witnesses, with two exceptions, were produced by the owners. A long succession of them affirmed their faith in the colliery's management and said attention to ventilation had been meticulous.

As he was quite sure all the witnesses would say the same thing, Roberts said he was not anxious to hear any more. But the coroner

[1] *The Haswell Colliery Explosion*, edited by W. P. Roberts, p. 3.

retorted it was his duty. "Mr. Roberts said he merely threw out a suggestion."

The third injustice at the inquest was the composition of the jury, carefully selected for its bias to the masters. Roberts later observed: "They were all farmers or shopkeepers—some directly, and many of them indirectly, under the influence of the owners. . . . One of them, at the close of the first day, remarked 'he could not see the use of examining any more; it was clear that it was all accident'." [1]

The inevitable verdict—accidental death—left Roberts and the union intensely dissatisfied. What made matters worse was that, within a month of the Haswell disaster, another explosion occurred. It was at the Coxlodge colliery, and the inquest opened at the Wellington Inn, Kenton, on 30 October 1844. The coroner, doubtless still smarting from Roberts' intervention at the previous inquest, decided to exercise tighter control over the Court. He refused even to permit Roberts to question witnesses. Roberts applied for an adjournment, in order to consult the Government. He referred to a recommendation of the 1835 Select Committee on colliery accidents that a proper party be sent to assist the coroner.

The coroner replied, "No attorney shall come here to interfere with me." Whereupon Roberts turned to his assistant: "Take that down." The coroner objected to Roberts making notes, but Roberts claimed the same privilege as reporters. In the middle of this altercation, Mr. Ryan, a mining engineer, added to the Court's confusion by jumping up and starting to explain his own system of ventilation which, he was sure, would prevent accidents. Martin Jude also joined in the free-for-all. Yet, despite all the anger, excitement and irrelevance, the coroner clung to one salient "fact"; Mr. Liddle, for the colliery management, had said the ventilation had been as good as possible and he (the coroner) told the Court he thought the ventilation was *always* as good as possible. The verdict was again: accidental death.

Commenting, the *Miners' Advocate* exclaimed: "Truly, Coroner's Inquests, as at present conducted, are a farce."

*   *   *

The miners' leaders can be forgiven their pessimism. Nevertheless, tangible progress was being made. The general public was genuinely shocked by the revelations of the Haswell disaster, W. P. Roberts rightly wrote: "Society is alive to the enormity of this event; the tone

[1] *The Haswell Colliery Explosion*, p. 10.

of the Press—all of them except two or three in the immediate pay
and proprietorship of the Coal Owners—is proof of this."[1]

One manifestation of public misgiving had been the formation of
the South Shields Committee for the Investigation of Accidents in
Mines. Its secretary, James Mather, who was extremely energetic and
well-informed, published the Committee's findings on the Haswell
tragedy.

Its report challenged the evidence at the inquest that Haswell was
well ventilated and free of gas. There were 40,000 cubic feet of passage
in this pit fouled to firing-point as far back as 1840, when the workings
were a third less than in 1844. On 17 August 1841, an explosion of
fire-damp killed two miners only 200 yards from the site of the
second explosion. Strong evidence of carburetted hydrogen abounded.
The managers had insisted on men working with Davy lamps, which
were not needed in a gas-free mine. Where gases did exist, the Report
continued, the Davy lamp was inadequate since the flame passed
through a red-hot gauze that could ignite some gases.

Support for the South Shields Committee's main contentions came
from Dr. J. Murray. He pointed out that more shafts were essential.
It took seven hours for air to pass through fifty to sixty miles of underground workings. In some places ventilation was sluggish, in others
rapid; currents and counter-currents made a combustible mixture.
At Felling colliery, where workings extended for seventy miles, he
thought it was a marvel there had only been two explosions in nine
months killing 130 men. Turning to the Haswell disaster, Dr. Murray
contended it was not a question of whether the pit was one of the best
in Northumberland and Durham, but whether it was the best knowledge could make it.[2]

Both Dr. Murray and the South Shields Committee did the utmost
to publicise their views through the press. Dr. Murray also presented a
memorial to the Queen, denouncing the Davy lamp.[3] James Mather,
for the Committee, sent two letters to the Prime Minister, Sir Robert
Peel, in which he said "it is a matter of surprise that these lamentable
occurrences, instead of being occasional, are not incessant and over-
whelming . . . while this imperfect ventilation is allowed to continue,

---

[1] *The Haswell Colliery Explosion*, p. iii.   [2] *Miners' Advocate*, 14 December 1844.
[3] As J. L. and Barbara Hammond state in *The Town Labourer*, p. 38: "The Davy lamp,
for which the inventor refused to take out a patent, renouncing an income of £5,000
or £10,000 a year, his sole object to serve the cause of humanity, was used in many cases
to serve the cause of profits. Deeper and more dangerous seams were worked, and
accidents actually increased in number."

the mining districts and the public must prepare themselves for the continual recurrence of these dreadful calamities." Mather maintained that legislation had become imperative: "We have shown that the system pursued will continue, while it is allowed to prevail."

Similar representations were made to the Prime Minister by W. P. Roberts. He seized an opportunity provided by a break between sessions of the Haswell inquest to journey to London and from thence to Brighton for a personal meeting with Peel. As a result of their discussion, the Government appointed two eminent scientists, Professors Lyell and Faraday, to attend the remainder of the Haswell hearing. According to one contemporary, "the appointment of the two professors caused almost as great a sensation amongst colliery-owners and viewers as the accident itself." But since Lyell and Faraday declined to associate themselves with the general denunciation of the Haswell colliery management, W. P. Roberts and the union reacted with chagrin. Even Dr. Murray saw them as part of "a coalition imbued with feverish solicitude . . . to exculpate the proprietors". W. P. Roberts who, according to Fynes, displayed "indomitable perseverance" throughout, again visited the Prime Minister to express dissatisfaction over the outcome of the Haswell inquest and inform him of their determination to ensure that the whole subject was brought before the next session of Parliament.

Notwithstanding, Lyell and Faraday did make an important contribution. While they were careful not to ascribe blame for the disaster, their report aroused considerable critical comment from all quarters. It was "criticised in pamphlets and newspaper articles in a tone more or less adverse to scientific suggestions in a matter so practical as coal-mining."[1] Yet, it was precisely on this point that the value of Lyell and Faraday's work lay: they produced the first scientific report on the causes of colliery disasters.

*   *   *

Progress, nevertheless, remained slow. Inquests continued to be whitewashing farces, designed to save the owners' faces rather than the miners' lives. A particularly bad example came after the Jarrow colliery disaster on 21 August 1845. Thirty-nine men had been killed by the explosion, and James Mather had been down the mine a mere two hours before it happened. He was, therefore, in a position to give expert evidence. Yet the coroner refused to postpone the inquest until

<hr>

[1] R. N. Boyd, *Coal Pits and Pitmen*, pp. 86–7.

Mather, who was suffering from the effects of gas, was well enough to attend. He even prevented Thomas Horn, the Chartist music-seller from Newcastle, from cross-questioning witnesses on behalf of the union.

Safety remained a preoccupation for miners. In 1854, when Jude promised to write three articles for the *Northern Tribune*, the first dealt entirely with the problem of mine disasters. It was indicative of the importance he attached to the subject. But, in their efforts, Jude and the union encountered immense obstacles: the owner's indifference to the miners' sufferings, an ingrained suspicion of any arguments emanating from the union, a tremendous amount of ignorance, and an incredulity that scientific procedures could be adopted to lessen the number of deaths.

The main obstacle, however, was finance. Owners were confronted with a choice: greater profits for themselves or greater safety for the men. Ventilation involved sinking fresh shafts and these, as John Buddle told the Select Committee in 1835, were very expensive. "It might not be convenient," he said, "to spend £20,000 more to sink another merely to avoid the chance of any accident that might eventually happen." Buddle pointed out a new pit might cost from £50,000 to £60,000; to add further expense would be prohibitive. Indeed, he suggested that, if Parliament imposed certain requirements, "it would tend to extinguish a very large proportion of our coal mines".

When, finally, Parliament took action, the provisions of the Act could easily be sidestepped and its intention disregarded. Owners simply had to follow the example of Lord Londonderry, who amalgamated Seaton colliery and Seaham colliery in 1864, "following legislation which required every pit to have two shafts. As the two pits were only 150 yards apart, it was not a difficult matter to unite them underground."[1]

[1] Lady Londonderry, *Frances Anne*, p. 229.

15

Politics and the Union

THE history of mining trade unions, probably more than any other section of the working class, has been one of intense political involvement. At one time, colliers were among the most reliable supporters of the Liberal Party. Today, the same kinship and solidarity makes them the most wholehearted supporters of the Labour Party. Coal-mining constituencies return Labour candidates with the largest majorities in the country; the biggest group of trade union sponsored M.P.s belong to the National Union of Mineworkers. This represents the culmination of a long road of political activity, many of whose landmarks are well known. The first town councillor to be elected with trade union backing was Yorkshire miners' leader John Normansell, at Barnsley in 1861. The first working men to be Members of Parliament were Northumbrian miners' leader, Thomas Burt, for Morpeth, and Alexander MacDonald at Stafford, in the general election of 1874. Both stood as Liberals. Once working people had gained the vote, miners became an important political factor. Occupationally concentrated in certain constituencies, their very weight of numbers made them dominant in these places. They were able to win a seat more easily than other sections of the working class, whose supporters were more diffuse and possessed less group loyalty. This showed itself at general elections: for instance, in 1885 six of the eleven working men M.P.s were miners. When colliers started to become disenchanted with the Lib-Lab alliance, miners' leaders like Keir Hardie were able to swing them over *en masse* to accepting the concept of independent working-class political action. Ever since the Labour Party's early days, the miners have constituted an important segment of its support.

All this is recounted in detail by other historians and need not be re-told by us. What is, perhaps, less well understood is how, much earlier, this process of political involvement began. In the 1840s all the pressures which led to these subsequent developments already existed. In fact, the way the Miners' Association responded to them helped to give a distinctive slant to future miners' unions. By the end of its days, it had become strongly impressed upon the mining community that one of the most hopeful means of redressing their manifold grievances was through legislative action. Indeed, in Northumberland and Durham, where the problem of safety was much more acute, the union's last fling, in 1849, was based on the call for government intervention, not just as one object among many but as *the* object of the organisation. At that stage, it was the industrial weakness, the lack of bargaining strength, which made the Association place such great store on political action.

Yet it would be wrong to regard political activity as an index of industrial inadequacy. When the Association was at its zenith, it was still very much concerned with what happened in Parliament. By its very nature, the coal industry appeared to have a natural need for State intervention. There were already, by 1825, nearly 200 regulations and statutes affecting the coal-trade.[1] It seemed a logical progression for this tendency to be extended from the coal-trade to the coal-industry. Miners and social reformers appreciated that, if conditions in the pits were to be improved, it would be necessary to formulate regulations and see they were enforced throughout the country. So, on such issues as safety, ventilation and inspection the miners looked to Parliament for the answer. They were also concerned with ways in which Parliament might secure the prosperity of the industry. The imposition of an export tax on coal, a serious blow, especially to the Northumberland and Durham coalfields, at least showed negatively that politics could directly influence living standards.

It is not surprising, therefore, that the inaugural meeting of the Miners' Association, in November 1842, was summoned for an avowedly political aim: "for the purpose of taking into consideration the distress of the coalminers and adopting a petition to Parliament." The first Wakefield conference also passed a resolution supporting Ashley's Mines Regulation Act and thanking the main sponsors of the Bill.

The Wakefield conference had taken place while the nation still buzzed with excitement caused by the publication of the First Report of the Commission of Children and Young Persons. As we have already stated, this Report focused public attention on the scandalous conditions prevailing in the pits. It conveyed the general impression that colliers were a poor and unfortunate section of society. Conditions that previously had been taken for granted, as part of the natural order

[1] E. Mackenzie; *A View of the County of Northumberland*, p. 156.

of things, were now seen as iniquities which ought to be ended. So, although not the intention of its authors, the Report provided a powerful impetus to the formation of the Miners' Association. It created the right mental climate for the union's birth; it gave an authoritative backing to miners' grievances; it helped the colliers to shake off the shackles of localism and see themselves as a whole—a class exploited throughout the country.

The Report had another important effect on miners. The nationwide expressions of horror and disgust that it aroused resulted in a clamour for legislative action. The Mines Regulation Act, introduced into Parliament by Lord Ashley on 7 July 1842, embodied an important new principle: it was the first direct act of State intervention restricting the supply of labour in coal-mines. Its importance was not lost on miners, who generally regarded it as a beneficial measure. The Act clearly showed it was possible, by Parliamentary legislation, to better the miners' lot. Therefore, it provided a strong stimulus among colliers to political interest.

*   *   *

But the fate of Lord Ashley's Bill—the opposition and obstruction of strong vested interests—showed this would be no easy task. In its passage through Parliament, Lord Ashley's Bill was watered down considerably. Originally, it embodied five major clauses: no females were to be employed underground; no boys under thirteen were to be employed in mines; no person under twenty-one was to be in charge of steam engines for lowering or raising colliers; the system of apprenticing young boys for long terms was to be abolished; and, finally, an inspectorate was to be established to enforce the Act.

The coalowners and their allies, opposing the Bill, were a powerful political force. In the upper house sat influential figures like Lord Durham, Lord Melbourne, Lord Granville and—most hostile and intransigent—Lord Londonderry. They were easily able to induce their fellow peers to pass amendments, limiting the scope of the Act. The Lords reduced the minimum age for being in charge of steam-driven winding gear from twenty-one to fifteen. Likewise, the apprenticeship system was only made illegal for boys under ten years. And, most important, the minimum age for working underground was lowered from thirteen to ten.

But this type of opposition, merely striving to weaken the Act's impact, was not enough for Lord Londonderry. He wanted, on principle, to oppose it all along the line. He did so for two main reasons. First, the Bill sought to interfere with the sacred rights of parents, their freedom to do what they thought was best for their children. He believed kindly colliers sent their young children to work underground simply out of dedication to their striplings' welfare, a desire to see them securely settled in a career. And, moreover, the children themselves positively revelled in their work which, to them, resembled a form of play.[1] So why should the State seek to disrupt these idyllic arrangements? It was in his self-styled role as "the miners' friend" that Lord Londonderry strode forth to do battle. In defending the right of children to work in mines, he was reassured by a letter he received from his friend and fellow Durham coalowner, Robert Brantling, who wrote:

"I understand, the Pitmen very naturally consider this measure not only as a most unjustifiable interference with their rights as parents but as separating them from their fellow-men and branding them as a class not only destitute of all moral sentiments, but even of the common feeling for their offspring possessed by the beasts of the field."

Lord Londonderry's second argument related to the employment of women. Some seams, he suggested, were naturally suited to female labour. Usually, coals were drawn along waggon-ways by ponies. However, in some instances, these passages, besides being very steep—as much as two feet in five—were also very low. Consequently, animals could not be used; women had to drag the loads. Lord Londonderry considered the coal industry would be seriously affected if the proposal to prohibit the use of female labour were introduced. He sought to convey the impression that supporters of the Bill were well-meaning but misguided, unacquainted with the intricacies of mining.

Lord Londonderry concluded his case by denouncing inspectors. He questioned the accuracy and probity of those responsible for the Report. He went on to attack inspectors in general as meddlesome busybodies, and thought a coalowner would be justified in telling an inspector, "You may go down the pit how you can, and when you are down you may remain there." Alas for his Noble Lordship, this remark had precisely the opposite effect to the one intended. With a vision of inspectors marooned at the bottom of mines all over the

[1] See Chapter 3, p. 47.

country, Parliament inserted a clause saying that owners must grant inspectors the necessary facilities to perform their duties.

Lord Londonderry's actions, in another respect, misfired. While he always regarded himself as "the miners' friend", they—misguided and ignorant, in his opinion—showed their base ingratitude by having an unparalleled hatred for him. The fact that he (and other coalowners) had opposed the Ashley Act did not pass unnoticed. Colliers were aware that he would like to see it repealed. Consequently, miners had to keep a watchful eye on Parliament, ready to mobilise the maximum pressure to scotch any such attempt. In other words, unwittingly he helped to increase their political involvement.

The miners' political commitment was further heightened because the struggle for the Ashley Act did not end by it being passed through Parliament. It had to be applied. Many owners simply disregarded the Act, employing skilful subterfuges. At Wigan, one owner, who was also a magistrate, installed ladders and look-outs so that women could make a quick exit if inspectors came around. Another Wigan owner dressed his women workers "in male attire, having jackets and trousers in place of the linsey petticoats and bedgown they formerly wore over their short trousers."[1] Tremenheere, in his 1845 Report, estimated that 200 of the 700 to 800 women in Wigan who worked down the mines before the Act still worked there. He commented, "the police cannot give up the whole of their time to this matter".[2] In Scotland the law was also violated. For instance, the Duke of Hamilton employed more than sixty women in his pits at Redend. One of them—a pregnant woman—was killed, along with her husband, when she was coming up the shaft and was struck by a descending tub. The incident led to a typical outburst; "Let his Dukeship look out; if he is a law maker, we are yet to learn if that qualifies him to be a law breaker."[3]

*   *   *

When W. P. Roberts became "the miners' attorney", it only served to stimulate further the union's political commitment. The ferocity and venom with which he fought their legal battles clearly emphasised the importance of the law. Colliers appreciated it was, as a first step, vital to gain in reality the rights they already enjoyed on paper under the law. Then, it was necessary to get Parliament to repeal obnoxious legislation. And, finally, it was essential, if miners' working and living

[1] *Northern Star*, 30 Spetember 1843.   [2] *The Inspector of Mines Report*, 1845, p. 5.
[3] *Northern Star*, 9 September 1843.

standards were to be improved, for Parliament to be persuaded to pass progressive measures, of which the Ashley Act would be the fore-runner.

The achieving of these objectives would necessitate a deep and abiding interest in politics. Parliamentary affairs had to be carefully scanned and the best means possible devised to bring pressure on M.P.s.

The union's first big political campaign began in March 1844. W. P. Roberts informed the Association's Glasgow conference that the Masters and Servants Bill, then before Parliament, constituted a very grave threat to their interests.[1] At first, the Bill had simply seemed a measure that extended colliers' rights to appeal to the magistrates court when an owner defaulted in paying their wages. But a clause was inserted that allowed any master or his agent sweeping powers against workers. It would permit a single magistrate to commit men to prison for two months if found guilty of any "misbehaviour concerning such service or employment" or to have absented themselves before they had completed the work they had contracted to do. W. P. Roberts contended this represented a great enlargement of the powers masters had over men and would lead to even greater injustices.

William Cloughan, of Holytown, disputed Roberts' view. He argued that the new measure was an improvement since it reduced the maximum period of imprisonment for this type of offence from three months to two. Roberts replied that this was a small gain. It was outweighed by conferring new despotic powers on a single magistrate. Conference sided with him, and agreed to launch a national campaign in an attempt to defeat the Bill. On Roberts' advice, thousands of leaflets were quickly printed and dispatched to other working-class organisations. All the delegates at the Glasgow conference, representing 60,000 miners, signed a petition deploring the Bill. They also contacted their friend, T. S. Duncombe, M.P., informing him of their views.

Until then, the Bill had been quietly passing through Parliament, arousing neither hostility nor interest. It had reached the Committee stage. Nevertheless, Duncombe was instrumental in obstructing the Bill, further consideration being postponed until after the Easter recess. Meanwhile, up and down the country mass meetings mobilised working-class opinion. Hostility ran high. The people were expecting a reform—Parliament then had the Ten Hours' Bill before it—not

---

[1] S. and B. Webb, op. cit., p. 183, wrongly locate the conference at Sheffield, not Glasgow.

repressive legislation. Two hundred petitions, representing two million workers, were sent to Parliament. Faced with this tangible expression of public disapproval, Radical M.P.s began to back Duncombe and Ferrand, the only two M.P.s who had vigorously opposed the Bill. With the mounting pressure, both in Parliament and outside, Duncombe succeeded in defeating the Bill.

Such organised trade union activity, aimed at influencing Parliament, was entirely new. That it was actually successful gave its sponsor added pleasure. The miners realised that, not only were they peculiarly subject to the law, but, in certain circumstances, could intervene decisively in the making of it.

Their first venture a success, colliers turned hopefully to Parliament to redress other grievances. They hoped for legislation that would lessen their disadvantages when conflicts occurred with employers. They wanted to end evasion of the Truck Act. They were eager to abolish payment by measure, a method easily manipulated by the masters, and substitute payment by weight, But all these matters, though pressing, were subordinated to a more urgent need—that of preventing accidents. Following the great strike, the death roll from explosions increased alarmingly.

The worst hit area—Northumberland and Durham—petitioned Parliament twice in 1845, asking for action to be taken. Duncombe spoke eloquently, but without avail. A bitter lesson had to be learnt; it was easier for the miners to block anti-trade union legislation than to induce the legislature to do something positive to alleviate the miners' lot. Confronted with opposition from high-ranking interest groups, parliamentary action was a slow and painful process.

In spite of this, Duncombe never stopped trying. He repeatedly brought the miners' plight to the notice of Parliament. In 1847, he introduced a measure that contained the bulk of the colliers' legislative ambitions. The Bill provided for inspection, accurate plans of mines, education for miners' children and payment by weight. While the House was considering the measure, a particularly poignant pit tragedy underlined its urgency. The disaster was at Kirkless Colliery, near Wigan. As the facts became known, tempers began to rise. For a long time, the pit had been notoriously unsafe; the owners apathetically refused to do anything about it. Even on the day of the explosion, men had remonstrated with the manager. Then, to make matters worse, after the explosion the owners refused to allow anybody to go down to see whether the men were dead or alive. Quickly, the news spread throughout Lancashire that six miners had been "walled up". Angry crowds surged through the streets; the authorities were lucky to avoid a riot.

In Parliament, Duncombe recited all these facts and demanded an enquiry by the Government Commissioners. Sir George Grey, for the Government, refused on the grounds that "the magistrates and local authorities ought not to be exempted from the duty". So the eventual outcome was a communication from the local magistrates to the Home Secretary. In their opinion, none of the men left in the pit could have been saved. There, unsatisfactorily, the matter was closed.

Partly because of these events, it became unfashionable to oppose Duncombe's measures directly and on principle. Popular support ran too high, the odium incurred was too great. So parliamentary opponents adopted a hypocritical tactic. They pretended to agree with the measures in principle, and then went on to complain of their lack of preparation or precise terminology. Feigning regret that the Bills were introduced so late in the session, the opponents went on to ask whether it would not be better to await the outcome of the Government's own enquiries.

Faced with this kind of manœuvre, Duncombe's Bills foundered. He had to re-think his whole approach. If a measure was too long and complicated, he would simplify it. If its demands were too large and vague, he would make them precise. Towards the end of 1847, Duncombe presented another Bill. This was stark in its simplicity. Parliament was simply asked to prohibit open lights or blasting powder where fire-damp was known to exist. Confronted with this clear choice, the House rejected the Bill. Undeterred, Duncombe tried again two years later, only to encounter the same fate. Yet, this war of attrition was having an effect. Growing public opinion demanded that Government do something to lessen the terrible death toll underground. In 1850, the legislature bestirred itself: the first Coal Mines Inspection Act was passed. While, by that time, the union had been pulverised, the Act can be regarded as a posthumous victory for the Miners' Association. For the union was responsible for launching the safety campaign; miners' eyes were firmly set on its achievement; and the 1850 Act, in the long run, merely quickened colliers' interest in political matters.

Jude affirmed the Act was inadequate. An insufficient number of inspectors had been appointed. He strongly urged miners to campaign for more inspectors. Notwithstanding the Act's limitations it was a progressive move, a fruit of political action, and miners were doubtless heartened by Lord Londonderry's reaction. He thought the Act was "the most mischievous and unjust measure that could possibly be imagined".

★   ★   ★

Throughout its entire life, the union could rely upon the tireless efforts of Thomas Slingsby Duncombe, M.P. for Finsbury, to champion its cause in Parliament. Duncombe had a strange, complex character. He was completely at home amid the luxury and elegance of high society; he loved to hear witty conversation at literary soirées; he frequented the underworld haunts of London. A man for all seasons, he was still completely at ease with weavers, engineers, miners, discussing how they could jointly further the struggle to improve their lot. They greatly appreciated his help. Meetings and banquets were held in his honour. After the Masters' and Servants' Act had been defeated, largely due to his tenacity, their praise knew no bounds.

As the *Northern Star* observed:

"In the month of May 1844, the Trades of London and the inhabitants of its vast suburbs were filled with admiration and delight at the manly and noble conduct of Labour's champion—T. S. Duncombe, Esq., M.P. The ability displayed by that gentleman in resisting legislation and his jealous untiring advocacy of the rights of labour were the common themes of all classes of Reformers."[1]

Even Engels could not resist joining in the paean of praise: "Thomas Duncombe, the representative of the working-men in the House of Commons, was the great man of the session." Engels continued: "This man was, except for Ferrand, the representative of 'Young England', the only vigorous opponent of the Bill."

Certainly, Duncombe fought hard for the working class. In 1842, he presented the second Chartist petition to Parliament, which was rejected by 287 votes to 49. During the general strike of that year, the Home Secretary opened his mail. In the aftermath of the strike, he pleaded for clemency for those imprisoned. In 1845, he became president of the National Association. When, in 1848, the third and final Chartist petition was presented to Parliament, meetings up and down the country affirmed their confidence in O'Connor and

[1] *Northern Star*, 29 March 1845.

Duncombe, the people's leaders. The fact that his name was so frequently linked with O'Connor's is an indication of his wholehearted support for Chartism and his work on its behalf.

The miners expressed their political kinship with Duncombe in numerous ways. Automatically, they contacted him when they had issues which they wished to be raised in Parliament. Frequently, they bestowed praise on him for his efforts on their behalf. We are left in no doubt that he was their ideal of what a Member of Parliament should be. When W. P. Roberts said, during his election campaign, that he wished to become an M.P. to augment the efforts of Duncombe, we can assume he had the complete endorsement of the Miners' Association.

Yet, Duncombe, who had the unique distinction of being, to use Engels' phrase, "the representative of the interest of the proletariat" in Parliament, enjoyed squandering money on fashionable clothes and disreputable pursuits. A contemporary journal, *Fraser's Magazine* wrote: "In Mr. Duncombe they saw one whose fame had reached through all classes as a distinguished supporter of the gaming house, the brothel and every haunt of vice."[1] Quite understandably, these activities, combined with attempting to maintain his niche in high society, meant he was incessantly living beyond his means. When working people, all over Britain, subscribed generously to a fund for Duncombe—as an appreciation of his work in opposing the Masters' and Servants' Act—almost certainly the money was immediately swallowed up by his debts.

His son's unsatisfactory biography of him omits mention of these aspects of his private life and makes scant reference to his connections with the Labour Movement. He tries to dismiss the latter by writing: "The greatest trial to his patience were deputations of working-men. These persons also came with 'bottled-up' speeches and insisted on wasting his time by delivering their crude notions." His son goes on to quote his father as saying to a deputation, "Will you hold your tongue? . . . I will not hear you."[2]

Even if true, this account is not typical of the way Duncombe treated working people. He showed them consideration; much of his time was devoted to their cause. Nevertheless, his son's biography, by emphasising the side of Duncombe's character that hankered after

---

[1] Quoted by P. W. Kingsford in his article, "Radical Dandy", in *History Today*, June 1964.

[2] *Life and Correspondence of T. S. Duncombe*, pp. 123–7.

cavortings with the aristocracy, does underline a significant fact about
the man: he represented the working class; he did not come from the
working class. He fought for their interests; he did not accept their
outlook. In this respect, and in many others, he was very similar to
W. P. Roberts. One battled in the Courts, the other in the Commons;
but both were staunch Chartists and had the miners' struggle at heart.

Roberts and Duncombe fit into a long lineage of middle-class
radicals in the early nineteenth century. In a perceptive characterisation
of this tendency, E. P. Thompson observes;

> "Only the gentlemen—Burdett, Cochrane, Hunt, Feargus
> O'Connor—knew the forms and language of high politics, could
> cut a brave figure on the hustings, or belabour the Ministers in their
> own tongue. The reform movement might use the rhetoric of
> equality, but many of the old responses of deference were still there
> even among the huzzaing crowds. Whenever a working man
> appeared to be rising 'above himself' even in the reform movement
> he quickly drew jealousy of many of his own class."[1]

Thompson argues that the influence of these middle-class Radicals
waned as the working class grew in strength and organisation. The
Miners' Association encountered this historic problem. Its efforts to
tame Roberts, to make him a servant of the Association, indicate the
intractable difficulties that then prevailed. Nevertheless, even though
its efforts were often fruitless, the union's strenuous attempts to assert
itself were not without significance. The days of middle-class maverick
in the Radical Movement were numbered.

*   *   *

The Miners' Association's involvement in politics did not stop with
applauding men like Duncombe. In the General Election of 1847, two
of its leaders, William Dixon and Roberts, actually stood as candidates.

William Dixon's fight was at Wigan, where he was well known as a
Chartist and trade unionist. During the 1842 general strike, he
addressed meetings there and in other parts of South Lancashire. He
told them how his brother had recently received four sabre-cuts in
clashes with the troops at a Manchester demonstration.[2] Although a
weaver by trade, after the general strike he appears to have devoted
his energies to the Miners' Association. Later, in 1843, immediately
after Swallow's lightning recruiting campaign, Dixon was appointed

[1] E. P. Thompson, *The Making of the English Working Class*, p. 623.
[2] *Manchester Guardian*, 24 August 1842.

as a union lecturer in North Staffordshire. In this capacity, he attended the Manchester conference. In December 1843, three weeks before the conference, he spoke at a Wigan public meeting, along with Feargus O'Connor.[1] He then journeyed alone to near-by Hindley, where he told "a large meeting of miners" of the need for the Charter and for abstinence.[2] After 1844, when the union fell into bad financial times and had to sack most of its lecturers, Dixon opened a temperance hotel in Manchester. William Grocott, county secretary, stayed there for a while and the premises appears to have been used as his headquarters. Handbills, advertising this establishment, were distributed at colliers' gatherings. Then, in 1846, Dixon played a prominent part in the largely unsuccessful Bolton strike. As this extended, in its initial phases, from Rochdale to Wigan, he would certainly have had an opportunity to renew contacts with Wigan workers—if they had ever been broken.

But 1847 was not Dixon's first parliamentary contest; in 1841 he had also fought Wigan. On that occasion, he wrote a gleeful report for the *Northern Star*.[3] It was the custom in Wigan, as in some other mining areas, for the coalowner to march his colliers to the polls as moral support for himself or his candidate. However, on that occasion, instead of behaving like a docile claque at a pantomime, they caused pandemonium. They strode to the hustings singing "The Rogues' March" and rapped in time on the polling station door. Yet, in spite of this fillip, Dixon's campaign in 1841 fell flat. His presence as the "People's Candidate" went comparatively unnoticed in the orthodox press, which regaled its readers with lurid descriptions of Tory thuggery and intimidation. Even at the hand-showing stage, which usually preceded the ballot, there was little indication of support for Dixon. The colliers' demonstration had largely been of opposition to the owners, not of approval for the Chartist candidate.

By 1847, things had changed. William Dixon, now a favourite of the Lancashire miners, had much greater popular appeal. Undoubtedly, this was due, in the main, to his exertions on their behalf. But also it signified a growing awareness among the masses; the miners had come to realise that their enemies and the Chartists' enemies were one and the same people. This was especially true in Wigan. In the 1847 election Colonel James Lindsay, the son of the Earl of Balcarres, was the Tory candidate, while the Whig candidate was Ralph Thicknesse, of Beech Hall, a local banker and coal-proprietor.

---

[1] *Liverpool Mercury*, 8 December 1843.   [2] *Northern Star*, 16 December 1843.
[3] Ibid., 23 September 1841.

Dixon, an eloquent and forceful speaker, spoke "at great length", according to newspaper reports.[1] The *Wigan Herald*, published as part of the *Preston Pilot*, quoted his speech in great detail.[2] From it, it is obvious Dixon wished to emphasise three main points. First, the appalling wretchedness of prevailing conditions:

"A great deal has been said about slavery, but he thought the starvation system of England was quite as bad as the slavery of America—the only difference was that the slave-owner always provided his slaves with sufficient food and raiment whereas the Englishman kept his workmen until he could find some starved out man to work a little cheaper, and then, if he would not have his wages lowered, off he must go to the work-house."

Second, he enforced the customary Chartist arguments and exposed the farcical nature of existing electoral arrangements:

"He thought every man that wore a head, and was of sane mind, ought to have a voice in electing members of Parliament. All of them could hold up their hands for him this day, but the next day came the old system of jugglery when only a few of them would be allowed to give their votes. He would merely refer to one fact in order to prove the jugglery. The friend who seconded him on the last occasion had, since that time, lost his £10 house, and although he had enough sense to vote at the last election, because he had lost his £10 house, he had now lost his sense and was not allowed to vote."

Third, he emphasised the need for the working class to gain representation in Parliament:

"He thought that labour ought as much to be represented as machinery, coal, the sticks and stones of the aristocracy, or the army and navy, for there were one hundred and forty officers in the last Parliament who voted for their own wages."

When it came to the vote, Dixon's prophecy proved correct. The mayor, as returning officer, asked the assembled crowd—estimated at 15,000—to vote by show of hands. Only about a dozen hands were

---

[1] Dixon, always an aggressive speaker, was never overawed by the opposition. On one occasion, he disrupted an Anti-Corn Law meeting in Preston, addressed by no lesser personages than Cobden and Bright. When proceedings reached the financial appeal, Dixon and his supporters mounted the platform, seized the rostrum, and proceeded to address the meeting on Chartist principles. Considerable confusion ensued. Respectable citizens left the hall, making no contribution to the League's funds. *The Struggle* (n.d.), Preston's Anti-Corn Law journal, indignantly reports the incident.

[2] *Preston Pilot*, 31 July 1847.

raised for Colonel Lindsay, followed by about a hundred for
Thicknesse, but "a regular forest of working men's hands appeared
in favour of William Dixon, whom the mayor declared to have a
majority."[1] Inevitably, "a poll was demanded by the Hon. Colonel,
accepted by Thicknesse, but declined by Mr. Dixon".[2] Polling, duly
arranged for the following day, gave Dixon a further opportunity to
make a long oration. The election, to him, was treated as a means to
demonstrate the farcical injustice of an electoral system that left most
people without the vote:

> "Should I, by an unjust system, be prevented from taking my seat
> in the House of Commons, I shall have the proud consolation of
> knowing I am the people's representative, an honour which, after
> this day, neither of my opponents will dare to lay claim."[3]

As anticipated, the poll resulted in a majority for Colonel Lindsay;
Dixon consoled himself that he was the people's choice.

★　　　★　　　★

In the 1847 general election, upwards of twenty candidates who
might be loosely classified as Chartist were nominated. They included
Feargus O'Connor, returned as the Member for Nottingham; Ernest
Jones, unsuccessful at Halifax; and Julian Harney, who contested
Palmerston's seat, Tiverton. The *Northern Star*, of 24 July 1847,
published the list of Chartist candidates. While it contained such a
highly dubious supporter of the cause as Sturge, it is noteworthy
Dixon's name was omitted. The most probable explanation is that the
Northern Star, still smarting from its row with the Miners' Association,
was continuing its practice of not reporting activities of the union or
its spokesmen. Yet, if the *Northern Star* did not publicise Dixon's
candidature, it made up for this neglect by showing great interest in
W. P. Roberts' contest at Blackburn. For a long time it had advocated
he should stand for Parliament; now he would have his chance.

In fact, this chance arose fortuitously. Before the election, Roberts
had never even visited the constituency. It must have come to him as
a surprise that he, with long-standing associations with the miners,
should be invited by a branch of the cotton workers' union to stand
for Parliament as a representative of labour. The approach to Roberts
was made as a result of a strike at Hopwood's Mill, Blackburn, at the

---

[1] *Preston Pilot*, 31 July 1847.　　　　[2] *Bolton Chronicle*, 31 July 1847.
[3] *Northern Star*, 14 August 1847.

end of May 1847. Among cotton operatives, Hopwood was considered a bad master, his house had been wrecked by rioting during the 1842 general strike; and still a lingering bitterness against him remained.

Besides being a mill-owner, Hopwood was returning officer for Blackburn. So, as the strike continued, the strikers suddenly hit on the idea of asking Roberts to stand. It was a golden opportunity to hurl defiance at their master, cause him the maximum annoyance, and at the same time show contempt for the undemocratic electoral system. Probably one of the leaders—William Beesley—suggested it.[1] Anyway, the union instructed him to go to Manchester and see if Roberts was prepared to stand. In high spirits, Beesley returned to Accrington and addressed a strike meeting on Sunday, 30 May. The Tory *Blackburn Standard* reported:

> "We pass over the objectionable tone given to some parts of the speeches of last Sunday, to notice a most wicked and dangerous attempt on the part of one of the speakers named Beesley to incite his hearers to a riotous attack upon the returning officer of the borough, Mr. Robert Hopwood Junior. This man declared to thousands assembled round him, that the returning officer was 'abominated, hated and detested' . . . if Mr. Hopwood did 'dare to show his face' during the election 'there would be sure to be a riot and probable sacrifice of life'."[2]

At a further strike meeting Roberts was billed to speak but did not attend. Beesley explained that his absence was due to his defending strikers at Warrington, and went on to make his own speech. By the middle of June the dispute was over, but the cotton workers were not prepared to let matters rest: Roberts was still invited to be their candidate for the constituency. The *Blackburn Standard* frothed with anger when it heard about it. Its editor wrote that he would have supported Roberts' candidature if "representation was to have been in a beer-shop or on the Moor". As that was not the case, however, it felt constrained to warn its readers:

---

[1] After the debacle in the North-east coalfields, Beesley returned to his native Accrington. As well as working as a weaver, he kept an eating-house in Abbey Street. Quickly, he became a prominent local trade unionist. In his spare time he developed the unusual hobby of knocking down walls. This caused much annoyance to Mr. Jonathan Peel, a local landlord, who paid to have them re-built. He wanted to enclose the park that surrounded his house; Beesley regarded the land as public property. In spite of police vigilance, Beesley and his confederates accomplished their demolition work three times. (*Men of Note*, by R. S. Crossley (Accrington Public Library) and W. R. Hindle's Collection (Oak Hill Museum, Accrington).)

[2] *Blackburn Standard*, 2 June 1847.

" If there be any ignorant of such facts as Mr. Prowting (an evident misprint for Spouting) Roberts and Mr. William Beesley, it may be well to mention that the one is a contract-lawyer for the Chartists, strikers, turnouts and unionists in this part of the country; and his associate is an operative weaver and chairman, fond of haranguing his 'fellow-labourers' on 'the points' and took a prominent part in the recent strike in this town."[1]

Accustomed to adverse publicity, Roberts contented himself with making his own position clear. He published his election address on July 5th, outlining his political platform:

1. He was a friend of the Ten Hours Bill, and would have rejoiced had it been an Eight Hours Bill. Nevertheless, he had no objection to grown men working as long as they thought fit.

2. He was a member of the Church of England, and favoured, the separation of Church and State for the sake of the Church.

3. He was opposed to the existing law of primogeniture.

4. He was opposed to all taxes on food, commerce and manufactures, wishing them to be replaced, in the main, by additional taxes on property.

5. He was opposed to capital punishment, war, and the Game Laws. Moreover, he strongly objected to the continual increase in the powers of magistrates, abrogating the principle of trial by jury.

6. He was opposed to the rate-paying clauses of the Reform Act and anything giving greater rights to wealth and property.

7. The House of Commons would never be as it should be till every sane man had the right to vote.

In conclusion, he dissociated himself from political parties— "never was there less of a party man than myself"—and announced his intention to incur no more election expenses than the law permitted.

Initially, Roberts appeared to have a reasonable chance. Newspapers took his challenge seriously. Only gradually did it dawn on them that, great as Roberts' popularity was, it was almost entirely confined to people without the vote. Local trade unions tried to help, but the restricted franchise proved an insuperable handicap. Even the Miners' Association gave what aid it could. Blackburn has a few coalmines.

[1] Ibid., 28 June 1847.

So the *Miners' Advocate* urged everybody to support Roberts' candidature and reprinted the whole of his election address in its columns.

During the election campaign, Roberts held a number of public meetings. Frequently, he reiterated the statement giving his reason for standing:

"It is time the working classes should be more adequately represented than they have been. This is the ground on which I appear before you. Popular principles are now and then brought before the House of Commons, but such principles are only regularly supported by one man—Mr. Duncombe."[1]

On election day, Roberts' support was swollen by textile workers and miners marching in from neighbouring Accrington. He was "a decided favourite with the populace", as even the hostile *Preston Chronicle* had to admit. Very conscious of this, Roberts posed as the champion of the disenfranchised masses. He made his "appeal for support to the non-electors of Blackburn chiefly, whom he trusted would one day let a people's Member of Parliament be returned. It was for them he came forward."[2]

Throughout his speech at the hustings, the crowd interrupted with applause:

"He was there to claim equal rights, powers and privileges, whether political, social or religious; and he was prepared to carry out those principles at all times, at all places, and under all circumstances. This was his political faith (cheers). He believed all men to be really brothers. Not in a mere hollow form of words, to be used in a parlour to a child on Sunday; but as a most solemn truth under all circumstances of life (cheers). He was called the People's Attorney in a sarcastic sense; but it was a term of honour to him.

"Looking back a few years, they could recall 140 Chartists being in prison simply, with one or two exceptions, because of their opinions. Dr. M'Douall, who was on that platform, had been sent to prison because of his opinions; and Feargus O'Connor because a speech was published in his paper but without his knowledge. So that, in fact, Whiggery had done all it could to oppose and oppress the peoples."[3]

Roberts then turned to attack the Tories. He was less scathing than when he dealt with the Whigs. For the Conservative candidate was John Hornby, an Anglican manufacturer, who had maintained the

[1] *Preston Chronicle*, 21 July 1847.   [2] Ibid., 24 July 1847.   [3] Ibid.

wages of his handloom weavers during the depression. He had been elected by a small majority at the previous general election. In Parliament he had supported popular measures—the Ashley Act, the Ten Hours Bill, and he had given a subscription to the campaign to free Oastler from prison. Therefore, it is not surprising Roberts was less severe. Even so, he characterised the Conservative Party's faith as being:

". . . there were two classes of men, a rich and a poor—the one to make the laws, the other to obey; one to levy the taxes, the other to pay them."[1]

The outcome at Blackburn was the same as at Wigan When it came to the poll, Roberts came bottom: Hornby 641, Pilkington 602, Hargreaves 392, Roberts 68.

In spite of Roberts' puny vote, a new pattern had been established. For the first time, a prominent spokesman of the trade unions had stood for Parliament as an independent labour representative, and the union for which he worked was a miners' trade union. From the days of the Miners' Association onwards, colliers became more attentive to, and later more active in, the political arena.

But it would be wrong to connect Roberts' efforts solely with the miners' struggle. Others were also probing the possibility of parliamentary action. The National Association, of whose nine-man executive Roberts was a member, seriously debated launching a Labour Party. Probably, it was only the persecutions of its leaders, like John Drury, who faced two trials in 1847, that deterred the National Association from taking the step. For the litigation left it temporarily leaderless and weakened. Cole and Postgate described the National Association's quandary:

"It is interesting to find that in the course of the struggle against economic recession and legal persecution, the Association for the Protection of Labour seriously considered the launching of a Trade Union political party. The debates on this matter at its conferences revealed strong differences of opinion. While some of the delegates argued that only political action would enable the workers to get their economic grievances redressed, a rival faction held that any introduction of politics into the Trade Union would fatally destroy working-class industrial solidarity, and lead to the disruption of the movement. In the end, after Drury's release, and the revival of trade

[1] Ibid.

had relaxed the immediate pressure, the project of Trade Union political action was abandoned—to be taken up by Ernest Jones in his attempts to revive the decaying fortunes of Chartism in the early 'fifties. But the Protection Association deserves to be remembered as the first body to suggest the creation of a working class party resting primarily on Trade Union support."[1]

It was to this discussion that Dixon and Roberts, two miners' leaders, furnished first-hand information by their electoral activity.

In view of the many forms of political activity indulged in by the Miners' Association, it may seem somewhat strange and inconsistent that the union had a "no politics" rule. To understand the significance of this, it must be realised that the rule was meant as a precaution, not a prohibition. It was there as a safety measure, to be enforced if discussions got out of hand. This situation would be considered to have arisen when the union's solidarity was being endangered or wild statements made that might lead to the authorities taking repressive measures. So the term "politics" was used in a special and original way. In no sense did it inhibit union members from attacking Tory or Liberal papers, petitioning Parliament or supporting Roberts' candidature. It was, however, used to prevent the union from becoming associated with passionate revolutionary utterances of the John Rayner Stephens type. Stephens, had been a popular speaker in the Lancashire and North-east coalfields. Many miners echoed his pleas for physical force.[2] To rough, tough workmen, fighting was just another form of self-expression, a method of underlining an important point. Union leaders, however, realised that the Association must remain completely free from violence, both in word and action. Consequently, whereas Stephens was regarded as "political", Feargus O'Connor was perfectly admissible.[3]

We have already mentioned how close the union's connections were with Chartism. Almost without exception, prominent union leaders also took part in Chartist activities. The closeness of the two

[1] G. D. H. Cole and Raymond Postgate, *The Common People*, p. 318.

[2] E. W. Jones, a Liverpool Chartist, says Lancashire miners gave him £150 to buy arms, but he declined and somebody absconded with the money (cf. T. Joff, *Coffee House Babble*).

[3] When a correspondent attacked O'Connor, the editor of the *Miners' Advocate* sprung to his defence: "We believe Mr. Feargus O'Connor to be a pure and incorruptible patriot, and a sincere, uncompromising, and devoted friend of the oppressed working man. The National Land Company, of which he is father and founder, will form a new era in the history of Labour's Redemption. . . . We are proud to say we are members of the National Land Company, and we say to our readers, if you respect yourselves and your families, 'go and do likewise' . . . " (February 1848).

organisations can be shown by a simple illustration. The Wakefield conference of November 1844 was addressed by W. P. Roberts, who urged the union to support the Chartist Land Scheme, and by O'Connor, who counselled them to remain independent from politics. That he construed the word in a different way to present usage can be seen from the fact that O'Connor then journeyed to Newcastle, where he addressed two public meetings jointly sponsored by the local Chartists and the union. At one meeting he spoke on mines inspection, but the other was devoted to Republicanism, hardly deemed a non-political topic today.

The wasteful extravagance of the Monarchy was frequently attacked by O'Connor and his journals. In 1847, *The Labourer*, organ of the Chartist Land League, stated: "From a recent number of the Court Journal we learn that the Queen, in consideration of her starving subjects, has been 'graciously pleased' that the crumbs of bread from the Royal tables should be given to the poor, instead of being thrown into the dust-bin." The monarchs' munificence was celebrated by a poem:

> "In Windsor Palace, 'neath plate and chalice,
> The many tables groan:
> The Queen has eaten and drunk her fill;
> And she thinks (thought cometh, do what you will)
> How the children of Famine moan."[1]

At the same time, similar thoughts were expressed by William Beesley. Only two months after the Blackburn election, a newspaper report gives a succinct account of the political attitudes of one of Roberts' main helpers:

"William Beesley addressed the meeting on Chartist principles. . . . He commenced his address as usual by a 'skit' at the police and a tirade against the Queen, Prince Albert and the Bishops, and all in authority. He said the Queen was a 'gilded butterfly' and 'useless' . . . and she must be a drunken woman as there was a great deal of money allowed for wine, etc."[2]

It would be possible to instance many other examples of Chartist utterances that were made by people who played an important part

---

[1] *The Labourer*, 1847, v. 1, p. 234. The *Miners' Advocate*, August 1847, also attacked the expense of royalty.

[2] *Blackburn Standard*, 15 September 1847. Beesley's remarks are consistent with his having edited a Chartist temperance journal in North Lancashire.

in the union. Throughout the organisation's existence, Commissioner Tremenheere remained convinced it was Chartist agitators who were responsible for industrial strife. While he undoubtedly underestimated the profound discontent that existed, the embittered feeling of being oppressed and exploited that prevailed among miners, there can be little question that Chartists helped to make this articulate. In this way, the Miners' Association gained the unique distinction of being the union most affected by Chartism.

16

The Final Collapse

WITH its national organisation totally shattered, large parts of the Lancashire stronghold decimated, and in the teeth of a raging economic depression the Miners' Association was singularly unfit to resist factious activities within its own ranks. But this it was obliged to do. The National Association was taking advantage of the weakness of the Miners' Union to spread its own alternative principles, and naturally the dispute became more bitter as time passed. The unhappy defection of the Scottish miners still rankled and the language of the quarrel grew more abusive.

On 8 January 1848 the *Northern Star* reported that Mr. Lenegan, of the National Association, had addressed the Rose Bridge Lodge of the Miners' Association at Hindley, advising them to make application for membership cards and he distributed copies of the rules of the consolidated body. The following week William Cloughan, who was by now one of its leading adherents, told the Holytown miners that the National Association was the most rational and practical form of organisation. A resolution was passed in favour of joining, and Cloughan was deputed to undertake a tour of the other mining areas to gain recruits. The *Northern Star* reported that there was a strong feeling in Lancashire in favour of the National Association, despite the report circulated by David Swallow, entitled "The National Association—A Delusion and a Snare".

At first, the line which Lenegan pursued in Lancashire was to suggest there was no incompatability between the two organisations. At Shevington, on 3 January, he had been at pains to deny that the National Association had any intention of subverting local unions. The Miners' Association's district secretary had been sufficiently impressed by this argument to pledge his support, and the local branch had carried a resolution in favour of supporting, and co-operating with, the National Association. In an effort to bring the issue to a head, a debate was held in the Ship Yard, Millgate, Wigan. The speakers were John Berry, lecturer for the Miners' Association, and John Lenegan, provisional agent for the National Association. Such was the intensity of mutual hostility that three officials were needed to maintain order. There were two chairmen; one, Ingham, who favoured the Miners' Association, and the other, Hancock, whose bias was the other way. A neutral umpire, Turrill, presided.

Lenegan spoke first and, predictably, made the point that his organisation did not propose weakening the existing miners' union but rather strengthening it. He found it strange that Berry and Ingham should be opposing him since both had been supporters of the idea of national association in 1845. He quoted from the *Miners' Magazine* of March 1845, which reported a meeting held in Wigan to consider the propriety of joining the National Association. Berry had been in the chair when Ingham had moved the following resolution:

"That, in the opinion of this meeting, Union is the only means whereby the working man can be emancipated; and we hereby pledge ourselves to do all that lies in our power to bring about, as soon as possible, a general organisation of those who live by their labour."[1]

This motion had been seconded by W. P. Roberts, whose speech in favour of joining Lenegan read out. He further claimed that there was a general tendency towards general union and rejoiced that "the miners of Lancashire had taken their proper place in this movement".[2] In sending Mr. Berry to the 1845 conference of the National Association in London they had done themselves and him an immortal honour.

Berry then stated the case against the National Association and professed himself sceptical about the practicability of organising such a union. He could not see how a mechanic or a weaver or a tailor could mediate between an employer and a miner. He also objected to the power of the Central Committee to impose what levies they pleased. If 33,000 men went on strike, as they had in Northumberland and Durham in 1844, it would take £20,625, the subscriptions of 2,475,000 men to support them at 12s. 6d. per week.[3] The Scottish miners, during their strike of 1847, had not been supported by the National Association. Because of this, Berry claimed, they had intimated to the last conference of the Lancashire miners their intention of rejoining the Miners' Association.

[1] *The Miners' Magazine*, March 1845.
[2] *Northern Star*, 29 January 1848.   [3] Ibid.

Lenegan explained his union's provisions for finance. In the first place money was saved on management costs. Whilst the expenses of the whole National Association for the quarter ending September 1847 was only £163 16s., the Miners' Association had spent £187 14s. 6d. on the lecturing department alone in two months from 6 September to 30 October. Secondly, the National Association would support only legal strikes by legal means whereas the Miners' Association, through the laxity of its laws, often supported illegal strikes. He concluded his argument by explaining the role of the National Association in providing for employment of labour.[1]

Berry responded by drawing attention to certain extravagances in the National Association's balance sheet—the Secretary's salary, the full committee meeting at Christmas, 1847, and the cost of postage for one quarter, £13 1s. 10d. Rather inconsistently, he also remarked, in passing, that he had done some work for the National Association for which he had not received a farthing. More important than anything else was the question of agents. The miners would never join the National Association unless they could keep their own agents. Lenegan replied that he did not care if the miners kept five hundred agents so long as they paid them.

The arguments were obviously inconclusive, but they had touched on the two major fears and differences which separated the two bodies. The Miners' Association was worried that their organisation and their agents, which they had paid large levies to support, might be used for purposes which had little to do with the needs of the miners. The National Association, on the other hand, strongly disapproved of the tendency towards illegality and sometimes even violence to which the miners' union was prone. When the motion was put: "That the Miners keep their agents; but approve of the National Association", the latter clause was rejected by a small majority.

The dispute continued on two fronts. On the ground, in the Lancashire lodges, the National Association carried on factional activity, preaching the need for a national combination and, at the same time, assisting the circulation of rumours concerning the probity and financial disinterestedness of the miners' leaders. Along with these activities, correspondence in the columns of the *Northern Star* further

---

[1] He was referring to the National Association of the United Trades for the Employ-ment of Labour, a sister body of the National Association of United Trades for the Protection of Labour until the two merged in 1848. The former was presided over by Thomas Duncombe, M.P., and devoted to the principles of self-employment and co-operative workshops.

inflamed the argument. In the issue of 5 February, William Grocott
wrote in reply to Lenegan's assertions concerning the expenses of the
Miners' Association. The General Secretary seemed to assume that
a general dismissal was all that was needed to refute the imputations.
He claimed that Lenegan's remark about the lecturing department was
"utterly without foundation" and a "wilful promulgation of a direct
falsehood".[1]

Lenegan returned to the attack a fortnight later. He suggested that
Grocott must have forgotten he had already published *A Two Months'
Report of the Miners' Association from September 6th to October 30th*
which, in reality, only went up to 18 October. In this "infamous
document" Lenegan claimed to find that £139 17s. 6d. had been paid
out of the General Fund for lecturers' and executives' wages and coach
fares. A further £32 19s. had been paid from the County Fund to
J. Berry and others of the Travelling Committee. This total reached
£172 16s. 6d., which would certainly have become £180 by the end
of October. Following these introductory remarks Lenegan warmed
to his task.

"There is one strange feature in this Association, viz., that the one
set of men are the Executive and the Travelling Committee. And
although a conference held on the 11th August, 1847, in St. Helens,
resolved 'that William Meadowes, Robert Marsh, and William
Cheetham be the Travelling Committee'; and 'that the above three,
in conjunction with the general secretary and the treasurer, do form
the Executive of the Miners' Association', still these three have been
drawing money from both funds, viz., the General and the County
Funds. . . . There are other items in this balance sheet that I do not
wish to mention at this time. Suffice it to say that, if I thought
proper, I would make any honest unionist wonder how men can be
so long duped by a few."[2]

Such accusations obviously required a reply and, a fortnight later,
one was forthcoming from the general secretary of the miners. Grocott
stated that he possessed the document which was referred to and found
that the "whole of the expenditure, including the payment of several
debts, together with salaries of the Executive Committee does not
reach the amount specified by nearly £50". As for the "extraneous"
matter concerning the Executive and the Travelling Committee being
the same, and the six-week balance-sheet purporting to be two months,

[1] *Northern Star*, 5 February 1848.   [2] *Ibid.*, 4 March 1848.

the Secretary again relied on rather vague assertions: "I can only say that you are involving yourself more deeply in the odiousness of wilfully perverting the truth, or writing deliberate falsehoods."[1]

But the National Association and its agents were intervening ever more actively in the day-to-day affairs of the Lancashire miners. The depression and consequent unemployment not only weakened the miners' union for economic reasons but also engendered discontent that the consolidated body could exploit. Addressing a public meeting of unemployed miners at Hindley, Lenegan declared that nothing short of a national combination could effectually secure the rights of the working classes. A committee was appointed to agitate for this aim in the district.

When strikes took place the National Association, with the aid of the *Northern Star*, sought to share responsibility and secure publicity for itself. At Darcy Lever, a reduction in wages was proposed similar to that in other trades. The miners decided to ask their employer whether he would emulate other employers in better organised Lancashire areas and bear half the cost of the reductions himself. A deputation was organised on 28 January but met with brutal treatment. The proprietor turned on the members and discharged them all. The *Northern Star* commented, "If a poor workman only dares to see his employer and to ask for a remnant of his rights; if he only does this, he must be discharged, victimised, branded as a union man, and be literally starved to death".[2] Two of the men thus treated obtained alternative employment and the Central Committee of the National Association stepped in to support the rest.

The depression had virtually killed the Miners' Association, and internecine strife was sufficient to finish the job. The pitmen's union was the loser whilst the National Association failed to win. By March 1848 the union had ceased to function and miners throughout the British Isles were unorganised. In any case, many of the activists had found more urgent calls upon their time. 1848 was the year of revolutions, and economic circumstances combined with news from Europe to create an explosion of political and revolutionary activities. The miners played their small part in this. An enormous meeting of Scottish miners at Airdrie soon after the revolution in France was addressed by a miner by the name of Lees who claimed that all the workmen's evils were due to political inequalities and warned the capitalists and aristocracy of the insurrection to come.

---

[1] *Northern Star*, 19 February 1848.   [2] Ibid.

The authorities were sufficiently impressed to feel alarm, especially since other meetings of the miners were planned. Yet a more important cause for the demise of the miners' union was the reign of terror which was unleashed on the Chartists in the summer and autumn of 1848. Many of the union's activists were caught up in the mass arrests which followed such incidents as the killing of a policeman during a riot in Ashton-under-Lyne. W. P. Roberts rushed from place to place, devoting his whole time to the defence of Chartists and, in connection with the incident just mentioned, appeared at Manchester Borough Courts on behalf of the fifteen who were arrested. In September, Grocott himself was arrested and committed for trial at the Assizes by the Manchester magistrates. He was tried in December 1848 at the South Lancashire Winter Assizes, along with seventy-five other Chartists, and given a year's imprisonment. The last recorded reference to Grocott comes in the following year. Nine prisoners in Kirkdale jail, including George White, William Dixon, James Leach and William Grocott, submitted a memorial to the Home Office on 23 January 1849. Of course, nothing came of it.[1]

The Miners' Association was dead but the principle of unionism insisted on kicking a little before it would lie down. On 18 August the *Glasgow Post* reported disturbances in the mining districts of Lanarkshire. Large meetings of colliers had taken place demanding additions of 1s. 6d. per day to the 2s. 6d. they were already receiving. There was no disposition on the part of the employers to comply with such a demand. In Lancashire the occasion was not one of demanding advances but of resisting further reductions. Indeed, the situation was not dissimilar to that in Northumberland and Durham after the great strike. Repeated assaults by the employers might revive memories and sometimes provoke sporadic resurrections of the union idea, which were, in turn, hailed as a return to the better days. But nothing more than isolated responses to particular grievances was forthcoming.

Such an incident was provoked by an attempted 10 per cent reduction in wages imposed by Mr. Pearse, the agent of the Earl of Balcarres. The miners were incensed, and a mass meeting was held on Aspull Moor on 4 September to concert counter-action.

"This reduction in wages is very different treatment from what might have been expected after the great promises made in the

---

[1] Home Office 45 (1849) O.S., 2,619. James Leach, who organised the distribution of the *Miners' Advocate* throughout Lancashire in 1843-4, is supposed to have introduced Frederick Engels to Julian Harney. (A. R. Schoyen, *The Chartist Challenge*, p. 91.)

speeches delivered a few weeks ago at the festivities and rejoicings at Haigh Hall so much paraded in the local papers in the neighbourhood. The men are beginning to think that they are to pay dear for the dinner his lordship gave them on Monday, July 31st, at well as the smiles so graciously bestowed by the Earl, Lord Lindsay, and the ladies. . . . Previous to the present reduction there were colliers working for one and sixpence or two shillings per day."[1]

The 10 per cent cut followed a 14 per cent cut a few months before and:

"has had the effect of driving the men to their union again; on Saturday last, three lodges were established and a great number of men enrolled. . . . The Miners' Association is spreading fast in all the principal districts in Lancashire."[2]

Dennett, Price, and especially David Swallow, the miners' greatest trouble-shooter and agent in times of adversity, were active in the attempt to promote and encourage the revival. On 30 October a delegate meeting, at the Fleece in Wigan, deputed these three, together with Meadowcross, to prepare statements for the next meeting so that a wage demand could be submitted as soon as possible. It was resolved that:

"It is the duty of every colliery and district to organise, and to appoint deputations from amongst themselves, to wait upon those men who may be out of the Union, and to invite them to join immediately."[3]

A week later, on 6 November, Swallow was again addressing a great demonstration of the miners of Aspull and Blackrod to demand the wages of '46 and '47. But, unlike the revival attempts in the Northern coalfield in the years after the strike, the Lancashire miners had no thriving outside centre to support and subsidise their efforts. The Northern miners had not managed to reorganise themselves even with this assistance; Lancashire could not survive without it. The *Northern Star* plaintively asked:

"What are the miners of the Tyne, Wear and Tees doing? Are they not coming to the rescue? During the past week meetings have been held at Ringley, Bury, Bolton, and Wigan."[4]

With a careful perusal of its own columns, it could have answered

---

[1] *Northern Star*, 9 September 1848. [2] Ibid., 9 September 1848.
[3] Ibid., 4 November 1848. [4] Ibid., 11 November 1848.

its own questions. By December, even the eternally hopeful Martin Jude had abandoned all his expectations and was appealing to the miners of Northumberland and Durham, not to join the union, but to contribute sixpence each to repay him the loan of over £100 he had made to the union during the 1844 strike:

"Having waited until this time with a full assurance that the organisation of the union would again be effected and thereby establish a proper channel for the collection of debt due to me and others, but from present appearances there is but slight hope of any effective organisation being brought round."[1]

★   ★   ★

Ironically, Jude, who had snatched hopefully at straws for many years, now reconciled himself to defeat immediately before the most genuine—though abortive—revival to occur in the Northern counties through all the long days since 1844. A contemporary record described this wholly unexpected upsurge of activity that occurred in the following year:

"On the 13th March, 1849, the tocsin of union was again sounded throughout the two counties by the Seaton Delaval men, who for several years past had taken an active part in all the leading movements for the emancipation of their fellow-men, and who were looked upon as the vanguard of liberty. Feeling once more that their own weakness constituted the strength of their opponents, they resolved to form themselves into one united body and have for their rallying cry 'The better ventilation of mines, and the Government inspection thereof'. Active measures were at once taken, and Mr. Robert Turnbull, of Seghill, was appointed as the first agent. . . . But such was the servile condition of the miners at this time that at several of the collieries visited by Mr. Turnbull they were afraid to go near him for fear that their masters should get to know of it, and they would be discharged. But very few of the old veterans that took an active part in the union of 1844, having felt the effects of the men's ingratitude, could be induced to come to the fore again. The old spark remaining, soon however began to blaze, and a large portion of the Northumberland miners got united and were determined to rouse up their brethren of the Wear and Tees. Mr. William Bell, of Seaton Delaval, was appointed secretary. Mr. John Hall and Mr. George Young (the father of Mr. Ralph Young, the respected treasurer of the Northumberland Miners' Association),

[1] *Ibid.*, 16 December 1848.

together with others, formed the first committee. They went to work in the two counties and succeeded in getting a large number of men both in the Tyne and Wear to join the union. It was difficult to get meetings at many places, and old Ben Embleton was seen on many occasions going about the collieries with a tin pan, or a sheet of iron, commonly called a 'bleazer', to attract the attention of the men and induce them to come out. His favourite speech was, 'Lads, I know the position the masters have you in, and nothing but your union will liberate you from the oppression you have to bear.' A favourite quotation of his was 'someone will have to bell the cat'. Ben Embleton and his other colleagues were ever ready to address the meetings, till the union began to get a firm hold. But, as in the case at the formation of the previous unions, no sooner were the men united, than they all wanted their grievances shook off at once, and the consequence was there was always a large number of collieries on strike at the same time. Seaton Delaval and Cowpen were on strike together and collieries in the County of Durham were out in the same way. This prevented many collieries from joining the union, as there was a heavy levy to pay to support those on strike. This action on the part of the men and that of the masters in turning the men off who belonged to the union, prevented the union of 1849 from reaching the dimensions of that of 1844.

"Cowpen Colliery was eleven weeks on strike, and resulted in a great loss to both masters and men as trade was very brisk at the time. It also led to a very unfortunate affair. A man named George Hunter, a pitman at Cowpen, on returning home was attacked by someone and injured so severely that he died in a few days. Hunter was not a union man, and was disliked by the men of the colliery. Some of the miners were apprehended, but as the authorities could not prove any charge against them they were discharged, and those who had caused his death were never found out.

"The cholera having broken out at this time with great violence in the colliery districts, the attention of both employers and employed was turned towards the improvement of the sanitary condition of the villages, and union matters were laid aside for a time, as great numbers of the workmen of the collieries were dying daily, struck down by the dire disease. Among those who fell victims was Mr. William Bell, the secretary of the General Union, whose death took place at Seaton Delaval."[1]

The stillbirth of the "Three Week Union" was ascribed by this observer to the cholera and to over-commitment at the start of its

[1] R. Fynes, op. cit., pp. 133-5.

life. Yet the underlying cause was the same as in Lancashire. A union was simply unable to operate at a time of falling wages. It could neither arrest nor interrupt the steady decline of wages and conditions. Jude, who had given the cause up for lost and took no part in the 1849 revival, wrote despondently to the *Northern Star*, concluding:

"Thus we have a brief history of the position of the general body of miners in the North and unless they bestir themselves and by union and combination seek to bring about a better state of things, they may rest assured their position will get worse."[1]

The miners had sought to do what Jude recommended and failed. An article, again by Jude, in 1851 complained that wages continued to plummet.[2] Indeed, he was right: their position was getting worse. In such a situation nineteenth-century unions stood little chance of surviving. A far better prepared and more solidly based union in Lancashire had also failed amid the gales of economic depression. They never attempted to claim more than a local basis and no attempt was made to solicit aid or even establish contact with other coalfields. The position was as dark as it had ever been by the end of March 1849.

The picture must have been made even gloomier by the demise of the *Miners' Advocate*. It appears to have ceased publication in the late spring of 1849.[3]

The great Miners' Association had finally staggered to a close, beaten at last by economic circumstance, faction, and the malicious hostility of the powers-that-be. It is not suggested that the union was free of faults on its side. On several occasions it was disunited and hopelessly uncertain of the path it wished to tread; on all occasions its organisation and degree of central control failed to match the great expectations and pious assertions of those who had built it. There had been a great experiment and decisive—sometimes irrevocable—slants had been given to the future of trade union development in this country. If historians have been too much obsessed by the working-class political movements of the period to read the lessons and draw conclusions from the story of the Miners' Association, there were lessons and verdicts alike for nineteenth-century trade unionists to find. Their conclusions need not all have been as uncharitable as those of the *Northern Star* to which we shall give the last word:

[1] *Northern Star*, 24 March 1849.   [2] *Notes to the People*, No. 23, 1851.
[3] The last reference to the *Miners' Advocate* was in *The Manx Liberal* of 21 April 1849. It stated that it continued to be printed at the Herald Office in Douglas. William Cubbon, in his *Bibliography of Works relating to the Isle of Man*, says it must have ceased publication with the withdrawal of special postal privileges.

Q

"THE COLLIERS OF NORTHUMBERLAND AND DURHAM.

During the management of the affairs of the Durham and Northumberland colliers by Mr. Roberts there was no class of labourers who stood in a better position to resist the aggressions of the strongest class of the masters, and to this fact is to be attributed the intense hatred of the latter class of him... As in the case of the Dorchester Labourers and the Glasgow Cotton Spinners, so it was with the colliers during their strike; we devoted our time, our money, and our space, to the advocacy of their cause, and our reward in all cases was the same—neither thanks nor gratitude. Nevertheless, as we ascribe all to system we will once again lend our aid to the reorganisation of the Colliers' Union which, while in its strength, was the most powerful Labour Union ever known in this country."[1]

[1] *Northern Star*, 27 January 1849.

17

Postscript

A DIFFICULTY in writing this history is to decide when to end. No clear end exists. It is impossible to say when the union ceased to function. In 1850 delegates purporting to be from the Association attended meetings in South Wales.[1] Again, with the revival of trade in the early 1850s went a revival of trade unions. Many of them adopted the name "Miners' Association" as part of their titles. This might be attributed to a remembrance of things past—exploits, struggles, songs still fresh in miners' minds—but, as well, it indicates how gradually the change took place. Almost imperceptibly, centralised control withered away. This was the crucial point. The Miners' Association of the 1840s was a national union, exercising varying degrees of direction over its constituent bodies, whereas the Miners' Associations of the 1850s were tiny, independent unions, operating on a coalfield or county basis. Occasionally, they met to discuss mutual problems. Yet little or no attempt was made to weld these small disparate bodies into a national organisation. When, eventually, this did occur at the Leeds conference of 1863, most delegates did not regard it as a new union, merely the resuscitation of the old. It took a further twelve years before a new title was generally accepted.[2]

We do not wish to become involved in a sterile argument over nomenclature. Nevertheless, the issue does serve to highlight two important points. The first is the prolonged and profound effect of the Miners' Association on the mining community. In 1849 the *Northern Star* described it as "the most powerful Labour union ever known in this country". It must have made a lasting impression if its title was still used in the 1870s, so long after its demise. The second point is that social and economic conditions made trade unions a necessary and

[1] *Mining Journal*, 22 September 1850. Also, J. H. Morris and L. J. Williams, *The South Wales Coal Industry*, p. 272: "In Monmouthshire in 1850 two 'strangers' who were sentenced to one month's imprisonment for breach of contract claimed to be organisers for a national miners' movement." The book mentions that W. P. Roberts "appeared in the district to demonstrate the advantages of the union by defending the colliers in the Courts in 1865. . . ."

[2] R. Page Arnot, *The Miners*, Vol. 1, p. 45.

enduring part of mining. Whatever the vicissitudes—setbacks caused by defeats and slumps—the organisation continued at grass-roots (or, rather, pit-face) level. Sometimes weakened, often informally, the men still met for combined action. Perhaps this can best be seen in Scotland, where miners determined "the darg" from 1825. It was a primitive and perennial form of unionism. Its existence, however, explains why many miners did not regard the Leeds conference of 1863 as an inaugural meeting: continuity had been maintained among the rank-and-file. Just as the amoeba when cut up continues to exist, each part functioning separately, so the miners' union continued to function, not as a whole, but as many disparate parts.

There can be no doubt that the small unions of the fifties were a regression compared with the Miners' Association. It may be enunciated, as a general rule, that the ability to transcend mere pit-level organisation, to incorporate it as a base for a more elaborate county or national structure, is indicative of progress. The greater the degree of confidence and strength felt among the workers, the greater are the possibilities for building a national union.

Notwithstanding, the local unions of the 'fifties often displayed aggressive militancy. In 1853, colliers in the Wigan coalfield struck for a 2d. in the shilling increase. The strike lasted eight weeks. It culminated in a riot. For almost a whole day, rioters were in control of the town while the police discreetly barricaded themselves in the police station. Law and order were only restored when the cavalry galloped down from Preston, where they had been helping to quell a textile workers' strike. Despite the severe repression that ensued in Wigan, some wage increases were won and the union remained intact.[1] A correspondent of the *Wigan Observer*, 3 December 1853, argued that the colliers' union had never achieved any permanent good for its members and referred to the agitation of Ernest Jones and W. P. Roberts. It is, perhaps, significant that when Ernest Jones wrote about the lessons to be drawn from the miners' struggle, he did not mention the need for greater unity among colliers throughout the country but of closer collaboration between sections of the working class:

"The game of the employers will be to starve or irritate the men in isolated places into violence—so as to dispense them in detail with a concentrated force—to arrest and imprison the leaders—to create a feeling against the working men—and to break in pieces the

[1] Tantalisingly, the union's records for the period up to 1855 were recently destroyed by a person who did not realise their significance.

first links of the majestic union about to take place among all sections of the working classes. But they will fail. The unpremeditated outburst in one place has not compromised our cause—but remarkably displayed the weakness of others—since they were obliged (of all places in the world) to draw troops from Preston to pacify the men of Wigan."[1]

Jones wanted unity of action between Wigan colliers and Preston weavers, part of a bigger unity encompassing all workers that would "strike terror to the employers". This idea found tangible expression in the Labour Parliament of 1854. But the miners, probably thinking that it bore too close a resemblance to the National Association that had inflicted so much damage on their own trade union, did not participate in this new venture.

★   ★   ★

Disputes appear endemic to mining, and the local unions of the 'fifties were not immune. Usually trouble remained confined to one area, but in 1858 it flared up in Yorkshire, Lancashire and the Midlands simultaneously. The strength of the Yorkshire unions (there were several) can be seen from their ability to resist successfully a proposed 15 per cent wage cut. At Oaks colliery, near Barnsley, "their Association has spent upwards of £2,000".[2] In West Yorkshire, where some pits were idle for twenty-seven weeks, the men out of work "were thrown . . . on the funds of the Miners' Association".[3] Colliers at pits not in dispute raised £3,600 in six months for the strikers. In South Staffordshire, where increasing numbers were paying the weekly subscription of 6d., the strike was for a wage advance from 2s. 9d. to 3s. 3d. And Lancashire and Cheshire, at a Bolton delegate meeting, decided to go for a general increase of 2d. in the shilling. A month later, a special meeting was informed that nine owners had granted the increase. But delegates thought it was necessary for it to be general; otherwise the nine would have a pretext for reducing their wages again.

After the disputes ended, organisational ties were strengthened. James Johnson, a leader of the South Staffordshire Miners' Association, journeyed to Yorkshire to establish contact with the various unions there. These were all amalgamated into the Yorkshire Miners' Association in December 1858.

[1] *People's Paper*, 5 November 1853.   [2] *Manchester Guardian*, 5 October 1858.
[3] Ibid., 11 October 1858.

During these strikes, as in all others, W. P. Roberts came in to help. In September 1858 he was the principal speaker at Shedon Hill. Martin Jude and Alexander Macdonald also spoke.[1] In the same month, Roberts defended ten miners at Dudley. He must have been on form, because the magistrate said that in twenty years on the bench he had never heard such language from an advocate; Roberts defended his right to use it. Then, in November, Roberts represented another ten strikers, this time at Hyde in Cheshire, charged with making a riotous and unlawful assembly. After a trial lasting six hours, the two to three hundred colliers present in Court happily heard the verdict: case dismissed. In December 1858 Roberts addressed the Manhood Suffrage Association in Manchester. In the New Year, he continued his legal battles for the colliers. Striking against a wage reduction when their Bonds were renewed, four Durham miners were prosecuted for breach of contract. Roberts' speech at the trial was inspiring. It led to a "solidifying of the whole of the workmen of the Wearmouth", to active support pouring in from other sections and, later in the year, the formation of the Durham Miners' Association.[2]

The events of 1858–9 have been recounted because they clearly show that local unions could be powerful bodies with strong financial support. It would be wrong to imagine that the period 1849 to 1863 was devoid of mining unions. Also, there is considerable continuity: colliers acting in the same way, organisations with the same name, familiar faces (like Roberts) playing the same old role. The Leeds conference of 1863 should be forgiven its error: it was easy to imagine that the Miners' Association was being revived, not a new union created.

*   *   *

Yet a profound change had occurred. Economic conditions had improved; it had become easier to wring concessions from the employers; different trade union tactics were required. Moderation rather than militancy was the keynote of the National Miners' Union in the sixties: the crude expression of class conflict doctrines, quite common among miners in the 'forties, became inappropriate.[3] Likewise the political climate had been transformed. Chartism, a revolutionary movement, greatly influenced the Miners' Association. Most of its prominent members had played an active part in Chartism. But to

---

[1] *Colliery Guardian*, 25 September 1858.
[2] John Wilson, *History of the Durham Miners' Association*, p. 5.
[3] R. Challinor, *Alexander MacDonald and the Miners*, p. 7.

leaders of a later age such beliefs would have been positively embar-
rassing. Not that they were uninterested in achieving reforms through
Parliament—men like Alexander Macdonald placed great store by
doing so—but their aim was to work within the existing system. None
had the least desire to alter the political set-up drastically.[1]

In discarding apocalyptic visions, revolutionary views and class
warfare attitudes, many may have thought they were drawing lessons
from the experiences of the Miners' Association. The leaders in the
'sixties all received their first-hand knowledge of trade unionism in an
earlier age. Alexander Macdonald, the first president of the National
Miners Union, knew the Miners' Association leaders personally.[2]
The vice-president, William Pickard, joined a local union in 1838, four
years before the formation of the Miners' Association. And Thomas
Burt, who, along with Macdonald, became the first miners' M.P.,
started down the pit at the age of ten in 1847. He must have been
well-acquainted with conditions in the Northumberland and Durham
coalfields, the repressions that followed in the 1844 strike. His father,
Peter Burt, suffered at Seghill pit and made a rhyme that became
popular among the men about the unjust system of payment for coal.
His uncle, Robert Burt, with Thomas Wakinshaw and seven others,
was prosecuted for breaking the Bond. So, to some extent, it might
have been from personal experience that the new leaders sought to
adopt a new course. They strove to avoid a confrontation with the
owners, aware of the trouncing the miners received in 1844.[3]

But the leaders themselves could not have accomplished this transformation had not the economic and social conditions, reflected in the
attitude of the mass of miners, also altered immensely. An age of
tranquillity—at least, comparative tranquillity—succeeded an age of
turbulence in the mining industry.

The new look is epitomised by Lord Elcho, a big coalowner, inviting

[1] Dr. Royden Harrison, in his admirable book, *Before the Socialists*, vividly describes
the transition from the second to third quarters of the nineteenth century: "The Co-
operative Movement did pass from community-building to shop-keeping; the Trade
Unions did become less like 'schools of war' and more like the workman's equivalent to
the public school . . . working-class politics became less a 'knife and fork' and more a
'collar and tie' question. In the first period the Labour leadership was largely recruited
from the crowded ranks of prophets, visionaries and demagogues; by the second it had
exchanged these 'outside' enthusiasts for 'great men of business' trained into 'carefulness'
through the management of the substantial institutions which they controlled." (p. 7.)

[2] Macdonald discussed the qualities of the various leaders of the Miners' Association
at a conference in 1873. He rated David Swallow as the most talented and outstanding.

[3] It is difficult to see how Page Arnot (op. cit., p. 53) says "Burt represented the break
with Chartism and Socialism"—Chartism, yes; Socialism, no. None of the leaders of the
Miners' Association had ever claimed to be Socialists.

union leaders to a champagne breakfast; Alexander Macdonald making his money from commercial speculation; William Pickard investing his money in the Wigan Coal and Iron Company, a firm well known for treating its men badly.[1] What a far cry from the times of W. P. Roberts! He never fawned on the masters or courted respectability. The coalowners had a deep and sincere hatred for him that Roberts bountifully reciprocated. During the 1844 strike, as Roberts rushed round the country denouncing the owners and raising money for the strike fund, the masters' abuse reached unparalleled ferocity. He was also depicted as a deserter, absent from his post in the hour of need. Where is Roberts, they howled, when he should be in Newcastle? Roberts replied with a quote from *Macbeth*:

First Witch: Where has thou been, sister?
Second Witch: Killing SWINE.[2]

Roberts' hatred for the rich was only matched by his love for the poor. He completely identified himself with them and their struggles. His legal ability was always at their disposal because he genuinely believed in the working class, right or wrong. He stated his position in an address to the Northumberland and Durham miners:

"When one of the POOR are injured very many others necessarily share in his suffering: you are not rich: you have no pictures, horses or gewgaws to divert you: to you, *your friends* are *ALL*. It is no exaggeration to say that for one man sentenced as a criminal (and it does not matter one straw whether he is guilty or not—nor whether what he is charged with is a crime or not) ten families are thrown into lasting grief. The evil thus done becomes incalculable."[3]

Roberts, prepared to defend workers, whatever the charges, whatever the facts, did not fit in with the new set-up, the National Miners' Union. He never attained the same status as in the earlier union. His utterances were too wild, his militancy too dangerous. For Roberts, the times were out of joint. He still liked to defend trade unionists in Court cases. He still took an interest in the movement. In 1866, Roberts' testimony before a Parliamentary Select Committee on the master and servant question was, according to Daphne Simon, the most outstanding of eleven which expressed the worker's viewpoint.[4]

[1] William Pickard asserted that union members threatened to dismiss him for preaching temperance and thrift. Evidence to the S.C. on coal, 1873.
[2] *Miners' Magazine*, June–July 1844.   [3] Ibid., June–July 1844.
[4] D. Simon, "Master and Servant", an essay in *Democracy and the Labour Movement*, p. 184.

In 1867, he defended Allen, Larkin and O'Brien, three Fenians—
sometimes referred to as "the Manchester Martyrs"—who were
hanged for killing a policeman. Roberts remained active right up to
the end: he attended the Trades Union Congress in March 1871, a
few months before his death. He was buried at Rickmansworth, near
to O'Connorville, the site of an abortive Chartist land project in
which he lost considerable wealth.

*   *   *

Other leaders, without the security Roberts gained from having a
professional occupation, did not last as long as him. Many were marked
men, denied work wherever they went. Either they made their peace
with the masters, capitulating as Hepburn had done, or they emigrated.[1]
But, whatever happened, the cadres of the Association were completely
eliminated. Martin Jude, in ailing health throughout the 'fifties,
witnessed this disintegration taking place. Always expecting a revival,
always his hopes were dashed. In 1850–3, a weak, much persecuted
union still existed in Northumberland and Durham. In many villages,
where suitable meeting places were denied them, clandestine meetings
took place in back alleys. Even so, if information got back to the
masters certain dismissals ensued. At Seaton Delaval, for example, the
colliery agents dismissed thirty prominent unionists. These included
Edward Richardson, a leader both in 1844 and 1849. His son, Matthew,
had been crippled in the pits and walked on crutches. He received
"smart money", a small pittance of compensation paid by the coalowners. Yet when his father was sacked this also was stopped. Edward
Richardson went round to the colliery office to plead for his son and
was told the company would have nothing to do with him or his son.
Edward Richardson then moved to South Shields, where he tried in
vain to support his family. Gradually, he sold all his possessions. A
noted scholar, he even had to sell his treasured collection of books.
Eventually, he died of starvation. Fynes comments, "he was too
independent in spirit to let his wants be known".[2]

---

[1] Many emigrated to Australia and New Zealand. A booklet giving advice on prospects
for gold mining in Australia was published in Newcastle in 1852. It contained, as well,
adverts for ten other booklets on emigration. But some returned disillusioned from
Australia. The *Disputes Tracts 1817–1844* (North of England Mining Engineers Library)
contains a letter from a miner who had returned from Australia. He reported, "Scores
have made fortunes; hundreds have done pretty well; thousands have done nothing—and
many have found a grave. Such is the result of gold mining." The letter ends: "I'll go no
more a-roving."

[2] R. Fynes, op. cit., p. 140.

R

Despite tragedies such as this, Jude, helped by a diminishing band, struggled on. While the miners were always his primary concern, he did his best to assist workers in other trades who were struggling to build their own unions. This was a more fruitful field of activity. Jude and Hall took part in the Northern Political Union, along with Cowan and Harney, advocating extension of the franchise. Yet he was becoming increasingly isolated. When he died, in August 1860, only a few miners bothered to attend the funeral and the most appreciative tributes came from other occupations. The *Chainmakers' Journal* bemoaned that:

"Martin Jude, the true friend of political and social reform, the veteran soldier in many a severe struggle of labour against capital, the earnest worker for the amelioration of the conditions of the miners in the North, is now no more."

The tribute continues: "For upwards of a quarter of a century Mr. Jude was an efficient labourer in various political agitations." This means he must have been active in Chartism almost from its inception. History has not accorded Jude the credit due to him: in so far as central organisation existed in the union, he was responsible for creating and sustaining it.

But if Jude has the credit for the central organisation, David Swallow must be acknowledged as the prime mover in the union's formation. Posterity has largely forgotten him. Yet there can be no doubt whatsoever that the *Northern Star* was referring to Swallow when it said "the flag was hoisted . . . by a working miner who had been discharged for locally advocating the right of himself and his fellow workmen to a good day's wage for a good day's work." His role was appreciated by his fellow union members. At the second Wakefield conference, held exactly two years after the inaugural meeting, Swallow was made the main speaker at the anniversary celebrations. He used the opportunity to remind his audience that "scarce two years have elapsed since the first meeting in Wakefield, which was attended by a few poor illiterate men". His statement that the union originated in Yorkshire and was later taken to the North-east would have been challenged by delegates at the second Wakefield conference were it not true. As it was, his remarks were published in the *Northern Star* and *Miners' Advocate* without a word of dissent.

Swallow also played a vital role in spreading the union, recruiting members, and making it a truly national organisation. When new area committees were formed, a similarity in the phraseology and thought-content of their appeals with that issued immediately after the union's formation at Wakefield suggests that Swallow, besides being the best organiser, played an important part in drafting public declarations. He struggled on, trying to keep the Association alive, until well into the 'fifties. The last time he was active appears to have been 1854, when he gave evidence to the Committee on Accidents in the Mines.

By the very nature of the labour movement, its strength, its exploits, its existence always depend on a multitude of people whose individual efforts go unrecorded by history. These are the mass that make the movement. It is only occasionally possible, with an outstanding individual, like David Swallow, to rescue them from oblivion. Another whose efforts were truly prodigious was Benjamin Embleton, who first joined a union in 1810 and remained active until 1849. Tremendous hardship and sacrifice, a dogged determination to continue despite repression and massive opposition from the employers, make Embleton a great pioneer, one of the unsung heroes of the trade union movement.

★   ★   ★

What were the historical achievements of the Miners' Association? In size, in duration, in power, it represented a fresh development, a new departure, for trade unionism in Britain. It left its imprint on subsequent unions, particularly of miners. In particular, its concern about Parliament and the need to secure legislation favourable to the working class has been inherited by successive generations of the miners right down to the present day.

While united on the importance of political action, the Miners' Association never had a clearly thought out industrial strategy. It wavered between conflict and conciliation. Prominent members reflected this indecisiveness by their own vacillations, swinging from moderation to militancy and back again. This might appear at the present time, when we are accustomed to being able to distinguish between right and left wings, as a lack of consistency. But in the 1840s trade unionism was still young, the fund of experience acquired was still small, and so workers were more likely to shift their basic attitudes as a result of some immediate happening. This fluidity and uncertainty was an indication of the Association's dilemma—the impasse that it quickly reached. The road to moderation, which exists for workers today, offered little hope. For arbitration and conciliation to take place the employers had to be prepared to accept the existence of the trade union and not try to destroy it. With a person who is attempting to kill you, little basis for friendly co-operation exists. But the alternative, a policy of militancy and strikes, was dangerous—or more accurately, fatal. The masters were far stronger than the men: their status, their wealth, their ability to call in blacklegs, all made it an unequal struggle. While the miners were handicapped by disunity, resulting from the diverse conditions prevailing in the various coalfields, combined action on a national scale was impossible.

So the Miners' Association was certain to collapse. Indeed, it was a great achievement that it endured as long as it did. Other, stronger and more enduring miners' unions have risen from the ashes, and the lessons of their brothers in the 1840s are there for them to see.

Bibliography

Accidents in Coal Mines, 1763–1863, North of England Institute of Mining Engineers, vol. 15.

ALLEN, V. L., "The Origins of Industrial Conciliation and Arbitration", *International Review of Social History*, vol. IX (1964).

"Ancient Mining Customs", *Gentlemen's Magazine*, vol. 36 (n.s.).

ANDERSON, D., *Blundells' Collieries: Wages, Disputes and Conditions of Work*, Lancs & Ches. Hist. Soc., vol. 117 (1965).

ANON, *Life among the Colliers*, London, 1862.

ARMYTAGE, W. H. G., *A. J. Mundella, 1825–1897: The Liberal Background to the Labour Movement*, London, 1951.

ASHTON, T. S., and SYKES, J., *The Coal Industry in the Eighteenth Century*, Manchester, 1929.

ASPINWALL, A., *The Early English Trade Unions*, London, 1949.

BAILEY, J., *The Coal Trade in Durham*, North of England Institute of Mining Engineers, vol. 2.

BANKES, J. H. M., *The Nineteenth Century Colliery Railway*, Lancs. & Ches. Hist. Soc., vol. 114 (1962).

BARKER, T. C., and HARRIS, J. R., *A Merseyside Town in the Industrial Revolution*, Liverpool, 1954.

BARNSBY, G., "The Working Class Movement in the Black Country, 1815–67" (Birmingham University M.A. thesis, 1965).

BEER, M., *A History of British Socialism*, London, 1920.

BOYD, R. N., *Coal Pits and Pitmen*, London, 1892.

— *Mines Inspection*, London, 1871.

BRIGGS, A. (ed.), *Chartist Studies*, London, 1959.

BUDDLE, J., *Accidents in Coal Mines*, Newcastle, 1810.

BURT, T., *From Pitman to Privy Councillor: An Autobiography*, London, 1924.

CARUS-WILSON, E. M. (ed.), *Essays in Economic History*, Vol. 3, London, 1962.

COLE, G. D. H., *Attempts at a General Union*, London, 1953.
— and FILSON, A. W., *British Working Class Movements. Selected Documents, 1789–1875*, London, 1965 ed.
COLE, G. D. H., *British Working Class Politics, 1832–1914*, London, 1941.
— *Chartist Portraits*, London, 1965 ed.
— and POSTGATE, R., *The Common People*, London, 1949.
COLLINS, H., and ABRAMSKY, C., *Karl Marx and the British Labour Movement*, London, 1965.
COOPER, T., *The Life of Thomas Cooper*, London, 1872.
CRAWFORD, EARL OF, *Haigh Cannel*, Manchester Statistical Society, 1933.
CROSSLEY, R. S., *Men of Note*, Accrington, n.d.
CUBBON, W., *Bibliography of Works relating to the Isle of Man*, Douglas, 1934.

DEVYR, T. A., *The Odd Book of the Nineteenth Century*, New York, 1882.
DUNCOMBE, T. H., *Life and Correspondence of T. S. Duncombe*, London, 1868.
DODD, A. H., *The Industrial Revolution in North Wales*, Cardiff, 1933.
DUNN, M., *Coal Trade of the North of England*, Newcastle, 1844.

EDWARDS, N., *The Industrial Revolution in South Wales*, London, 1924.
— *History of the South Wales Miners*, London, 1926.
ENGELS, F., *Conditions of the Working Class in England, in 1844*, London, 1892.
EVANS, E. W., *Miners of South Wales*.

FORSTER, J. M., *Children of Darkness*, Wigan, 1889.
— *The Pit Brow Lassie*, Wigan, 1893.
FAWCETT, H., *The Miners' Doom*, Newcastle, 1844.
FYNES, R., *The Miners of Northumberland and Durham*, Sunderland, 1873.

GALLOWAY, R., *Annals of Coal Mining and the Coal Trade*, 2 vols., London, 1902.
GAMAGE, R. G., *History of the Chartist Movement*, London, 1892.
GROVES, R., *But We Shall Rise Again*, London, 1928.

HAIR, P. E. H., "The Social History of British Coalminers, 1800–1845", Oxford University Ph.D. thesis, 1955.
HALLAM, W., *Miners' Leaders: Thirty Portraits and Biographical Sketches*, London, 1894.

HALEVY, E., *The Age of Peel and Cobden*, London, 1947.

HAMMOND, J. L. and B., *Lord Shaftesbury*, London.

—— — *The Age of the Chartists*, London, 1930.

—— — *The Town Labourer*, London, 1918.

HAMMOND, W., *The Explosion*, Newcastle, 1844.

HARRIS, J. R., *The Hughes Papers. Lancashire Social Life 1780–1825*, Trans. of Lancs. and Ches. His. Soc., Vol. 103 (1951).

HARRISON, R., *Before the Socialists*, London, 1965.

HOLYOAKE, G. J., *Sixty Years of an Agitator's Life*, London, 1892.

— *Life of Stephens*, London, 1881.

HOVELL, M., *The Chartist Movement*, Manchester, 1918.

HOWELL, G., *Labour Legislation, Labour Movements, and Labour Leaders*, London, 1902.

— *The Conflicts of Labour and Capital*, London, 1890.

HOBSBAWM, E. J., *Labouring Men*, London, 1964.

JEVONS, H. S., *The British Coal Trade*, London, 1915.

— *Progress of the Coal Question*, British Association Report, 1875.

JOHNSON, W., *The Miners' Grievances*, Newcastle, n.d.

JOFF, T., *Coffee House Babble*, Walton, 1915.

KINGSFORD, P. W., "Radical Dandy", *History Today*, June, 1964.

KOVALEV, Y. V., *An Anthology of Chartist Literature*, Moscow, 1956.

LLOYD, W., *Strange Tales of Colliery Life*, Wigan, n.d.

LONDONDERRY, MARCHIONESS OF, *Letters to Frances Anne, 1837–61*, Marchioness of Londonderry, London, 1938.

MACKENZIE, E., *A View of the County of Northumberland*, Newcastle, 1825.

MACHIN, F., *The Yorkshire Miners*, Barnsley, 1958.

Marx and Engels on Britain, Moscow, 1953.

MARX AND ENGELS, *Selected Correspondence*, London, 1934.

MATHER, F. C., *Public Order in the Age of the Chartists*.

MATHER, J., *Coal Mines, their Dangers and Means of Safety*, London, 1853.

Mining and Miners and Diggers and Priggers, by a Shareholder, London, 1854.

Mining Sketches and Tales, Sunderland, n.d.

MORRIS, M. (ed.), *From Cobbett to the Chartists, 1815–1848*, London, 1948.

MITCHELL, W., *The Question Answered: What do Pitmen want?*, Bishop Wearmouth, 1844.

NEALE, R. S., "Class and Ideology in Bath, 1800–1850", *Our History*, Summer, 1966.
NEF, J. U. *The Rise of the British Coal Industry*, London, 1934.

Our Coal and Our Coalpits: the people in them and the scenes around them by a Traveller Underground, London, 1859.
O'CONNOR, F. (ed.), *The Trial of Feargus O'Connor and Fifty-eight Others at Lancaster*, London, 1843.

PAGE ARNOT, R., *The Miners*, London, 1949.
— *The Years of Struggle*, London, 1953.
— *History of the Scottish Miners*, London.
— *South Wales Miners*, London, 1967.
PARIS, COMTE DE, *Trade Unions of England*, London, 1869.
PEEL, F., *The Rising of the Luddites, Chartists, etc.*, London, 1880.
PELLING, H., *A History of British Trade Unionism*, London, 1963.
PRESSNELL, L. S. (ed.), *Studies in the Industrial Revolution*, London, 1960.

RAYNES, J. R., *Coal and Its Conflict*, London, 1928.
ROBERTS, W. P., *The Haswell Colliery Explosion*, Newcastle, 1844.
ROSTOW, W. W., *British Economy of the Nineteenth Century*, Oxford, 1948.
ROWE, J. W. F., *Wages in the Coal Industry*, London, 1923.

SAVILLE, J. (ed.), *Democracy and the Labour Movement*, London, 1954.
SAVILLE, J., *Ernest Jones, Chartist* London, 1952.
SCHOYEN, A. R., *The Chartist Challenge*, London, 1958.
SCOTT, HYLTON, The Miners' Bond in Northumberland and Durham. Pro. of Soc. of Antiq. of Newcastle, 1947.
SWEEZY, P. M., Monopoly and Competition in the English Coal Trade, 1550–1850. Harvard, 1938.

TAYLOR, A. J., "The Miners' Association of Great Britain and Ireland", *Economica*, February, 1955.
— *The Wigan Coalfield in 1851*, Trans. of Lancs. & Ches. Hist. Soc.
TAYLOR, R. C., *Statistics on Coal*, London, 1848.

TAYLOR, W. C., *Notes on a Tour of the Manufacturing Districts of Lancashire*, London, 1842.

THOMPSON, E. P., *The Making of the English Working Class*, London, 1963.

THOMPSON, F. M. L., *English Landed Society in the Nineteenth Century*, London.

THOMPSON, J. B., *The Collier's Guide*, Bishop Wearmouth, 1843.

TUFNELL, E. C., *The Character, Objects and Effects of Trade Unions*, London, 1834.

TURNER, H. A., *Trade Union Growth, Structure and Policy*, London, 1962.

WARBURTON, W. H., *History of Trade Union Organisation in the North Staffordshire Potteries*, London, 1931.

WARD, J. T., *The Factory Movement, 1830–1855*, London, 1962.

WATSON, A., *A Great Labour Leader: The Life of Thomas Burt*, London, 1908.

WEARMOUTH, R. F., *Methodism and the Struggle of the Working Classes, 1850–1900*, Leicester, 1954.

— *Some Working Class Movements of the Nineteenth Century*, London, 1948.

WEBB, S., *Story of the Durham Miners (1662–1921)*, London, 1921.

— and B., *The History of Trade Unionism, 1666–1920*, London, 1920.

— — *Industrial Democracy*, London, 1897.

WELBOURNE, E., *The Miners' Unions of Northumberland and Durham*, Cambridge, 1923.

WEST, J., *History of the Chartist Movement*, London, 1920.

WILLIAMS, D., *John Frost*, Cardiff, 1939.

WILLIAMS, D. J., *Capitalist Combination in the Coal Industry*, London, 1924.

WILLIAMS, J. E., *The Derbyshire Miners*, London, 1962.

WILSON, J., *History of the Durham Miners*, London, 1907.

WILSON, T., *Putman's Pay and Other Poems*, Gateshead, 1843.

Collections of Documents

Accrington, Oak Hill Museum: W. R. Hindle Collection.

Liverpool, Picton Library: A History of the Coal Trade (12 vols.).

Newcastle-on-Tyne Central Library: The Cowen Collection.

North of England Mining Engineers' Library, Newcastle-on-Tyne: Bell Collection; Buddle Collection; The Disputes Tracts (1817–1844).

Sheffield Reference Library: Wentworth Muniments.
Wigan Public Library: Pitman's Strike Collection; Pamphlets relating
    to Mining and Manufacture (20 vols.).

Official Reports

Select Committee on the State of the Coal Trade, 1830.
Parliamentary Report from Committee on Bill to regulate Labour of
    Children in Factories, etc., 1833.
Select Committee on Accidents, 1835.
7th Report on Public Petitions.
Children Employment Commission, 1842.
The Inspector of Mines Reports, 1844 onwards.
The Midland Mining Commission, 1843.
Parliamentary Report on Accidents in Coal Mines, 1849.
Select Committee on Colliery Accidents, 1854.
Royal Commission of Trade Unions, 1867–9.
Select Committee on the Scarcity and Dearness of Coal, 1873.
Home Office Papers.

Newspapers and Journals

*Blackburn Standard, Bolton Chronicle, Bolton Free Press, Chainmakers'
Journal, Charter, Chartist Circular, Colliery Guardian, Cooper's Journal,
Derbyshire Courier, Durham Chronicle, Durham Gazette, Flint Glass
Makers' Magazine, Gateshead Observer, The Labourer, Leeds Times,
Leeds Mercury, Liverpool Mercury, Manchester Guardian, Manchester
Courier, Manx Liberal, Miners' Advocate, Miners' Journal, Miners'
Magazine, Morning Herald, Newcastle Chronicle, Newcastle Courant, North
of England Magazine, North Staffordshire Mercury, Northern Liberator,
Northern Star, Northern Tribune, Notes to the People, The Potters'
Examiner, Preston Chronicle, Preston Pilot, The Labourer, Sheffield
Independent, Sheffield Journal Staffordshire Advertiser, The Struggle, The
Times, Tyne Mercury, The Union, Whitehaven Herald.*

Index